MAKE CHINA GREAT AGAIN

Make China Great Again

ONLINE ALT-HISTORY FICTION AND POPULAR AUTHORITARIANISM

Rongbin Han

Columbia University Press
New York

Columbia University Press
Publishers Since 1893
New York   Chichester, West Sussex
cup.columbia.edu

Cataloging-in-Publication data is available from the Library of Congress.
ISBN 9780231220545 (hardback)
ISBN 9780231220552 (paper)
ISBN 9780231563291 (epub)
ISBN 9780231566438 (PDF)

LCCN 2025047987

Cover design: Elliott S. Cairns

GPSR Authorized Representative: Easy Access System Europe,
Mustamäe tee 50, 10621 Tallinn, Estonia, gpsr.requests@easproject.com

To time and history,
and to my daughter, Audrey Zhiyan Han, and my wife, Yi Fu

CONTENTS

ACKNOWLEDGMENTS ix

Introduction: Online Fiction, the Chinese Dream, and Pop Hegemony 1

Chapter One
Internet Literature in China: A Commodified Political Field 19

Chapter Two
Dancing with Shackles On: State Intervention as Coproduction 39

Chapter Three
Make China Great Again: Alt-History Fiction and the Chinese Dream 59

Chapter Four
The Variety of Chinese Dreams: MCGA and Ideological Interpellation 79

Chapter Five
More Than Audience: Reader Participation in MCGA 102

CONTENTS

Conclusion: Pop Hegemony in the Making 123

APPENDIX 141

NOTES 153

BIBLIOGRAPHY 187

INDEX 209

ACKNOWLEDGMENTS

Writing an academic book often sounds like a lonely journey, as the author endeavors into the unknown with their own imagination and creativity. However, such a mission can hardly be accomplished singlehandedly. I want to take the opportunity to express my gratitude to people who have accompanied me during this time, briefly or throughout the process. And I must apologize for the inevitable omissions in advance given how challenging this task is.

Above all, glories belong to internet literature and its producers and consumers. I owe my deepest gratitude to the writers and readers of internet literature, who have made this research possible in the first place. I became and remained an avid reader of various genres of online fiction long before realizing my interest in studying the phenomenon. Such experiences and passion made me feel accompanied and inspired during the research and writing process.

I have received invaluable academic and emotional support necessary for the project from colleagues and scholars who share similar research interests. I am particularly indebted to Ashley Esarey, Min Jiang, and Daniela Stockmann who have read and provided feedback on each of the chapters in detail. Cas Mudde, my faculty mentor when I arrived at the University of Georgia (UGA) in 2013, thoroughly read the book, nearly line editing it and offering many constructive comments. My adviser Kevin

O'Brien encouraged me to pursue the project very early on, even when I was not quite sure whether internet novels were political enough to study from a political science perspective. Michael Hockx and Guobin Yang, both pioneers in studying internet literature in China, provided me with guidance, sources, and useful tips at multiple occasions.

I also had the privilege of being invited to present the project at the Taipei School of Economics and Political Science, Hamilton College, China Research Center in Atlanta, Zhejiang University, and East China Normal University. I am particularly thankful for Alexsia Chan, Zongshi Chen, Juan Du, Xiang Gao, Han-chao Lu, Li Shao, Bolun Zhang, James Schiffman, and Chung-min Tsai for inviting me over and then commenting on and offering concrete suggestions to improve this book.

I have also presented earlier drafts of several chapters from the book at the annual conferences of the American Political Science Association, Association for Asian Studies, and Midwest Political Science Association and received highly constructive feedback from the panelists and audience. Among others, I would like to thank Bruce Dickson, Kecheng Fang, Gengsong Gao, Jonathan Hassid, Lincoln Hines, Jean Hong, Qian Huang, Xian Huang, Aram Hur, Xinru Ma, Suzanne Scoggins, Hong Shen, Dan Slater, Filippo Trevisan, Jeremy Wallace, Jessica Chen Weiss, Angela Wu, Yuan Yao, and John Yasuda.

I am forever indebted to many scholars who have served as my role models and continuously nourished my academic growth, including especially my advisers at Berkeley: Chris Ansell, David Collier, Thomas Gold, Kevin O'Brien, and Rachel Stern. Many other scholars, including but not limited to Timothy Cheek, Dan Chen, Wenhong Chen, Zifeng Chen, Martin Dimtrov, King-wa Fu, Mary Gallagher, John Garver, John Givens, Christian Göbel, Heike Holbig, William Hurst, Jieun Kim, Genia Kostka, Lizhi Liu, Yawei Liu, Liang Ma, Andrew MacDonald, Melanie Manion, Blake Miller, Andrew Mertha, Jean Oi, Jennifer Pan, Maria Repnikova, Yipeng Shen, Kristin Shi-Kupfer, Christoph Steinhardt, Denise Van Der Kamp, Yicheng Wang, and Susan Whiting, have offered me invaluable comments and encouragement at different stages of the project.

I would like to express my gratitude to colleagues at the Department of International Affairs, who have provided a nurturing environment for research and writing. In particular, I would like to thank Amanda Murdie, my former my department head and current dean of the Ivan Allen College of Liberal Arts at Georgia Tech, and Justin Conrad, my current department head, for being incredibly supportive and providing financial assistance to facilitate publication of the book.

Sheldon Liu, Lainey Lyle, and Elise Trubey offered valuable research assistance. Sheldon helped with coding, and I am impressed by his dedication and diligence. I asked Lainey and Elise, my UGA Young Dawgs mentees, to edit earlier drafts of the book to ensure that it is as accessible as it can be. Now it is time for you, my dear readers, to test whether we have achieved this goal.

I had the opportunity to visit the University of Hawai'i where I finished the final revision of the book. I thank Kristi Govella for making this visit possible and Cathy Clayton for being such a wonderful and supportive department chair during my visit.

As always, I am deeply grateful for the constructive yet critical feedback from the reviewers of this book. Their comments and suggestions have certainly improved it in multiple ways. My editor at Columbia University Press, Caelyn Cobb, has been wonderful, once again. She has seen me through the whole process, literally as I approached her very early about the project at the 2018 Association for Asian Studies annual conference. Since then, I have received nothing but support and encouragement from her. I would thank Marisa Pagano for carefully editing the final draft.

My parents, Suoxiao Han and Yindi Zhang; parents-in-law, Xiulin Fu and Qirong Wu; wife, Yi Fu; and daughter, Audrey Zhiyan Han, are unsung heroes behind my academic endeavor. I cannot acknowledge their support and sacrifice enough.

MAKE CHINA GREAT AGAIN

INTRODUCTION

Online Fiction, the Chinese Dream, and Pop Hegemony

While discussing an alternate history of China in the context of the late 1980s leading to the Tiananmen movement, political scientist Andrew Nathan once asked, "Could Beijing have taken a different path?"[1] The question is tempting. As a keen reader of Chinese internet novels, I also find the question quite familiar. In the past few decades, millions of Chinese have explored similar speculation by way of a specific genre of internet literature called alt-history fiction. Through engaging in the production and consumption of the popular genre, writers and readers have fantasized about going back in history and transforming China militarily, politically, economically, and socially. For instance, in *Pointing South* (*Zhinan Lu* 指南录), the writer takes readers on a journey to save the Southern Song dynasty (1127–1279 CE) from the Mongol invasion and transform China into a capitalist society with a parliamentary system. Another popular title, *Red Dawn* (*Chise Liming* 赤色黎明), imagines a contemporary Chinese young man born in the 1980s traveling back to 1905 to launch a communist revolution even before the Communist Party of China was founded. Through thousands of such works, Chinese writers and readers hypothesize, (re)examine, and (re)interpret changes to history, especially at critical junctures and in response to historical crises. I argue that, in doing so, they engage in an ideational process to Make China Great Again (MCGA), which not only resonates with the state narrative of national revival but also interestingly echoes the Make America Great Again (MAGA) phenomenon in the United States and populist movements around the globe.

With a reported 528 million users (or 49 percent of the internet-user population in China) as of June 2023, internet literature provides an excellent window into the politics of digital cultural consumerist experiences and their implications.[2] Such experiences, mainly produced and consumed by citizens and mediated by the techno-market mechanisms with state intervention and regulation, represent a special form of commodified expression that is political in nature. The specific genre of internet literature that I focus on, MCGA alt-history fiction, is straight-out political in that it deals with history and engages in discussion of an ideal China and potential developmental paths of the nation. At the core of this genre is the nationalist quest for China revival, a theme that directly interacts with the state ideological construct of the "Chinese dream." Thus, studying the production and consumption of these works illuminates not only how the party-state, market, and citizens negotiate digital experiences and the landscape of China's ideational realm but also how these multifaceted negotiations may affect authoritarian rule and its legitimation.

In this book, I investigate internet literature in China as a commodified political field in which the party-state, market, and citizens partake in ideational contestation through daily digital experiences. I find that the production and consumption of MCGA fiction represent a technology- and market-mediated process of societal imagination and construction of an ideal China, which in turn bears significant implications for authoritarian legitimation and ideological governance. Although this process can both confirm and challenge the party-state in the ideational realm, it may ultimately lead to the rise of a paradigm of authoritarian governance I call "pop hegemony," under which authoritarian rule is popularly constructed, negotiated, and legitimized.

Based on both in-depth and guerrilla-style online ethnography with systematic content analysis, I address several questions: How can we make sense of the ever enriched, dynamic, and complex digital experiences in the context of an adaptive high-capacity authoritarian regime? More specifically, given the trends of both full-speed digitization and increasing state control, how do the state, society, and market negotiate everyday digital experiences? And, finally, what are the implications for authoritarian rule?

Instead of taking an "activism-focused" perspective that pays special attention to how the internet empowers social activism and how the state controls digital mobilization, I focus on mundane experiences in the more latent virtual field and the habitus of internet literature.[3] I explain not why or how people participate in collective mobilization, but rather how they engage in politics through everyday experiences. As my analysis shows (chapter 1), internet literature is a commodified political field in which ideological contestation and digital consumerism processes take place simultaneously. Such digital experiences, although challenging the state, enable popular participation in the negotiation and justification of authoritarian rule, which, borrowing the Gramscian idea of cultural hegemony, ultimately contributes to the rise of "pop hegemony."[4] Unlike Gramsci's analysis, however, which assigns the state (and ruling class) the more active and dominant role, my analysis, joining some of the latest studies, highlights the societal and market agency in China's digital governance, especially in the building up and contestation of ideational hegemony.[5] Put it simply, in this book, I explore how an ideology can be negotiated into dominance among the state, society, and market in the digital age.

By emphasizing the role of social and market actors in authoritarian legitimation, I avoid a state-centric framework. Completely dismissing the critical influence of the state would be a mistake, however, as the Chinese state has actively engaged with the production and consumption of internet literature (see chapter 2). With a three-layered strategy of censorship, co-optation, and promotion, the state sets the permissible zone of online writing and encourages the works it prefers. Thus, although the state does not directly create any internet literature works, it is an indispensable coproducer. In other words, although I highlight the agency of the market and citizens in relation to the state, I also reveal how they have together coproduced these digital experiences and their political consequences (i.e., authoritarian legitimation).

I offer an alternative intellectual or ideational history in another light. Instead of privileging political elites, intellectuals, professionals, or those who are traditionally considered "thinkers" or "literati," I observe how digitally empowered citizens share their views, reflections, and visions of the past, present, and future of China and the world through everyday practices.[6] These "*minjian* intellectuals," as Sebastian Veg puts it, include those who are unofficial, unaffiliated, and among the people.[7] Although one may question if such actors would produce any profound knowledge, insight, or thought comparable to the traditional intelligentsia, I show they deserve our attention as a group whose political expression takes the everyday consumerist format, as Michel de Certeau eloquently points out in *The Practice of Everyday Life*.[8] Their active participation in imagining an ideal China represents a grassroots intervention in the oftentimes elite-oriented grand narrative of "the world according to China."[9] By directing scholarly attention to everyday digital experiences, I reveal how authoritarian legitimacy augmentation and erosion occur quietly in our everyday socioeconomic and cultural lives.

FROM AUTHORITARIAN RESILIENCE TO AUTHORITARIAN LEGITIMATION

The phenomenon of enduring authoritarianism has attracted much scholarly attention. Existing studies largely fall into two camps. The first camp by and large posits explicitly or implicitly that authoritarian regimes are plagued by a legitimacy deficit as they are not granted the right to rule through open, fair, and competitive elections.[10] But they can remain in power through coercion, control, and co-option of the opposition and potential challengers. In a nutshell, these studies essentially advance an "authoritarian power" argument that emphasizes the capacity of the state in relation to society. The second camp does not assume away the legitimacy of autocracies but sees it as contested and something to be earned or lost. Autocracies can buy citizens off or even win their minds and hearts by resorting to other sources of legitimacy than democratic elections. The Chinese state, for instance, has adjusted its government structure, institutions, and policies for "performance legitimacy" by delivering economic growth, improved living standards, and better government-citizen interaction.[11] In addition, it has turned to nationalism and other symbolic resources, such as compassion, morality, and traditional culture, to legitimize its rule.[12] This line of reasoning can be labeled as "authoritarian legitimation."[13]

In the digital age, autocracies face even greater challenges. The internet and digital media have facilitated social mobilization to overthrow several entrenched Middle Eastern and North African autocracies, shocking the rest in the region.[14] In high-capacity authoritarian or illiberal regimes, such as China and Russia, digital media has enabled citizens to better organize, coordinate, and mobilize collective action, to more effectively hold the state and its agents accountable, and to voice their discontent more freely.[15] Despite the challenges, strong authoritarian regimes have survived and may even thrive in the digital age. Why? Current explanations echo either the "authoritarian power" or the "authoritarian legitimation" argument. Many scholars have investigated how so-called high-capacity autocracies can effectively tame and utilize digital technologies to their advantage. In particular, observers have highlighted the state's capacity to control and manipulate information flows in virtual space.[16] For instance, in China, state agencies, service providers, and other intermediary actors, as well as participating citizens or social groups, have formed a formidable content censorship machine that is equipped with rich technological, administrative, and legal tools to control and manage citizens' online expression and content access.[17] Examination of censorship motives and tactics further show that the party-state not only selectively targets online information—out of purposes such as preserving regime legitimacy and defusing collective action—but also fine-tunes the censorship strength and tactics based on topical, temporal, and situational factors.[18]

In addition, authoritarian states have used digital technologies to their advantage. Autocrats across the globe have devised innovative digital propaganda and information strategies, such as flooding cyberspace with state information, wrapping propaganda in appealing packaging and framing (also known as ideotainment), and conducting astroturfing to sway public opinion at home and abroad.[19] The rapid digitalization of socioeconomic life has also enabled autocracies to effectively monitor citizens and penetrate deeper into society, as embodied in the social credit system as well as digital monitoring and tracking practices in China, to the extent of "total surveillance," according to some observers.[20]

The authoritarian power argument is insightful but explains digital authoritarian resilience only partially, especially given the burgeoning cyber-activism in autocracies. After all, state control and manipulation over information are never perfect and are often met with resistance and protest. Chinese citizens have developed rich "digital hidden transcripts" to evade censorship and to express and mobilize.[21] Even innovative information tactics, such as ideotainment and astroturfing, may fail to work because official narratives do not often resonate with the public, not to mention that traces of state manipulation can cause immediate backlash.[22]

Other scholars question the "state control versus social resistance" framework. Their studies, echoing the "authoritarian legitimation" literature, find that the internet has empowered not just regime critics but also regime supporters, such as the popularly known "voluntary fifty-cent army" and "little pink," which actively defend the regime against critics and promulgate proregime voices.[23] Further studies find that nationalism serves as an important source of proregime discourse; and citizens may defend the party-state not because they support the regime, but because they dislike the opposition force.[24]

These digital authoritarian legitimation studies explain well the coexistence of authoritarian rule and the empowering internet. However, they tend to focus narrowly on expressions on popular social media sites that feature more direct state-society confrontation, thus overlooking the variety, complexity, and richness of digital experiences. As Cara Wallis insightfully points out, "Within a highly commercialized and more liberalized sociocultural environment, new media technologies have opened up new spaces for multiple modes of expression, and as such, they are constitutive of complex processes of social change."[25] In addition, although scholars have probed into the sources of digital authoritarian legitimation, more in-depth studies are needed to investigate the specific conditions and dynamics of how digital experiences, political or nonpolitical, may affect regime legitimacy. For instance, it is unclear whether the seemingly symbiotic relationship between cybernationalism and regime support is deeply grounded or more contingent (as reacting to foreign hostile forces) in nature.

I explore how state, market, and societal forces interact in the production and consumption of online literature, and the subsequent implications for authoritarian politics. Such a focus on everyday cultural consumerist experiences and the accompanying technological, social, market, and political dynamics allows us to better map the pervasiveness of state influences and reveal the agency and active roles of the market and citizens in the process. More specifically, by examining the MCGA genre of fiction, I refine the conception of Chinese authoritarianism, highlighting its historical roots (ancient time glories and humiliations in the modern era), contemporary relevance (national revival and China rise), and social origin (as reflected in popular involvement in the state-championed national rejuvenation ideology). My argument is neither one of "authoritarian power" in which the state triumphs with coercion, nor a simple "authoritarian legitimation" thesis of the state unilaterally persuading citizens that it has the right to rule. Rather, it is a story of the citizenry, mediated by the market and digital media, building authoritarian legitimacy together with the state.

Recognizing the role of nonstate actors in authoritarian legitimation is crucial to explaining digital authoritarian resilience and to understanding where China is headed politically. Indeed, as mentioned earlier, digital media has empowered regime supporters who defend the regime against criticism and help manufacture proregime discourses. Such groups include the "voluntary fifty-cent army" and "little pink," noted earlier, often out of nationalism or a distaste of regime critics.[26] Little scholarly attention, however, has been paid to other, oftentimes interrelated, proregime voices, such as the "industrial party," a coherent online ideological group that proposes a blueprint for China to achieve great power status through continuous industrial and technological advancements.[27] Such a discourse affirms the party-state's historical role, including that of the first thirty years under Mao. The more recent Ruguanism narrative compares modern China to the Manchus before they cracked and replaced the Ming dynasty (1368–1644) and sees the United States like the Ming, which appears to be strong and affluent but is actually a "paper tiger" going downhill.[28] Justifying China's rise as a story of counterhegemony, and anticipating China to replace the United States, like the Manchus defeating Ming, this conception entails a proregime tendency acknowledging the party's role in national revival, and directly echoing President Xi's notion of the rising East versus the declining West (*dongsheng xijiang* 东升西降).[29] It is much more aggressive than those entertained by other proregime groups given the confrontational strategy it advocates to achieve rejuvenation of the nation.

The evolution of such discourses illustrates two critical mechanisms of authoritarian legitimation that I will further elaborate. First, the development is evidently driven by the reflection, debate, and transformation within proregime groups as well as by the contestation with regime critics, all digitally mediated. To a significant extent, internet literature, as a commodified political field in which cultural consumerist dynamics drive public expression, functions as an incubator for the discursive evolution. Indeed, proregime discourses and internet literature share some of the original hosts and have nurtured each other from the beginning. For instance, online forums such as SonicBBS (expired) and Dragon Sky (lkong.com) were both strongholds of proregime nationalist discourses, and they were also sites where some influential internet literature works germinated. An example is the popular *Morning Star of Lingao* (Lingao Qiming 临高启明), which tells the story of five hundred contemporary Chinese people time traveling to the late Ming period to change history through modernization and industrialization (see chapter 3). This title, often seen as imbued with "industrial party" narratives, is the collective brainchild of these noted online forums.

Second, authoritarian legitimation, and digital politics in general, must be contextualized in the socioeconomic and political transformations occurring across China and around the globe.[30] For instance, Guobin Yang, when discussing phenomena such as the rise of "China's wolf-warrior diplomacy" and "COVID nationalism," argues that these developments should be understood "in the context of an already emerging culture of cybernationalism and global populism."[31] China's ascendance and its global influence are shaping the "structure of feelings" among contemporary Chinese, conditioning the evolution of nationalist proregime (and opposing) discourses.[32] If China's rise is more about the growth in hard power, then the discursive evolution reflects more an ideational quest to sustain the nation's development (the industrial party) and pursuit of its international status as a great power (the Ruguanism narrative) as well as a process of China as a polity seeking "consent" from both within and outside. Therefore, these discourses are more than, or have grown beyond, simply being nationalist or proregime. They represent the ongoing explorations, debates, reflections, and speculations of the past, present, and future of the nation, which also bear global implications given China's ascending global influence. What is even more interesting, as I will highlight, is that the process is not necessarily driven by the elite.

DIGITAL CULTURAL POLITICS AND AUTHORITARIAN RULE IN CHINA

We know culture and politics are closely intertwined.[33] The role of culture in digital authoritarian politics, however, has yet to be sufficiently researched, with scholarly attention often drawn to topics of digital empowerment and online activism versus state control and repression. Instead of adopting a digital contention perspective of state control versus social resistance, I study digital cultural consumerist experiences as a field to explore how the state, market, and society interact in cyberspace as well as the subsequent political implications.[34] In particular, through this multi-interactionist framework, I reveal how discursive and ideational contestation in China, while challenging the party-state, may help negotiate the social consent, beyond the passive acceptance, of authoritarian rule.[35]

Digital cultural consumerism is understudied among political scientists, likely because it is often deemed nonpolitical in nature. Yet, ignoring such a trend and the politics of the seemingly more mundane experiences is problematic because it implies a narrow understanding of politics.[36] As Guobin Yang puts it, "to see politics only in the higher echelons of power or as its outright subversion, and consequently to think of political change only as regime change, has its limits."[37] Therefore, this approach fits a growing body of scholarship on the lively and dynamic internet culture and the politics of popular culture in China.[38]

Indeed, the cultural consumerist realm has always been an important one in which politics takes place and the state and society negotiate governance and dominance. Studies have found that cultural consumerist experiences play an instrumental role in social mobilization and resistance.[39] These experiences have also functioned as weapons of ideational dissent, the power of which is evident in works such as *Animal Farm* and *1984*, as well as in Chinese "scar literature" that reflects on, questions, and criticizes totalitarianism (especially of the Maoist era).[40] States have actively controlled, coopted, and exploited cultural consumerist experiences for their purposes. The Soviet Union and China, for instance, have produced massive amounts of literature, opera, arts, and other cultural products to mobilize the public and promulgate state-preferred norms, values, and practices.[41]

In addition, cultural consumerist experiences can be political, because their production and consumption are deeply embedded in, and interact with, the existing sociopolitical structure and order. On the one hand, literature projects popular perceptions and reflections of sociopolitical realities, rendering them political in nature regardless of genre or content. On the other hand, the production and consumption of literature often involves overcoming sociopolitical constraints; thus, the process often reflects one of production, counterproduction, and alter-production.[42] This is not just about politically threatening content. As Michel Hockx points out, the Chinese state "considers itself obliged to regulate culture in all its aspects."[43]

Even seemingly nonpolitical cultural consumerist experiences can serve political functions. In *Brave New World*, Aldous Huxley describes an alternative or opposite dystopian world to what George Orwell projected in *1984*. Unlike the Orwellian scenario of political order being maintained through harsh control, censorship, and suppression, the world Huxley envisions would mediate citizens socially and technologically into bliss so that they voluntarily give up resistance.[44] Both scenarios are highly worrisome, but more so the latter, as Neil Postman nicely summarizes in the foreword of his famous *Amusing Ourselves to Death*:

> What Orwell feared were those who would ban books. What Huxley feared was that there would be no reason to ban a book, for there would be no one who wanted to read one. Orwell feared those who would deprive us of information. Huxley feared those who would give us so much that we would be reduced to passivity and egoism. Orwell feared that the truth would be concealed from us. Huxley feared the truth would be drowned in a sea of irrelevance. Orwell feared we would become a captive culture. Huxley feared we would become a trivial culture, preoccupied with some equivalent of the feelies, the orgy porgy, and the centrifugal bumblepuppy. As Huxley remarked in *Brave New World Revisited*, the civil libertarians and rationalists who are ever on the alert to oppose tyranny "failed to take into account man's almost infinite appetite for distractions." In 1984, Huxley added, people are controlled by inflicting pain. In *Brave New World*, they are controlled by inflicting pleasure. In short, Orwell feared that what we hate will ruin us. Huxley feared that what we love will ruin us.[45]

Although Huxley and Postman did not set the context of their discussion in an autocracy, a study on China finds that entertainment media may "amuse citizens to loyalty," because it helps undo citizens' sophistication, making them more susceptible to state propaganda.[46] This echoes the propaganda strategy under the German Nazi Joseph Goebbels, who believed in the mission to "work on people until they are addicted to us."[47]

This "amusement to death or loyalty" reasoning, while inspiring, prescribes a relatively passive instrumental role of entertainment media, which functions by distracting, depoliticizing, or enticing citizens to state control. Rather than seeing internet literature as a tool that amuses the citizenry to passivity or loyalty (or provokes resistance and dissent), I treat it as a commodified political field in the Bourdieusian sense, in which the state, market, and citizens coproduce and contest digital experiences, as well as the political meanings they carry and embody.[48] Although the outcome of such contestation depends on many factors, I argue that citizens can play a more active role in the process and socialize themselves in a way that is to the advantage of the party-state.

POP HEGEMONY AND INTERNET LITERATURE

Current studies tend to assume implicitly or explicitly that authoritarian rule is imposed, and thus costly to maintain, as citizens constantly resist and rebel against it (the authoritarian power thesis) or that citizens in autocracies are tricked or bought into compliance (the authoritarian legitimation thesis).[49] I, however, show that citizens may play a far more active role in constructing and maintaining the state dominance they are subject to than current studies suggest. The eventual outcome, while yet to be created, can be a "pop hegemony" under which authoritarian rule is a result of popularly negotiated consent that is complied with and justified among citizens.

From Cultural Hegemony to Pop Hegemony in China

The notion of cultural hegemony, rooted in the Marxist theory of class dominance, was further developed and brought to prominence by Antonio Gramsci in his well-known *Prison Notebooks*. According to Marxism, a society's dominant ideology reflects the interests, values, and beliefs of the ruling class. But how can the ruling class establish the dominance of its ideology? Gramsci provided an answer, arguing that the ruling class achieves ideological dominance by socializing citizens with its beliefs, values, and mores through institutions such as schools, churches, courts, and the media. When its ideology becomes the accepted one, the ruling class establishes "cultural hegemony," effectively winning "the consent of subordinate groups to the existing social order," and thus it does not have to rely exclusively on domination or coercion.[50]

While devised to "address the relation between culture and power under capitalism," cultural hegemony as a concept serves nicely, if not perfectly, to capture the dynamics among power, market, and culture in contemporary

China, which features a highly capitalist economy, a booming cultural industry, and a reformed socialist regime in dire need of justifications for its rule.[51] Indeed, since its founding in 1949, the People's Republic has undergone major socioeconomic and political transformations that make the cultural hegemony concept more or less relevant at different times. Overall, before the reform era, China had a totalitarian regime that brought society under almost complete control, albeit not without resistance.[52] Cultural, educational, and ideational institutions, such as the media, schools, and churches, were largely part of the "state ideological apparatus," as Louis Althusser puts it.[53] The rule of the party-state, therefore, was more imposed and backed by coercion, with little non-state mobilized social participation, not to mention that of the market, which was essentially absent.

From 1978 until the end of the 1980s, China experienced economic reform and limited political liberalization. The process was accompanied by a "high culture fever" featuring "the revived status of intellectuals as social elites, the burgeoning of serious artistic pursuits [. . .], and the massive introduction of Western cultural works to China."[54] Even the party-state was very much confused, with many doubting the socialist road from within, as reflected in the influential documentary *River Elegy* (He Shang 河殇) produced by the party-state's mouthpiece, China Central Television, in 1988, which depicted traditional China as a "land-based civilization" that had its glorious time but was subsequently defeated by Western "maritime civilizations" in the modern era because of its isolation and conservatism.[55] The underlying message was that China must join the US-led Western order rather than stick with communism for national revival and development. The apex, and the end of this period, was the 1989 Tiananmen student movement, which almost collapsed communist rule. The state's ideational dominance was thus at its weakest.

After the Tiananmen crackdown, China in the 1990s witnessed the decline of "high culture" and the rise of popular culture, with continued economic reforms and technological development causing deep structural shifts in society. After more than four decades of reforms, China seemingly has concluded its process of "crossing the river by touching the stones,"[56] having established a market economy with Chinese characteristics and a relatively stable governing regime based on performance, nationalism, and stability maintenance. Concurrently, the Chinese society, shocked by the Tiananmen suppression and converted by the market, by and large have avoided challenging the party's right to rule directly. The status and role of culture and cultural elites have also dramatically changed. Since the 1990s, the influence of high culture and elitist literati-style intellectuals has declined in relative sense, with popular culture and grassroots (or *minjian*) intellectuals playing a more prominent role in the cultural and ideational realms, thanks to the rise of consumerism and digital media.[57] For example, none of the traditional writers can compete with top online fiction writers in terms of readership. As the prominent Chinese Literature professor Chen Pingyuan puts it: "The most tragic fate of the Don Quixotes [i.e. traditional cultural elites] in modern China may not only be that they would be punished by political authorities for deviance, but that they are abandoned by the market due to their 'morality,' 'idealism,' and 'passion.' Replacing them are the all-powerful players who 'avoid the sublime' and thus appear more 'popularized,' and who in Wang Meng's words, 'have well-adapted to the Four Cardinal Principles and the market economy.'"[58]

This transition was greatly facilitated by the rapid expansion of digital technologies. The internet, by breaking state monopoly over the media, has empowered societal actors, providing ordinary citizens opportunities to voice grievances and mobilize while creating a new dissenting space. Like the impact of the market, however, digital technologies have similarly sidelined critical literati intellectuals and have given rise to more pluralized grassroots forces. Facing such challenges, the party-state, after initial panic and exploration, has gradually figured out how to regulate, control, and exploit online expression and digital experiences in general.

China, under President Xi Jinping, has entered a new era in many aspects, some of which can be attributed to the president, while others demonstrate continuity from previous administrations.[59] Of particular interest to me is the ideational evolution that features a nationalist turn, heightened social control, and the rise of China and its adoption of a more assertive foreign policy. As soon as President Xi assumed power, he coined his governing philosophy as the "Chinese dream" of the "great revival of the Chinese nation."[60] The state has since promoted the ideological construct fiercely, including fabricating seemingly spontaneous supporting comments on social media sites.[61] Considering how China has significantly enhanced social control under Xi and its attempt to assert itself as a rising power in the international community, the "Chinese dream" is clearly an ideational effort of authoritarian legitimation, but to what extent it is effective depends on whether and how citizens resonate with it. It is against this background of time and space that cultural hegemony becomes more relevant.

Building on Gramsci and other thinkers, as well as by empirically examining how ordinary Chinese citizens imagine an ideal China in MCGA alt-history fiction, I propose "pop hegemony" to conceptualize how the Chinese state, the market, and various social actors negotiate the consent that helps legitimize the state's dominance in the digital age. In particular, the MCGA theme indicates popular resonance of the Chinese dream, suggesting that authoritarian legitimation through nationalism is working. These titles, however, also produce a variety of Chinese dreams that may be at odds with the official ideological construct, implying that consent negotiation is in process.

My concept of pop hegemony differs from Gramsci's original notion of hegemony as a form of state dominance that does not rely on coercive force.[62] I use the term *pop* to highlight the more active role and important agency of the citizenry and market in consent negotiation and construction. It is not just that the state (or the ruling class) imposes its ideology over citizens (the ruled) through indoctrination or amusement. Rather, social consent is popularly negotiated, with the state often making concessions to societal actors and absorbing social norms, values, and beliefs to its advantage. Moreover, *pop* indicates better the role of the market and platforms in internet literature as part of the pop culture in today's China, as well as the somewhat populist nature of the MCGA phenomenon, as I elaborate in the concluding chapter.[63]

Internet Literature as a Commodified Political Field

Pop hegemony is essentially a form of digital cultural hegemony as the consent negotiation process is embodied in, and mediated by, digital experiences. Such experiences range from direct state-society confrontation, such as the struggle over censorship, to everyday consumerist activities, like internet literature, which for analytical purposes, I conceptualize as a commodified political field. It is in such a field that the party-state, market, and citizens contest relative positions, negotiate power relations, and ultimately shape the ideational realm of China (for details, see chapter 1). On the one hand, internet literature has evolved into a hype-commercialized industry, creating a commodified field in which production, distribution, and consumption activities feature dynamics of supply and demand, competition, and the rule of attention economy. On the other hand, this process is embedded in the field of state power, which reflects the authoritarian nature of the Chinese regime and sets the boundaries of and shapes the digital experiences. As these two fields overlap and interact with each other, they create a commodified political field that hosts the power contestation between the state, market (especially the digital platforms), and citizens, as well as ideational negotiation toward pop hegemony. These three key actors have different goals and play different roles.

First, the state, with its coercive capacity and massive resources, can and will attempt to control, regulate, and manipulate digital experiences to maintain and legitimize its rule. Because the state is largely a foreigner to cyberculture and can no longer control cultural producers like it did in the past through institutions such as the China Writers Association and traditional media, it primarily intervenes in rather than actively produces digital cultural consumerist experiences. From the pop hegemony perspective, this means the state can promote or block the norms, values, and cultural symbols, but it cannot decide what is produced or how it is consumed within the permissible zone it prescribes.

Second, the market and digital media platforms, while subject to state control and regulation, serve as the incubator of pop hegemony. In particular, platforms (and the capital behind them) function to monitor, aggregate, and filter the produced norms, values, and cultural symbols for profit and to satisfy state power. This is crucial for pop hegemony: Fierce digital market competition fosters consent negotiation by creating winning ideations that are bound to be well-received and influential, which by definition would facilitate wide acceptance.[64]

Third, social actors—writers and readers of internet literature in this case—are the main contributors to pop hegemony as the actual producers and consumers of the norms, values, and cultural symbols. The fact that they are subject to state intervention and market dynamics does not mean that they play only a passive and receptive role. Chinese netizens are known for their creativity and effort to evade and challenge state control and manipulation, as well as for their agency and ability to condition and shape market dynamics. In the realm of internet literature, writers, as the primary producers, decide what is available on the market (within the state-sanctioned scope), and readers act as prosumers, who actively engage in the production of digital experiences (see chapter 5). In addition, through activities like clicking, voting, and commenting, they also help sort out and reinforce the more popular, salient, and conforming set of cultural norms, values, and symbols.

In sum, although they may pursue different goals in the commodified political field, through digitally mediated mass production and consumption of the cultural experiences of the internet literature, the Chinese party-state, market, and citizens together produce, contest, and ultimately agree on a set of values, norms, and cultural symbols that the state approves, the market sells, and the citizenry readily embraces. In this process, political socialization takes place and social consent about the accepted form of politics is negotiated, which may ultimately contribute to pop hegemony, under which given the active popular participation in the consent negotiation, authoritarian rule is neither Orwellian, nor Huxleyan, but a mixture of both. That said, because it is still in the making, the societal agency legitimizing and reinforcing authoritarian rule can also subvert or convert it in the future.

DATA AND METHODS

This project has been an academic and methodological challenge for multiple reasons. First, because of the COVID-19 pandemic, my initial plan to conduct fieldwork and interview platform personnel, writers, and readers had to be postponed again and again, until I realized that, with some adaptation, the project could be done based exclusively on online sources. I even decided not to conduct remote interviews. Because my primary purpose is to study digital consumerist experiences and ideational contestation, what people think in their mind (the type of data to gather through interviews) is much less relevant than what they have expressed and done (which could be observed online). Although this is not ideal—for instance, it would be useful to hear what writers and readers think about state intervention—the project is not hurt as much as I feared. In addition, remote interviews can be tricky in that the digital traces they leave behind may cause concern for interviewees given the somewhat sensitive nature of the project.

Second, the numerous titles, and the many platforms these titles appear on, have made it virtually impossible to identify the population of the study. Therefore, I have combined online guerilla and in-depth ethnography with more focused content analysis of works and reader comments of a selected sample.[65] The most important data sources include influential literature portals like Qidian (qidian.com), reading apps such as WeChat Reading, and literature forums and commenting platforms, such as Dragon's Sky (lkong.com) and Yousuu (yousuu.com, now expired). In addition, I observed online forums like Tianya (tianya.cn, now expired) and NewSmth (newsmth.net). They not only have dedicated literature boards but also allow me to observe how far and deep internet literature penetrates everyday online life. The ethnographic sites also include popular social media sites, such as Baidu Tieba, Zhihu, and Douban, where readers and writers share their experiences and views.

In addition to digital ethnography, I relied on content analysis of selected works and reader comments. I personally read through more than seventy MCGA and dozens of non-MCGA titles. This process was extremely time-consuming. The average word count of the 238 MCGA titles that I identified was 2.88 million characters, roughly equal to the Chinese version of the entire *Harry Potter* series. Yet doing so was highly rewarding. It allowed me to gain firsthand experience by immersing myself into these fictional worlds as a reader and to develop a map to code and analyze MCGA works as a researcher (see chapter 4). To examine how readers engage the works, I then analyzed user comments on MCGA and non-MCGA titles, using computer-aided techniques and manual close reading of the text (see chapter 5).

A PREVIEW OF WHAT FOLLOWS

This book has six more chapters. In chapter 1, I examine the rise of internet literature as a digital cultural consumerist phenomenon in China. After introducing its evolution from primarily a hobby to a booming entertainment industry, I explain how internet literature has become a commodified political field that is contested and shaped by the state, writers, readers, and market forces. Such multiple-actor interactions in the complex online environment, I argue, function as a consent negotiation process that may contribute to the rise of pop hegemony.

In chapter 2, I examine how the Chinese party-state has intervened in the production, circulation, and consumption of internet literature using a combined strategy of censorship, co-optation, and promotion. In doing so, the regime acts as a coproducer by setting the bottom line and preparing the ground for platforms, writers, and readers to negotiate the consent.

In chapters 3, 4, and 5, I zoom in on the specific genre of MCGA fiction and the implications for authoritarian legitimation and consent negotiation. In chapter 3, I introduce the plethora of titles that describe, interpret, and change history to save China from crises or glorify the nation. This shared MCGA theme, I argue, represents the collective ethos in the era of China's rise and echoes well the state ideology of the Chinese dream. The production and consumption of these works, therefore, embody the convergence of societal and state ideations and narratives, showing the prospect of pop hegemony.

In chapter 4, I continue the discussion by systematically investigating the reforms MCGA fiction have proposed for national revival, as well as the personal desires they pursue. I show these works present different Chinese dreams that may deviate from official ideology. Rather than truly threatening the regime, however, they represent more a form of "constructive destruction" by (1) enabling popular participation in consent construction; (2) validating, enriching, and popularizing state norms, values, and beliefs; (3) promoting pro–status quo tendencies; and (4) sidelining and weakening more critical cultural elites.

In chapter 5, I shift focus to the readers and explore how they serve as the driving force of internet literature and the pan-entertainment industries as consumers while engaging in the coproduction of digital experiences. I show how their active role and influence in the cultural ideational realm, mediated and empowered by attention economy logic, can both work to the advantage of and challenge the state, thus bearing intriguing implications for the negotiation of pop hegemony.

In the conclusion, I emphasize again how contemporary Chinese connect the history, present, and future of the nation through MCGA fiction and how they have together revealed a popular political vision based on which pop hegemony may emerge. The social origin of pop hegemony projects a potential path of China becoming a *Brave New World* of *1984* that combines amusement to death and total surveillance. I then further situate China within broader trends by linking MCGA to MAGA and global populism and by discussing the implications of China's pop hegemony for the world.

Chapter One

INTERNET LITERATURE IN CHINA

A Commodified Political Field

In 1999, as a college freshman, I read *The First Intimate Contact* (*Diyici de Qinmi Jiechu* 第一次的亲密接触) by Tsai Jhi-hsin 蔡智恆 during a class on the *Introduction to Mao Zedong Thought*. I thoroughly enjoyed the fiction, which tells the story of a young man finding his love through the internet but ultimately losing her to a fatal disease. I did not realize that this was my first experience with internet literature—the novel was originally released in installments posted on a bulletin board system before being published in print. I certainly did not foresee myself writing a book on the politics of internet literature in China one day.

Scholars studying authoritarian cyberpolitics often adopt a digital contention perspective, focusing on how digital technologies have empowered social actors to express discontent, to mobilize online and offline, and to challenge authoritarian rule, as well as how autocratic states may control and manipulate information and conduct digital repression.[1] Although such a perspective produces much insight, it implies a narrow binary framework of state control versus social resistance and limits the scope of scholarly explorations to certain issues, platforms, and activities, thus underappreciating the richness, complexity, and dynamic nature of digital experiences, such as internet literature, as well as their subsequent sociopolitical implications.[2] In particular, because politics often takes the form of cultural consumerist experiences, which have long served as vehicles for social dissent and mobilization, as well as a means of state control, cooptation, and indoctrination, it would be a mistake to overlook this realm when studying politics in any society, not in the least China.

In this book, I shift the focus to internet literature, which has so far been understudied by political scientists. Borrowing from Guobin Yang's multi-interactionism framework and the conception of "field" from Pierre Bourdieu, I treat internet literature as a digitally mediated commodified political field in which involved actors—the state, market forces, writers, and readers—coproduce the digital experiences while contesting and negotiating China's ideational governance, a process through which "pop hegemony" is being incubated.[3]

Indeed, as a popular digital cultural consumerist phenomenon, internet literature can be studied as both a commodified field and a political field. It is a commodified field because it has evolved from a literary hobby and a form of personal expression into a cultural consumerist industry occupying the upper stream of China's burgeoning panentertainment industries, subjecting involved actors (primarily writers, readers, and platforms) to market rules of supply and demand, competition, and attention economy. The state, although not absent in this commodified field, plays largely a regulatory role. But internet literature is also a political field, deeply embedded in China's sociopolitical structure, because literature is ultimately still a form of expression. Expression, no matter what form it takes, is inherently political, and the Chinese state is known for its strong capacity and will to control and manipulate it. Therefore, despite being commodified, internet literature features a nonstop political process of the state, market forces, and social actors (writers and readers) negotiating expression and digital experiences. The overlap and interaction between the two fields have rendered a commodified political field, which I believe can serve as a useful framework to investigate internet literature as a digital cultural consumerist phenomenon through which the state, digital platforms, market, and citizens engage in power and ideational negotiation and contestation in China.

In the sections that follow, I will first briefly introduce the history of internet literature in China and then discuss how internet literature functions as a commodified political field that is contested and shaped by the interests, motives, capacities, and strategies of the state, writers, and readers, as well as market forces and digital platforms. In doing so, I aim to clarify why it is both necessary and rewarding to study everyday digital cultural experiences despite appearing consumerist, quotidian, and seemingly nonpolitical.

INTERNET LITERATURE IN CHINA: FROM IDYLLIC DAYS TO HYPERCOMMERCIALIZATION

According to Michel Hockx, Chinese internet literature, either "in established literary genres or in innovative literary forms," is "written especially for publication in an interactive online context and meant to be read on screen."[4] Similarly, Guobin Yang defines internet literature as "all Web-based writings that are viewed as literature by their authors or readers."[5] Both definitions suggest that unlike electronic literature in the West, internet literature in China is less about innovation in writing styles or techniques and more about how these literary works are produced, delivered, and consumed through digital media.[6]

Regardless of the definition, internet literature has become a highly popular form of digital cultural experiences in China. According to China Internet Network Information Center (CNNIC), as of June 2023, 528.25 million (49%) of China's 1.08 billion internet users were consumers of online literature.[7] A 2019 report by CNNIC shows that internet literature apps account for about 9 percent of Chinese mobile internet users' online time, ranking only after instant messaging (14.5%), video streaming (13.4%), short video services (11.5%), and online music (10.7%).[8] Figure 1.1 captures changes in the user base and penetration rate of internet literature since 2013, confirming its significance in Chinese digital life.

Before diving into the discussion of its political relevance, however, it is necessary to briefly trace how internet literature has evolved from largely a literary hobby and means of personal expression into a hypercommercialized industry.

The Idyllic Days of Internet Literature

Internet literature took root in China almost as early as the internet itself, with Chinese netizens turning to the brave new world of cyberspace to share literary works ranging from classics to their own writings. In addition to overseas platforms, such as *China News Digest* (cnd.org, Huaxia Wenzhai

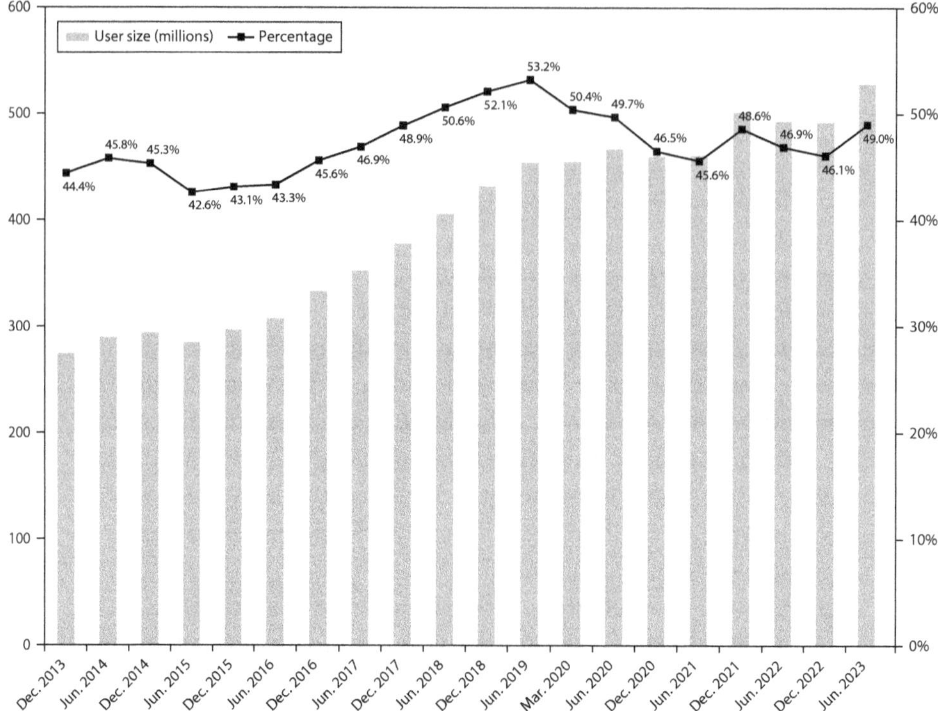

FIGURE 1.1. Internet literature user base and penetration rate. (*Source:* Data from CNNIC Statistical Reports on the Internet Development in China, https://www.cnnic.cn/index.html.)

华夏文摘, US-based e-magazine founded in 1991) and *New Threads* (xys.org, Xin Yusi 新语丝, a US-based site founded in 1994), which publish original literary works by Chinese across the globe, early bulletin board system (BBS) forums that popped up in China from 1994 onward almost all featured thematic boards for users to create, share, and discuss poems, prose, novels, and other literary writings.[9] For instance, among the very first group of discussion boards set up on SMTH, one of China's earliest and most popular university BBS forums, were Literature, Poetry, Reader, and StoneStory (Honglou Meng 红楼梦, a board dedicated to the Chinese classic fiction *Dream of the Red Chamber*). Other influential BBS forums like BDWM and YTHT also featured similar literature boards. Meanwhile, university literature associations, such as Peking University's We Club, learned to take advantage of the internet, setting up websites or discussion boards on campus forums to boost interaction among members and to reach a wider audience.[10]

Internet literature flourished when portal websites such as Sina.com expanded in the realm and when commercialized forums like Tianya (tianya.cn) became popular in the early 2000s. In January 1999, Sina.com and *China Business Times* launched a writing relay together, inviting netizens and readers to complete a novel started by a few young writers.[11] In the same year, another portal website, Netease (163.com), hosted an internet literature contest with well-known professional writers Wang Meng 王蒙, Liu Xinwu 刘心武, and Mo Yan 莫言 as the referees. Although observers debated the motives and influence, such contests revealed online portals' attempt to ride the popularity of internet literature for traffic.[12] And their involvement undoubtedly also contributed to the development of internet literature.

Tianya, founded in 1999 and once China's largest and most vibrant online community, was another important incubator for Chinese original internet literature. Inspired by the popular online romance *The First Intimate Contact* mentioned at the beginning of the chapter,[13] Hao Qun 郝群 (aka 慕容雪村 Murong Xuecun) published his famous *Leave Me Alone: A Novel of Chengdu* (*Chengdu, Jinye Qing Jiang Wo Yiwang* 成都，今夜请将我遗忘) on Tianya in 2002 and two other online communities.[14] The novel went instantly viral with millions of reads and was soon published by the print press, which was widely interpreted as a sign of being recognized as a serious professional writer.[15]

With the expansion of the internet in China, specialized literature sites began to emerge, with one of the earliest being *Under the Banyan Tree* (*Rongshu Xia* 榕树下, *UBT* hereafter).[16] *UBT* was launched in December 1997 by Chinese American entrepreneur and literary enthusiast William Zhu as a personal website to share his writings. It then began accepting public submissions via email and was soon corporatized as it grew exponentially. The platform attracted many literary enthusiasts, including future big names, such as Li Jie 励婕 (aka Annie Baby 安妮宝贝), Chen Wanning 陈万宁 (aka Ning Caishen 宁财神), and Lu Jinbo 路金波. *UBT* later extended its influence to traditional literature circles. It hired established author Chen Cun 陈村 as its chief artistic officer in 1999, serving until 2002, who invited well-known writers like Wang Anyi 王安忆, Jia Pingwa 贾平凹, and Yu Hua 余华 to serve on the referee team of its First

Original Internet Literature Contest. During its peak in 2005, the platform boasted 4.5 million registered users and more than five thousand daily submissions.[17]

The case of *UBT* is of particular interest, because besides being the most influential literature portal around the year 2000, it also embodied the transformation of Chinese internet literature from the idyllic days of literary enthusiasm and personal expression to the age of commodification and profit-seeking. William Zhu started the portal out of passion rather than commercial interests. As he recalled, "At that time, the entire society was about extravagant feasting and revelry, luxury and dissipation. People had particularly strong desires to make money. . . . But we still need to save a little room for spiritual aspirations."[18] Moreover, internet literature was taken as an opportunity to express oneself, free from state censorship and other socioeconomic constraints. For Zhu, "mass literature" online could bypass the censorship of publishers and print media editors.[19] As one of the earliest online writers Xing Yusen 邢育森 put it, "Before I got online, much in me was suppressed by my social roles and the mundane daily life. It was the internet and communications online that enabled me to feel and ultimately unleash something about myself that is pure, and to become my style of life."[20]

This notion of internet literature as a form of expression was well in line with that of early netizens who wrote, shared, and read literary works in online communities like SMTH or Tianya. Making money was not their drive. Rather, inspired by successful examples like *Leave Me Alone*, many literary enthusiasts viewed sharing works online as a shortcut to building reputation, which might then attract traditional publishers to help realize the "literature dream" of becoming a professional writer. Meanwhile, at this stage, platforms like university forums and personal websites devoted to hobbies were not profit-driven. Even *UBT*, which was corporatized, functioned more like a literature community because it had yet to figure out a feasible business model. The platforms had limited options, and the obstacles were multiple. Besides selling ads on their webpages, early literature platforms such as *UBT* primarily relied on cashing works that they managed to publish with traditional presses. This did not work well because only a small number of online works could get published in print; and even those largely did not sell well. As a result of the limited internet penetration rate, online writers were often not known offline, and readers of print literary works were generally picky.[21] *UBT* also tried to sell e-books, but failed as no reliable online payment system existed yet, and netizens were unwilling to pay for something readily available for free online.[22]

The community environment that these early platforms provided enhanced authors' and readers' experience and facilitated the growth of the market, which in turn created new business opportunities, ultimately leading to the successful commercialization of Chinese internet literature.[23] This tension, however, between literary enthusiasm and commercialization remains. Many literature platforms, such as Literature or Poetry boards on BBS forums, still primarily cater to netizens' expressive and literature needs, with little intention or capacity to capitalize. As one Tianya user commented, "Tianya Literature still maintains its original literary qualities. At a time when fantasies, time-traveling, romance, and other genres dominate, Tianya Literature forum continues serving as a platform for new and old-style poems, couplets, prose, book discussion, etc."[24] This probably explains why, despite the commercialization trend, Tianya, before it ultimately went out of business, was able to attract talented writers and produce popular works, such as *The Story of the Ming Dynasty* (*Mingchao Naxie Shier* 明朝那些事儿).

Note that this early stage of internet literature has important cross-border components, especially from the United States and Taiwan, where digital technologies developed earlier than in Mainland China. Even after Mainland-based platforms such as SMTH were set up, they initially relied on transposting original works from overseas and Taiwanese platforms. Taiwanese writers and platforms also served as examples for commercialization, including *The First Intimate Contact* mentioned earlier, which mapped the model of gaining online fame first to get published in print and to be adapted further for television and film.

From Commercialization to Hypercommercialization

In the early 2000s, many literature portals emerged, among which were Qidian (then cmfu.com, i.e., Chinese Magic Fantasy Union; from 2008 onward, the domain name has been qidian.com), Huanjian Shumeng (hjsm.net), and Dragon Sky (lkong.net). Largely because of its successful new business model, Qidian came to lead the pack. First introduced in August 2003, the portal separated works into free and VIP categories. To access the VIP content, readers, after an initial free trial period, would pay a small fee, which would be directly shared between the platform and its writers.[25] This model frees internet literature from the traditional publishing industry and its dependence on online advertising.[26] Other literature portals quickly followed suit. As writing became potentially lucrative for platforms and writers, internet literature found a way to achieve successful commercialization and was ready for explosive growth.[27]

The commercialization of internet literature continued and deepened. In 2004, Qidian was acquired by Shanda Interactive Entertainment, a Nasdaq-listed online gaming company, which annexed two other literature portals, Hongxiu (hongxiu.com) and Jinjiang Literature City (jjwxc.com), in 2008 to form Shanda Literature.[28] This signified a wave of hypercommercialization, characterized by capital operations and digital panentertainment expansion. Through a series of moves, Shanda nearly built up a monopoly with a reported market share of more than 90 percent during its heyday.[29] In 2015, information technology (IT) giant Tencent acquired Shanda Literature, merging it with its own Tencent Literature to create China Literature (aka Yuewen) as part of its panentertainment strategy.[30] Tencent was not the only tech giant turning to internet literature and the burgeoning panentertainment industries. The NASDAQ-listed search engine company Baidu acquired Zongheng (zongheng.com) to establish Baidu Literature in 2013.[31] In April 2015, Ali Literature (aliwx.com.cn) was formed as part of Alibaba's Mobile Business Group, an apparent effort to take a bite of the expanding market of mobile internet.

Under this panentertainment strategy, internet literature grew far beyond just a booming publication business with millions of writers updating their works daily and even more readers following the updates.[32] It thus became a phenomenon of transmedia storytelling and the upstream industry of other cultural entertainment industries, as successful works have been further adapted to film, television, games, and comics.[33] Intellectual property (IP) transactions, other than the paid reading fee, soon became the major revenue source for portals like Qidian, the IT giants behind them, and popular writers. Reportedly, internet literature is the most important contributing source of China's original cultural IP works. Of the 309 most popular television dramas and films in 2018 and 2019, 21 percent were adapted from internet literature works (primarily online fiction); among the top one hundred, the portion is as high as 42 percent.[34] Thanks to the panentertainment trend, successful writers now earn millions of yuan a year from royalties and IP transactions, as well as fees and tips from readers. For example, Zhang Wei (pen name *Tangjia Sanshao* 唐家三少) earned 110 million yuan in 2015.[35] Although most of these online writers earn much less, stories like Zhang's are nevertheless inspirational.

Moreover, internet literature by Chinese writers has grown beyond the Chinese market and has gained an international audience. According to Jianwei Zheng, as of August 2017, at least fifty-eight websites based in the United States, Germany, Netherlands, India, and Canada were dedicated to the translation and distribution of Chinese internet novels for foreign readers—the top ten translating sites alone have translated at least 364 novels.[36] And these ten sites, along with a few major distributing platforms, attracted about four million readers and two hundred million views around the globe as of July 2017.

INTERNET LITERATURE AS A COMMODIFIED POLITICAL FIELD

The previous section traced how internet literature evolved from a literary hobby to a hypercommercialized digital industry, with a focus on the platforms. As Guobin Yang insightfully puts it, multidimensional interaction is "an increasingly important condition of social dynamics in the age of information and globalization" as online experiences often involve "multiple parties, and the influences go in multiple directions."[37] Therefore, I adopted a multidimensional interactionist analytical framework to effectively capture the complex dynamics between cultural and consumerist needs of the writers and readers and the business logics of platforms and writers, as well as the political motives of the state.

In addition, to examine how these multidimensional interactions take place, I propose to see internet literature as a commodified political field that hosts such interactions. Originally a concept from the natural sciences, the term *field* has been widely applied by social scientists to study human society, among which the conceptualization by sociologist Pierre Bourdieu is perhaps the most influential. To Bourdieu, a society is composed of a variety of fields, and a field refers to "a network, or a configuration, of objective relations between positions objectively defined, in their existence and in the determinations they impose upon their occupants, agents or institutions, by their present and potential situation (*situs*) in the structure of the distribution of species of power (or capital) whose possession commands access to the specific profits that are at stake in the field, as well as by their objective relation to other positions (domination, subordination, homology, etc.)."[38]

Put more simply, "field" is a defined realm in which actors compete for valuable resources (e.g., status, power) and contest positions and power relations. Fields can overlap and interact with each other, and their relations can be hierarchical, with one nestled in the other, especially the large field of power and class relations.[39] Field theorists use the term in several interrelated senses: Some treat field as an analytical area, others see it as an organization of forces, and still others define it as a battlefield for contestation.[40] The richness and expandability of the concept make "field" a particularly useful theoretical lens to study cultural production.

Bourdieu also explains the necessary steps in field analysis, arguing that it is crucial to analyze (1) the position of the field in relation to the field of power, (2) the objective relational structure between the positions of the agents, and (3) agents' habitus (i.e., "the system of dispositions they have acquired").[41] I follow these guidelines and show how internet literature is both a commodified field of cultural consumerism and a political field of expression and ideational contestation, and thus ultimately a commodified political field. Specifically, commercialization has transformed the production, distribution, and consumption of internet literature, rendering it a commodified field in which the agents—the state, platforms, writers, and readers—occupy different positions and negotiate their relations largely following market logics. Yet, this commodified field is embedded in, and subordinates to, the field of power, in which the state occupies the dominant position. In this political field, while constrained by the technological, market, and social forces in one way or the other, the state sets the basic rules of the game for other main agents. As the commodified and power fields overlap and interact, a commodified political field emerges, with both commercial and political dynamics that position involved actors and condition their behavior within different incentive structures (see figure 1.2).[42]

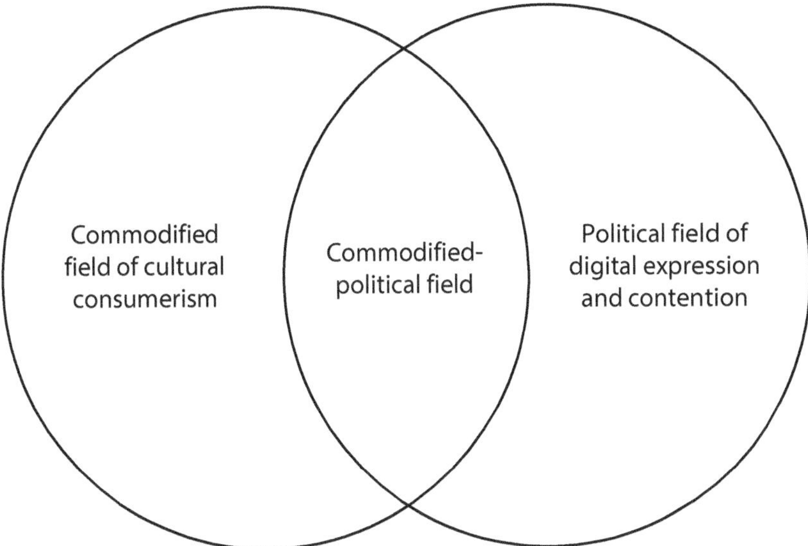

FIGURE 1.2. Illustration of commodified political field.

The Commodified Nature of Internet Literature

The commodified nature of the internet literature field prescribes that the positions of agents and their relations are primarily conditioned by market mechanisms of competition (between platforms and between writers) and supply and demand (between writers and readers, writers and platforms, and platforms and readers). The resources that agents pursue are capital (by platforms and writers), fame (by writers, maybe secondary), and cultural consumerist experiences (by readers), all mediated digitally. The currency that motivates actors in this commodified field, however, is "attention" and the interactions among agents are largely defined by the rules of the "attention economy," with platforms and writers trying to attract and capitalize on readers' attention, while readers channel their attention into shopping and voting for platforms and writers.[43]

Market, especially attention economy dynamics, have significantly shaped the production and consumption of internet literature. It is not a coincidence that long genre fiction published in installments has dominated the industry.[44] The pay-to-read model means that both platforms and writers directly benefit more from long novels than from any other literary form, and publishing daily in installments can effectively glue readers' attention. In addition, genre fiction is also friendly for adaptation to comics, television, film, and games, thus allowing platforms and writers to capitalize the attention of a broader audience in more ways and across a longer time span. As a result, despite reader complaints about writers (and platforms) prioritizing quantity over quality, literature portals like Qidian are still full of various genres of fiction with hundreds, even thousands of chapters.

In addition, a plethora of genres has flourished, catering to the pluralized taste of readers and panentertainment consumers. Table 1.1 lists the genres available on Qidian and the counts of complete titles with two million characters or more for each genre.[45] I do not use statistics displayed on the portal's homepage, because they do not seem to be up to date; and the two-million-character threshold is set to obtain the complete data for a sample (Qidian only shows up to one thousand titles for each search; if a genre has more one thousand titles, we will not know the actual number; data for mythical and reality fiction genres, which exceeded this limit, are obtained by adding their subgenres). The top genres, such as male-oriented mythical fantasies and urban fiction, as well as female-oriented ancient and contemporary romance, are not only relatively safe from state control (as will be discussed below) but also best fit in the panentertainment ecology, because they are easily adaptable to other entertainment formats. Mythical fantasies, for instance, are among the most popular IP sources for digital games, since they are often written following the role-playing game logic: The hero starts from a humble background and makes his way up; in the process, the hero overcomes many obstacles, each of which can be a game scenario for the hero (or the player in the game) to fulfill tasks or fight the evil boss. In fact, mythical fantasies are often inspired by these games. Such reciprocity also exists at the consumption end, as the popularity of the novel can feed into the reception of the derivative game (and panentertainment products in general) and vice versa.

Table 1.1 reveals how gender mediates the production and consumption of internet literature. Qidian directs readers to gender-specific content with separate male and female channels. In fact, some literature portals such as Jinjiang Literature City (jjwxc.net) cater primarily to female readers.[46] Writers also show a gender preference for specific genres. According

TABLE 1.1
Genres on Qidian

	Genres	No. of Titles	Percentage (%)
Male-oriented works	玄幻 (Mythical fantasy)	1,512	19.99
	奇幻 (Epic fantasy)	271	3.58
	武侠 (Martial arts fiction)	131	1.73
	仙侠 (Fairy-epic fiction)	767	10.14
	都市 (Urban fiction)	1,654	21.87
	现实 (Reality fiction)	41	0.54
	军事 (Military affairs)	109	1.44
	历史 (History)	929	12.29
	游戏 (Gaming fiction)	506	6.69
	体育 (Sports fiction)	189	2.5
	科幻 (Sci-fi)	364	4.81
	诸天无限 (Supernatural fiction)	419	5.54
	悬疑 (Suspense)	132	1.75
	轻小说 (Light fiction)	538	7.11
	Subtotal	**7,562**	**100**
Female-oriented works	古代言情 (Ancient romance)	837	40.24
	仙侠奇缘 (Fairy-epic romance)	93	4.47
	现代言情 (Contemporary romance)	831	39.95
	浪漫青春 (Romantic youth)	15	0.72
	玄幻言情 (Fantasy romance)	147	7.07
	悬疑推理 (Suspense mystery)	27	1.3
	科幻空间 (Sci-fi)	108	5.19
	游戏竞技 (Game and competition)	14	0.67
	轻小说 (Light fiction)	6	0.29
	现实生活 (Reality and life)	2	0.1
	Subtotal	**2,080**	**100**

Source: Completed titles from Qidian with two million characters or longer, qidian.com (as of April 22, 2025).

to a 2016 survey, nearly 24 percent of male writers prefer writing history/military genres while only 2.3 percent of female writers select this option.[47] Meanwhile, about 67 percent and 60 percent of female writers favor ancient and contemporary romance, respectively, while less than 4 percent of male writers have a preference of these two genres.[48] The survey results confirm what table 1.1 shows: The female channel is dominated by romance genres, whereas the male channel appears to be more diverse, with historical fiction being the third most popular genre. Although it is not the focus of this book, it is important to acknowledge the gender factor. In fact, Make China Great Again alt-history titles, which often involve traveling back in time to save or glorify China (discussed in chapters 3–5), are often written by male writers and attract male readers; time-traveling titles produced by female writers for female readers typically fit the romance genre and rarely attempt to change history.

In this commodified field, the behavior of, as well as the relations between platforms, writers, and readers, are shaped by market competition. Given the nature of digital media, this often boils down to the competition for readers' screen time. Attention is the currency. Such competition takes place between different platforms, and a larger market share means more profit. The success of Tencent in the panentertainment industry testifies to this reasoning.[49] Writers also compete to attract and maintain a reader base, as well as host resources, such as platform promotion opportunities, which include access to the homepage of the portal or many of the ranking lists that channel readers to their works.

The rules of the attention economy and the competition between platforms give popular writers some extra leverage, enabling them to negotiate with the platforms for resources and better contracts, including securing a relatively fair share of IP transaction profits. An exodus of popular writers (typically called gods or *dashen* 大神) can cause a problem even for dominating platforms like Qidian, as these writers could take their readers to competing platforms. Compared with writers, however, platforms overall are in a much stronger bargaining position: They can manipulate attention by directing users to selected works—not to mention that writers are typically locked in a disadvantaged contractual situation, because they can hardly foresee their success when signing the contract.

Predictably, conflicts arise between writers and platforms. In 2020, Yuewen, the owner of Qidian, attempted to revise their contract with writers and caused popular resentment. The new contract prescribed that Yuewen would own all translated, adapted, and other derivative products the platform develops based on the writers' original works. Moreover, should a contracted title fail to meet Yuewen's publishing requirements, the platform could take over and continue its production with exclusive copyrights.[50] The platform also reportedly tried to do away with the pay-to-read model, as a response to the fierce competition of other fee-free platforms, including pirate sites that generate revenue via online ads, and to overcome the quantity-over-quality incentive problem.[51] Many writers complained that such a change could affect their income.[52]

The production and consumption of internet literature can, of course, be understood as a process of supply and demand, with writers and platforms more on the supply side and readers on the demand side. Again, the rules of the attention economy apply. For platforms, this means competing to attract and retain popular writers and trying to improve the experiences of readers. For writers, popularity affects their income in many ways—the pay-to-read fee (or online ad revenue that also depends on user traffic), potential for IP transactions, and tips from avid readers. Thus, writers are motivated to win over and keep readers. For instance, because frequent updates help retain readers, many writers today publish at least five thousand characters daily, with more diligent authors doubling or even tripling that number.[53] This competition among writers has turned writing into intensive labor and offers extra incentive for writers to sacrifice quality for quantity. Moreover, many have criticized online genre fiction for becoming "fast food" purely to entertain and please readers, just like the popcorn movies or pulp magazine writing of the early twentieth-century United States, depriving readers of fiction's literary, intellectual, and aesthetic values.[54]

Writers (and platforms) have deployed other means to glue readers. One way is to increase writer-reader interaction. Online writing by definition will be influenced more directly by readers, especially for writers who are based in virtual communities, as digital platforms typically have built-in functions to facilitate user interactions.[55] In addition to engaging readers in comments sections, another common approach for writers is to address readers at the beginning or end of their daily installments, expressing gratitude (especially to loyal followers and generous tippers), soliciting support (such as votes that will decide the ranking), addressing complaints (e.g., why they fail to update regularly or why the plots develop in certain ways), or simply sharing their thoughts or life experiences. For instance, the author of the popular alt-history fiction *My Heroic Husband* 赘婿, often writes extended (a few thousand characters) essays sharing his views on public affairs, as well as reflections on writing in response to user comments. Therefore, increased writer-reader interaction is not purely a means for writers to profit from readers.[56] Instead, reading and writing have become interactive, adaptive, and improvisational, as well as hyperintimate and personalized, with opportunities for readers' inputs, comments, and other forms of "value-enhancing labor," which in turn transform readers into prosumers of digital experiences (see chapter 5).[57]

The Politics of Internet Literature

As explained in the introduction, cultural consumerist experiences, digital or not, are inherently political because they not only serve as vehicles of social mobilization and resistance but also facilitate state control, co-optation, and indoctrination. In addition, their production, distribution, and consumption are embedded in, reflect, and are politicized by their sociopolitical setting, especially an authoritarian one. In particular, scholars have shown the Chinese state to be intertwined with the market in the information and communication technology (ICT) sector.[58] Therefore, although internet literature demonstrates features as a commodified field, it is also a political field, and in this field of power, the state has attempted to subjugate all other agents with its massive capacity and resources. However, platforms, writers, and readers, while having to comply with the ground rules the state sets, are not passive subjects. They instead actively negotiate and contest state dominance.

First, by allowing writers, estimated to be more than twenty million as of 2021, to publish, and many more readers to read and comment, internet literature provides Chinese citizens with an alternative approach to realize their literary dream, and more important to express themselves, which is politically significant.[59] Given its expressive nature, internet literature features discursive struggles and ideational contestation, which are not simply about state-society confrontation but also include the broader rivalry and competition of different voices from within society.

Indeed, internet literature works often convey writers' (and readers') ideas, values, and beliefs about the nation, the state, and politics, whether directly or indirectly. Many works, like fiction belonging to the history and military genres, are straight-out political. Even seemingly nonpolitical or less political works can include political elements in one way or another. Take the martial arts genre. Although such novels concern the nonstate realm of "rivers and lakes" (*jianghu* 江湖), they often touch on political topics. As the prominent martial arts novelist Jin Yong 金庸 wrote in *The Return of the Condor Heroes*, "those for the nation and the people are the greatest heroes" (*weiguo weimin, xiazhi dazhe* 为国为民，侠之大者). With such a view of the hero, Jin's works are instantly politicized, inspiring discussions on Chinese history, national identity, and state-society relations.[60]

In cases in which writers (and readers) intentionally shy away from being overtly political, the works, besides implications such as "amusement to death" and helping map the boundaries of politics in everyday experiences (by indicating where politics is absent), may unexpectedly become political, should they transgress moral, aesthetic, or other implicit boundaries that the state patrols. China scholars have long ago learned that the Chinese party-state takes on moral and aesthetic obligations and attempts to shape cultural production by, for example, banning erotic and certain political content.[61] State intervention, politically driven or not, politicizes writing and reading, especially when writers and readers do not see how they have crossed the red line between permissible and nonpermissible zones.

Moreover, the specific production-consumption mode of internet literature bears political significance that is currently understudied. In particular, the chapter-by-chapter writing and reading style, as well as digitally enabled writer-reader interactions, have made internet literature a form of long-term, stable, and focused interactive experiences. This has allowed readers and writers to exchange ideas, values, and beliefs in a systematic, in-depth, and often instantaneous way that can hardly be found in traditional literature or other types of digital experiences.

In short, although internet literature is driven more by market dynamics, it is political in nature. Although it is qualitatively different from online discursive activism relating to official scandals, protests, and other forms of dissent, internet literature as a form of digital consumerist experiences has similarly developed outside of the existing "ideological state apparatuses" and has upset them.[62] The state is evidently aware of the challenge and has adjusted: Unlike traditional publishing, when state control is primarily enforced ex ante at the publication stage, the state now closely monitors and intervenes in the whole process through which internet literature is produced, distributed, and consumed, as it does with other forms of online expression. Because of the fusion of politics and cultural consumerist experiences and the fact that the former is often buried and blurred into the latter, the state reveals more of its time- and place-sensitive control capacity to intervene the writing and reading process constantly on a variety of platforms and scenarios, as will be discussed in the next chapter. The bottom line is that staying away from the state's taboo zone has become the prerequisite for writers, platforms, and readers to have such digital experiences in the first place.

Although the state sets the red line and can incentivize market and social actors to behave, its influence shall not be overestimated. Despite its strong capacity and rich resources, the state does not enforce content control all by itself. Rather, it relies on intermediary actors such as literature portals to intervene in the production and consumption of internet literature works, which gives platforms, writers, and readers some room to maneuver. Moreover, state control is often effective in setting the boundaries, but it can hardly prescribe the forms and content of online experiences. Ultimately, it is the writers, readers, and platforms that together make sharing, commenting, and "transmedia storytelling" possible.[63] Despite the state's influence, these actors are pursuing their literary dreams, fame, entertainment, and leisure purposes, as well as economic interests, that the state often cannot provide. Their agency, in addition to market and technological dynamics, explains why internet literature as a political field is highly contested, even given the state's tight control and active manipulation, and why the ideational contestation happens not just between the state and society but also among and within various groups of writers and readers.

The power relations in the field of internet literature are mediated by the market and by digital media dynamics. The fact that writers' income is directly tied to market success conditions their choices of topics and writing strategies, leading them to adopt genres that appeal to the market and shy away from genres subject to tighter state control. This, however, does not mean that writers do not touch on politically risky genres. On the one hand, individual writers' motives and strengths matter. Some are especially interested in and better at writing certain genres than others, not to mention that some write to express themselves. On the other hand, market incentives are sometimes in conflict with the state's preferences. The rules of attention economy mean that if readers have an appetite for certain genres, writers will produce them, even though it may have to be done in a careful way to avoid state penalties. For this reason, erotic fiction has persisted, and soft erotic elements can still be easily found in many writings even though the state repeatedly censors such content.

Notably, market dynamics and the agency of nonstate actors can also buttress and legitimize state domination. On the one hand, the mass social and market participation of cultural politics serves the state by diluting the influence of China's more critical, traditional elite intellectuals, a group represented by writers who "enjoyed a unique moral aura in the 1980s."[64]

Although its influence has declined since the 1990s, this group has been a constant source of regime challengers and critics. On the other hand, the expressive and ideational contestation in the internet literature field may contribute to "pop hegemony" by enabling a more covert, penetrating, pervasive, and much more effective mechanism of authoritarian legitimation by being popularly constituted and negotiated (as I will discuss further). In other words, the commodified production, distribution, and consumption of literary works online not only cover and sugarcoat state dominance but also generate voluminous content and experiences that socialize citizens to accept, embrace, and even actively champion authoritarian rule.

According to Gramsci, the notion of hegemony differs from dominance in that it relies not on coercive force.[65] Seeing internet literature as a digitally mediated commodified political field that features both market dynamics and power logics reveals how social consent can be popularly constructed and negotiated. This perspective suggests that although the authoritarian state prescribes the permissible boundaries of what is acceptable and what is not, it also makes a compromise, maybe involuntarily, by allowing citizens and the market to participate in creating digital experiences and the making of norms, values, and beliefs. In other words, the state meets the market and society in the middle and negotiates with them to reach a shared understanding, if not consensus, which might accommodate, normalize, and ultimately legitimize authoritarian rule even as it differs from the state's original ideological constructs.

CONCLUSION

In this chapter, I traced the evolution of internet literature in China from a literary hobby and exercise in personal expression to a hypercommercialized digital industry. Such cultural consumerist experiences have formed a commodified political field for multiple actors, including the state, market actors such as various literature platforms, and citizen groups like writers and readers, to interact with each other on multiple dimensions following a complex set of market, societal, and political logics.

In chapter 2, I shift the analytic focus and explore how the state controls, manages, and co-opts internet literature to set up and patrol the permissible boundaries and to engineer such digital cultural consumerist experiences to its advantage. I will argue that the state, although not the primary creator of such experiences, or the norms, values, and beliefs they carry, can be seen as an indispensable coproducer in the process that sets the bottom line and basic tone of ideational contestation. It is within the state-sanctioned permissible zone that platforms, writers, and readers demonstrate their agency in negotiating and contesting ideological governance and social consent for authoritarian rule.

Chapter Two

DANCING WITH SHACKLES ON

State Intervention as Coproduction

In 1942, at the Yan'an Forum on Literature and Art, Mao Zedong asserted that among the various fronts in the struggle for the liberation of the Chinese people is the cultural front, or the front of the pen.[1] On October 15, 2014, President Xi Jinping convened the highly symbolic Beijing Forum on Literature and Art, in which he emphasized that both literature and art constitute an important undertaking and a critical battlefront for the party, as together they play "a unique role in cultivating and spreading socialist core values," which he has advocated since he assumed power.[2]

Clearly, then, for the Chinese state, the cultural realm of literature and art is not only an important front of the Communist Revolution but also an indispensable part of its contemporary "ideological governance."[3] From the state's perspective, literature, art, and other cultural products serve the function of indoctrination, mobilization, and education. But they can also be used for protest, resistance, and ideological dissent, and thus must be carefully managed. The party's history is filled with internal struggles along this front, as well as those with cultural elites, particularly writers who intentionally and unintentionally question, resist, and contest the party's ideological constructs, norms, values, and narratives.

A case in point is *Liu Zhidan*, a biographic novel about the life of communist leader Liu Zhidan, who founded the revolutionary base that later grew into the Yan'an Soviet. After his death in a battle in 1936, Liu was remembered as a martyr by the party, until his biographical novel by his sister-in-law Li Jiantong became the example and evidence of an antiparty conspiracy in 1962.[4] "The use of novels for anti-party activity is quite a great invention," commented Mao at the Tenth Plenary of the Eighth Communist Party of China (CCP) National Congress, allegedly citing Kang Sheng who opposed the publication of the novel.[5] Mao then continued, "Anyone wanting to overthrow a political régime must create public opinion and do some preparatory ideological work. This applies to counter-revolutionary as well as to revolutionary classes."[6]

President Xi's father, Xi Zhongxun, who worked with Liu Zhidan before his death, was a victim of the *Liu Zhidan* case, because he supported the novel, thus standing against Kang Sheng (and Mao).[7] Bearing this in mind, the 2014 speech by President Xi is an even stronger reminder of the state's desire to control and shape the cultural realm, "as arbiter of what is or is not healthy and appropriate for mass audiences to read."[8]

How does the state control and arbitrate the production and consumption of internet literature? How do the platforms, writers, and readers react to state interference? What are the subsequent implications?

In this chapter, I explore how the state governs internet literature through a combined strategy of censorship, co-optation, and promotion. In many ways similar to state-society struggle over the control of online expression, there are nuanced but critical differences as a result of the commodified nature of internet literature, its extended production and consumption process, and the relatively stable platform-writer-reader relationship. Overall, I argue that, although the state cannot replace platforms, writers, and readers as the creators, it has demonstrated time- and place-sensitive capacity to set the bottom line for what is acceptable and to engage in the coproduction of digital consumerist experiences. Therefore, although market and societal forces have considerable agency and creativity (as will be discussed in chapters 3 through 5), this is the starting point for the negotiation of China's pop hegemony.

GOVERNING THE INTERNET AND GOVERNING INTERNET LITERATURE

The Chinese party-state has demonstrated strong adaptability to digital challenges by establishing a sophisticated censorship apparatus and by devising innovative propaganda and social control tactics. China's censorship machine involves state agencies at different levels, with the Cyber

Administration of China at the top directly reporting to President Xi Jinping.[9] In addition, service providers and other nonstate actors are held responsible for implementing state censorship directives, surveilling users, or conducting self-censorship and peer-censorship.[10] These state and nonstate censors, equipped with technological, legal, administrative, and coercive means, together implement the rigid, yet subtle, coordinated, and fine-tuned control over online expression and information access.[11]

In addition to control and censorship, the Chinese party-state has also attempted to work the new technology to its advantage, notably by turning cyberspace into a venue of propaganda, information gathering, and surveillance. On the one hand, the party has pushed state media outlets online to propagate preferred content, while embracing innovative tactics like "ideotainment" and "astroturfing" to sugarcoat its propaganda or conceal its traces.[12] Combined with censorship and information manipulation, such tactics allow the state to shape citizens' thoughts, emotions, identities and imaginations.[13] On the other hand, digital media is used to more effectively reach out to the public and penetrate the society.[14] This certainly means that China is moving closer toward a "surveillance state," although closer monitoring of the society also enables the state to provide better governance, deliver services, and address public concerns, which in turn enhances regime legitimacy.[15]

Given the significant function of literature in ideological governance, it is not surprising that the state has attempted to intervene in the production and consumption of online literature.[16] But how has the state done so? In this section, I introduce a three-layer strategy of censorship, co-optation, and promotion. Through censorship, the state prevents the works it dislikes from being produced, distributed, and consumed online; through co-optation, the state embeds platforms and writers into the system, so that they become more compliant and cooperative, or at least less deviating; and through promotion, the state boosts titles it prefers and signals to involved actors its preferences. In doing so, the regime, although not directly involving itself in the creation of any of these works, becomes a critical coproducer.

Censorship

The mode of production and consumption of internet literature in China today, primarily composed of genre fiction, is a long-term process because it typically involves long novels published daily in installments for readers.

This allows the state to intervene at various stages in different ways, including banning certain topics or specific novels entirely, interfering with the writing whenever it is deemed necessary, and screening manuscripts in real-time or post hoc to filter out taboo content. This renders state intervention a repeated game that shapes the behavior of the platforms, writers, and readers, oftentimes making them more inclined to accept and live with state control when possible, as will be discussed.

The state imposes constraints over certain topics or specific titles by banning them entirely. Although such control can be exercised post hoc, it is often preemptive and self-censoring in nature, as writers and platforms, aware of the restrictions through direct experiences or "control parables," shy away from these topics.[17] Yet, under certain circumstances, the state may interrupt the production and distribution of a fiction that has been tolerated, leading to its complete removal, unexpected ending, or storyline adaptation. Such intervention can come from the state or the portal that hosts the fiction. In fact, literature portals often provide micromanaging advice to writers to avoid triggering state censorship—in particular, the more abrupt and disruptive intervention that can be from the state. If the first type of control aims at prohibiting writing on taboo topics, the second is more about preventing writers of nontaboo genres from touching such topics as they are writing. Third, censorship of internet novels also includes keyword filtering, a mechanism that works in the same way as it does in other types of online expression, forcing writers (and platforms) to use alternative forms of expression to get the content through.

As far as topic censorship is concerned, the state can be driven by multiple motives. Ideologically subversive works are, of course, not permitted.[18] But topic censorship also reflects well the state's aesthetic and moral concerns. One particularly noticeable yet currently understudied category of censorship targets is "obscene and pornographic" (*yinhui seqing* 淫秽色情) fiction titles and their hosting sites.[19] This censorship is consistent with the state's efforts to censor online profanity and to contain literature and art works about sex, violence, and drugs. For example, in response to the sexual scandal of a hip-hop singer who was accused of having an affair with a married celebrity, the state launched a massive campaign targeting hip-hop culture and actors with tattoos in early 2018. The authorities explicitly outlined four types of celebrities to be banned, namely those with "low moral values," those with "vulgar and of low taste," those "whose thoughts and style are not refined," and those "involved in scandals."[20]

What are the more political topics that the state seems to be most wary about? My research suggests that several topics are more tightly controlled than others. First, the state imposes stricter control over writing on modern and contemporary history rather than on ancient history. Because of such differentiated treatments of historical periods, writers and readers joke about the censorship system being the Time-Space Administration Bureau (*shikong guanliju* 時空管理局). Because modern history overlaps with the Communist Revolution, free writing, from the state's perspective, may result in the disclosure of the dark sides of the regime, thus endangering its legitimacy. After all, many political crises, such as the Great Famine, the Culture Revolution, and the Tiananmen protest, happened during this period. Moreover, even if the writers can avoid mentioning these dark moments, which in itself is tricky, as readers may wonder why certain pieces of the history are missing, the state also does not want internet novels to "change" the history too much, to obliterate its own existence, or to lead writers and readers to discuss and question the official narrative of its role and the history in general—a propensity the state dubs "historical nihilism."[21] This is the primary risk of alt-history novels, which, after changing the past would logically end up changing the "now" given the "butterfly effect."[22] This is why some regulators seem to prefer a "pure" history and regard historical novels as deviating and distorting; it is also why, in April 2011, the director of the SARFT Television Drama Management Department, Li Jingsheng, commented at a conference of television drama directors that "time-travel dramas do not respect history and culture, thus should not be promoted."[23]

The second topic the state seems highly nervous about includes writings on communism. In this genre, the fiction *Red Dawn* mentioned earlier is probably the best known among readers. Originally published on Zongheng (zongheng.com), a major internet literature portal, the novel tells the story of a young man named Chen Ke who was born in 1980 but travels back to 1905, where he launches a communist revolution by way of Maoist ideations, strategies, and practices. The widely read work is both highly regarded and harshly criticized, generating heated debates on forums and other social media sites such as the Quora-like Zhihu (zhihu.com).[24] Although many people regard the novel as proregime, it nevertheless was removed from Zongheng in 2014, and its circulation is also censored. Figure 2.1 shows the error message when trying to access the novel.

Red Dawn is not the only case of communism being a target of censorship. Another example is the female-oriented fiction *Talented Martial Arts Girl* (*Tiancai Guoshu Shaonü* 天才国术少女). Although this genre is typically nonpolitical, the writer suddenly started to write about Marxism and the resurrection of Mao and relentlessly criticized modern China for deviating from socialist principles. It is unclear why this writer became politicized, although the writing suggests state interference triggered the shift. The fact that the work was censored signals explicitly that when communism serves as a tool to criticize the current regime, the party-state will not allow it. This is again reflected in the case of *Red Flag over the*

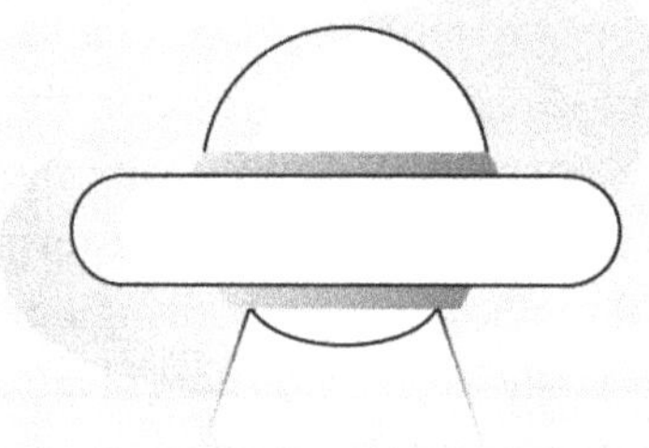

FIGURE 2.1. Censored message from Zongheng: "The page you're trying to access is currently 'binge-reading' elsewhere~ 500: This book does not exist or has been deleted!"

Wasted Land (*Hongqi Chabian Feitu* 红旗插遍废土), a fiction that depicts a true believer trying to practice communism in a postapocalyptic world. Likely because of the writer's caution—not directly mentioning "communism" but instead referring to it as "the-tabooed-ism" (*bukeshuo zhuyi* 不可说主义)—the title survived for quite some time, until it began discussing labor movements and religion. The fact this work casts communism as a "taboo" is quite ironic. It mocks not just state censorship but also the party-state's betrayal of its ideology, which has become a citizenry weapon to criticize the regime and to mobilize.[25]

The third topic the state has been cautious about includes religious topics, especially those that relate to Islam and Christianity as well as relevant minority groups. For instance, a popular writer, Author A, became tangled up in state censorship while writing a mythical fantasy. Although the story is set in an alien world, thus deemed completely nonpolitical by the writer and his readers, the work landed on the regime's radar amid the state's antiterrorism campaign of 2014, launched after several violent attacks took place in Xinjiang and elsewhere. Author A was first told not to write about religious splits—even in an alien universe—especially between moderate and extreme factions, as that may allude to Islam. After making the revision, he was then told that using religion as the basis for a power struggle was not acceptable. In the end, the storyline became so twisted that the writer decided to finish the otherwise highly successful title in a rush.[26] Another writer was told by his editor that his work was "pinpointed by above levels to be banned," because it "touches upon both politics and religion." He reasoned, "I thought it over. The 'politics' should be that I wrote about how the people's representative system can be more democratic and scientific than the parliamentary system in the last few chapters; 'religion' should be about the discussion on the Christian liberation theology movement and the comparison between early-day Christian communities and labor unions."[27]

Overall, confirming existing studies, state censorship targets political topics that bear implications for regime legitimacy and social stability.[28] My findings also add some nuances to our understanding of state control motives. Evidently, the state imposes limits over titles about modern and contemporary China because it does not want accounts of history that deviate from the official narrative or disclose its dark sides. When it comes to communism, the state worries that citizens may use the ideology to mobilize or hold the state against its socialist promises. The control over religious topics reveals the state's fear of rising ethnical and religious tensions, especially in cases of religions and ethnic groups with perceived higher risks of separation and political instability.[29]

In addition to topic control, the state imposes microlevel censorship that works similarly to key word filtering of other types of online expression. Evidently, erotic terms, even relatively neutral ones such as "flesh body" (*routi* 肉体), are prohibited. Political taboo words like "Tiananmen," "Tibet," and sometimes "democracy," are also banned. Moreover, literature portals in recent years have discouraged the use of real place names, because the state does not want readers to link the stories, especially negative ones, to reality. Some blocked terms, however, such as "doves" (*gepai* 鸽派), may surprise writers and readers, triggering serious complaints (more on this later).

Platforms matter in both topic control and keyword filtering, as in the case of general censorship.[30] The state normally does not deal with writers directly. Rather, editors from the platforms (or the producers, when the works are adapted to other formats) are the ones who continuously work with writers. In the case of Author A, the author constantly fielded small revision requests from editors before finally giving up on the novel. Portals tend to overreact, Author A noted: "When they find one work tagged by state censorship, they will warn all other writers who may step into the minefield, too."[31] The attentiveness of platforms is understandable politically, because they must comply with censorship to avoid state punishment. As far as market incentives are concerned, for a platform, the loss would be substantial should a title, especially a popular one, be censored, which would negatively affect readers' experiences, and thus their revenue, not to mention other repercussions, such as when deviations trigger a state censorship campaign that would require the platform to suspend operations.

Despite the general inclination to collaborate with the state, literature platforms vary in terms of control levels, just like social media platforms, as they go to different lengths to balance censorship and user experiences.[32] For instance, different platforms have different taboo word lists. Although some portals may manually correct the collateral damage caused by automatic filtering, others do not. Moreover, when shared beyond portals where the work originally appeared to other platforms like forums, Weibo, and WeChat, internet literature works also must go through filtering mechanisms on these sites. In other words, a work may go through multiple layers of keyword filtering before arriving at a reader's screen, leading to huge variation in censorship experiences for readers.

State censorship also varies over time, which is best exemplified in censorship campaigns.[33] In such times of emergencies, platforms can become very busy. For instance, during the 2014 antiprofanity campaign, literature portals had to purge erotic, profane, and vulgar content. Besides removing violating titles and shutting down risky channels directly, platforms mobilized writers to "desensitize" their writings. In an interview, a writer explained how the campaign affected her novel: "My novel *Powerful Young Master of The Red Family: The Petite Wife Strives for Favors* (*Hangmen Quanshao: Duochong Xiaojiaoqi* 红门权少：夺宠小娇妻) has been renamed *One Generation of Favors: Beauty Lilac* (*Yishi Shengchong: Meiren Dingxiang* 一世盛宠：美人丁香). Moreover, terms like 'Party chief' and 'mayor' are now replaced with No. 1, No. 2, etc. Now I can barely recognize my own writing."[34] The quote reveals that the target of censorship can go far beyond profanity.

State content control expands beyond the realm of internet literature and covers the entire panentertainment industry, which has a much larger audience. In the popular *My Heroic Husband* (*Zhui Xu* 赘婿), the main character was married to several women. But when adapted into a television drama, he has only one wife, evidently a compromise to conform with the mainstream value system.[35] In this case, state control affected the adapted work rather than the original writing, but such pressure is often channeled to writers. Author A, mentioned earlier, who has several adapted works, revealed how literature portals, publishers, and producers can actuate censorship: When censorship stings, everyone in the process gets hurt, and thus all involved pressure the writer, who then faces a moral obligation to comply because failing to do so will cause consequences not just for himself, but for others.[36]

Co-optation

Authoritarian regimes often utilize softer means of control, such as co-optation. Typically understood as an elite strategy to consolidate or broaden the supporting base, co-optation works by providing particularistic benefits or power-sharing arrangements to make targeted groups a stakeholder in the status quo.[37] Compared with patron-clientelism, co-optation targets groups instead of individuals and involves long-term credible commitments for both the elites and the supporters.[38]

I broadly interpret the effort of the Chinese state to bring involved actors, such as platforms and writers, into the governance structure as co-optation. Such a relatively broad definition includes measures such as delegation of censorship responsibilities to platforms, which are coercive in nature. In a highly repressive regime, although market and social actors oftentimes have no choice but to comply with the state, their compliance gradually results in a tacit cooperative relationship, which, however involuntary and unequal, helps integrate them into the regime. In this relationship, the state recognizes the legitimate status of the platforms and writers in exchange for their loyalty and compliance. This perhaps explains why campus bulletin board system (BBS) managers seemingly volunteered to participate in state censorship by asking for a keyword list when meeting with the Chinese Communist Youth League.[39]

Indeed, the state has made serious efforts to hold online literature portals and writers accountable and turn them into an arm of state control. In 2015, the State Administration of Press, Publication, Radio, Film and Television (SAPPRFT) issued the *Guiding Opinions Concerning Promoting the Healthy Development of Online Literature*, stipulating that online portals should "enhance online literature editorial staff management mechanisms; implement appointment qualification systems; establish and improve systems such as the real-name registration of writers, the responsible editor system, the publishing unit undersigning system, etc."[40] The motive, clearly, was to establish a responsibility system, which not only enables the state to track deviating writers and portals whenever necessary but also reminds platforms and writers that they are stakeholders in the "healthy development" of internet literature—meaning that, if it becomes unhealthy, big brother may have to directly intervene.

Another state co-optation strategy has been to task literature portals with "social responsibility." In June 2017, SAPPRFT introduced the *Provisional Methods for Evaluating Social Benefits of Online Literature Publication Service Platforms,* which proposed to evaluate the social impact of literature portals to "improve the quality of published works, regulate the market order, optimize the development environment, and guide internet literature publishers . . . to constantly produce excellent works that organically integrate ideology, artistry and readability, to better meet the people's spiritual and cultural needs."[41]

This document sets up a complete quantified scheme to rate literature portals (captured in table 2.1), which includes five prime indicators, twenty-two subindicators, and seventy-seven specific scoring criteria, for a total of 130 points.[42] The criteria promote content the state desires and suppress what it dislikes (as reflected in the indicators of "quality of publications" and "social and cultural impact," accounting for forty-five and thirty points, respectively), and to embed platforms and writers (the primary indicator of institution building, assigned thirty points). Portals are graded into four categories, excellent (scores ninety or above), good (eighty to eight-nine),

TABLE 2.1
Prime indicators used to evaluate social impact of online literature portals

Indicators (scores)	Evaluation criteria
Quality of publications (45)	Whether or not the internet literature portal "publishes works that uphold the direction of advanced socialist culture and actively promote socialist core values" and "puts efforts to publish works spreading the mainstream melody and positive energy;" and whether or not the [published works] "have healthy and uplifting ideological style and aesthetic taste, and bear positive impact on value orientation, spiritual guidance, aesthetic enlightenment, and so forth."
Propagation capacity (15)	Whether or not the literature portal actively "promotes outstanding original works, continuously improves communication methods and the means of delivery, improves the timeliness of the delivery of excellent works and user satisfaction, and expands the coverage of outstanding online literary works."
Content innovation (10)	Whether or not the literature portal "has an innovative spirit, values and takes measures to reverse the trend of homogenization like story duplication, plagiarism and imitation, and clichéd writing; promotes innovations in theme, genre, and form; forms specialties in concepts, content, and styles; and actively publishes personalized and creative works."
Institution building (30)	Assesses the literature portal's "rules and regulations, the construction and implementation of internal institutions," as well as "the professional quality, structure, and personnel training of its team, etc."
Social and cultural impact (30)	This item offers extra points and the assessment "combines expert evaluations, readers' word-of-mouth appraisal, market responses, etc.," and "gauges outstanding achievements and social influences" achieved by literature portals in publishing excellent works.

Note: All quotes are translated by the author from State Administration of Press, Publication, Radio, Film and Television, "Guanyu Yinfa Wangluo Wenxue Chuban Fuwu Danwei Shehui Xiaoyi Pinggu Shixing Banfa de Tongzhi" [Notice on Issuance of Provisional Methods for Evaluating Social Benefits of Online Literature Publication Service Platforms], National Press and Publication Administration, June 27, 2017, https://www.nppa.gov.cn/xxfb/tzgs/201706/t20170627_666172.html.

acceptable (sixty to seventy-nine), and failing (sixty or below). They will be vetoed (i.e., fail) should they (1) publish any works with "severe political mistakes" or "negative social impact"; (2) promote on the front page or key channels works with "problematic orientations"; or (3) violate "political discipline and political rules."[43]

This social responsibility strategy is not completely new as a state tool to integrate intermediary actors into internet governance. Rather, it is a time-tested practice to co-opt content and service providers into control and regulation structures, making them more compliant, at least in the effort to balance profit with being politically acceptable. According to the official document, those failing the social responsibility evaluation will be punished, whereas those excelling (total scores equal to or greater than ninety) for two consecutive years will receive priority support when it comes to award selection, work promotion, and external exchange opportunities, as well as publication funding and other special grants.[44] This clearly means that in addition to sticks, the state also offers carrots.

The state has also made efforts to co-opt writers. Most notably, it has set up internet writers associations and absorbed reputable internet writers into the corporatist China Writers Association (CWA). CWA further set up its special Internet Literature Committee in 2015, which it boasts as the home organization for "internet literature writers, websites, critics, and scholars."[45]

Another approach of state co-optation is to grant online writers state recognition, absorbing them directly into the regime. At the 2014 Beijing Forum on Literature and Art, for example, President Xi lauded two internet writers, Zhou Xiaoping 周小平 and Hua Qianfang 花千芳, for spreading positive energy.[46] Zhang Wei 张威 (pen name Tangjia Sanshao 唐家三少), one of the most successful internet writers, has become a delegate to the Thirteenth National Committee of the Chinese People's Political Consultative Conference.[47] By 2021, the United Front system had held four symposiums for internet celebrities, including writers. Reportedly, attendees of the 2018 symposium unanimously agreed that the study helped them "deeply realize the changes and development of the world, the nation, and cyberspace in the new era" and enhanced their "identity with the path, theory, system and culture of socialism with Chinese characteristics."[48] They vowed to "unite more closely around the Party Central Committee with Comrade Xi Jinping as the core" and to "continuously improve political grasp, public opinion guidance, innovation and creativity, and unity promotion" to achieve "the grand Chinese Dream of national rejuvenation."[49] These quotes are not merely propaganda clichés expressed in a collective manner; individual trainees also expressed similar sentiments, indicating voluntary or involuntary compliance, if not catering to state co-optation.[50] Evidently, internet writers have become part of the United Front, not just as targets of state co-optation but also as the extension of the state apparatus. Even if their expressed views are not sincere, the gesture is sufficient to indicate their open standing with the state.

Promotion

In addition to censorship and co-optation, the state has promoted the works it likes, often by recognizing writers and their works through various awards.[51] Since 2015, the SAPPRFT (and the succeeding National Press and Publication Administration, NPPA) has selected and recommended "outstanding original internet literature works" annually, evidently based on the "socialist values" that the state promotes.[52] By 2019, a total of 112 novels had been recommended (appendix table A.1 presents a frequent word analysis of the official introduction to these works).[53] Local authorities have established similar awards. Since 2015, the Beijing Bureau of Press, Publication, Radio, Film and Television has started awarding internet novels it deems as outstanding annually.[54]

Scholars find that the Chinese state can be innovative in promoting its ideological constructs.[55] In particular, the state in the reform era has taken advantage of China's booming entertainment industries to make propaganda more interesting and appealing, and as a result, popular on the market.[56] Thus, the state has instrumentalized both artistic and market forces to shape the internet literature it prefers. Take the "2019–2020 Internet Literature Film and Television Adaptation IP [Intellectual Property] Potential Evaluation Report" as an example.[57] In the guise of a professional market assessment—namely, that authored by the China Film Association Screenwriting Education Working Committee and Chinese Film Screenwriting Research Institute of Beijing Film Academy—the report's evaluation criteria explicitly followed "core socialist values," and the results strongly favored "main melody" works. Two specific titles—*Great Power Heavy Industry* (*Daguo Zhonggong* 大国重工) and *Ladder to Heaven* (*Tianti* 天梯)—both ranked higher in the first tier than many other more popular works, evidently reflecting the state's preference. In fact, *Great Power Heavy Industry*, which is about a contemporary young man who time travels back to 1980 and helps China better develop its industries, has won several government awards. It made the list of the "25 Themed Online Literary Works" jointly recommended by NPPA and CWA for the Seventieth Anniversary of the PRC celebration and the "2019 List of Excellent Online Literary Original Works."[58] In June 2022, it won the "Online Publication Award" of the "Fifth China Government Publishing Award," the first time for an online literature work.[59] Similarly, *Ladder to Heaven*, which tells a straightforward story of the Chinese officers who helped develop the People's Liberation Army (PLA) air force, has received government awards.[60] In addition to popularizing works that are already recognized and praised by the state, the report also highly ranked two COVID-related titles, *Healers of the Republic* (*Gongheguo Yizhe* 共和国医者) and *Republic Against the Epidemic* (*Gongheguo Zhanyi* 共和国战疫), which rode with the state's pandemic control campaign. By juxtaposing these state-preferred works with truly popular titles and by highlighting their potential to be adapted into movies and television series, the state not only enhances the popularity and potential market value of these works but also clearly signals to the market its preferences.

FROM ALTER-PRODUCTION TO COPRODUCTION

Through the three-layered strategy of censorship, co-optation, and promotion, the state flexes its dominance in the commodified-political field of internet literature. As we have seen, literature portals and writers have no choice but to comply with state control and co-optation or to at least avoid open deviance. This by no means implies that state power is not contested. Of course, one option is to exit. For instance, in response to the antiprofanity campaign of 2004, which specifically targeted erotic and sexual writings, many platforms hosting adult content had to either remove violating content, shut down, or move outside of China, leading a large number of platforms and writers to migrate to Taiwan.[61]

State control can be highly frustrating for writers, especially for those who consider their writings nonpolitical. Author A's experience is relevant: Censorship not only forced him to abandon a successful novel but ultimately also led him to quit writing for an extended period. He posted quite a few posts on Baidu Tieba, venting his frustration. Finding that the term "doves" (*gepai* 鸽派) was censored, an enraged mythical fantasy writer grumbled, "All I can say, eh, is that life is much more mythical than novels. We just keep silent and wink to each other!"[62] This is quite a scathing criticism of the regime, given that "wink to each other" (*daolu yimu* 道路以目) is an idiom that describes how people under the brutal Li King of Zhou, who killed to stop complaints, expressed their hatred of him: by winking to each other.

Writers can be politicized further than just complaining to readers. Hao Qun (aka Murong Xuechun), author of the popular internet novel *Leave Me Alone: A Novel of Chengdu* serves as a good example. Hao's works primarily deal with sociopolitical issues in China, and often touch on sensitive themes, such as corruption, sex, and underground life. Although he initially worked with the system through self-censorship, his experiences, especially what happened when he tried to publish his works in print, gradually transformed him into an internationally known anticensorship advocate and a "public intellectual."[63]

State Intervention and Alter-Production

State intervention sometimes forces platforms and writers to give up, or politicizes them, but it often does not end the production process. Rather, as Thomas Chen has argued, state intervention often results in "alter-production," through which writers and readers contest and negotiate the cultural production with the state.[64] Indeed, the struggle over internet literature has some nuanced but critical differences compared with the similar effort to suppress expression on social media. Although it is still largely a cat-and-mouse game, internet literature works are more visible and easier to control because their production and distribution typically happen on specific platforms in a repeated fashion. Moreover, as a profitable industry, platforms and writers have a stronger incentive to comply because they have much more to lose when hit by censorship (compared with when a social media post is censored). The market incentive and these stable, long-term relationships, however, have made involved actors—platforms, writers, and readers—more resilient to state control. They are unlikely to give up easily but rather will adapt. In fact, several of the examples discussed earlier show that keyword filtering is now simply part of the daily experience with the platforms, writers, and readers almost accustomed to it. Because of the market incentive, erotic content, a constant target of state censorship, has never been fully removed from the Web. According to deputy executive editor-in-chief at Qidian Liao Junhua, "There are tens of thousands of internet literature products, and the competition is fierce. To attract readers, generate more clicks, and have more paid subscribers, erotic elements, just like oil and salt for cooking, are necessary."[65]

For portals and writers, state intervention, especially control, which brings about inconveniences, is something that they live with. Writers, for instance, play with the censorship system, as Chinese netizens in general often do, thus accepting censorship as part of the writing process.[66] Simple tactics include breaking down taboo words, replacing them with symbols, or using guarded and indirect expressions. For instance, a fairy-epic fiction inserts "censorship prevention" (*fang hexie* 防和谐) in-between sensitive words and uses "applaud" (guzhang 鼓掌 or *pa pa pa* 啪啪啪) instead of any direct description of sexual activities.[67] Although such tactics may be perceived as passive "avoidance" rather than active "negotiation" of censorship, I argue they contest state power by bypassing it and producing the content the state intends to prohibit.

In addition, readers and writers often do not give up a title even when it is censored. Compared with censored social media posts, censored internet literature works often leave behind more traces that allow curious readers to follow. For instance, *Red Dawn*, although no longer available on the portal where it was initially published, can still be found online, and discussions on social media suggest that it is still alive. The same can be said about erotic novels. At least, many banned novels can find a haven beyond the Great Firewall. Writers may also continue writing despite censorship. An example is *Reborn as a Contemporary of the People's Republic* (*Chongsheng zhi Gongheguo Tonglingren* 重生之共和国同龄人), an alt-history fiction about the first thirty years of the People's Republic of China (PRC). The work is not quite subversive overall (to survive, it cannot be) but does touch on taboo themes like the Great Leap Forward and the Culture Revolution, and thus it was ultimately censored. The writer continued to update the work on platforms such as the QQ group and Baidu Tieba, with interested readers continuing to look for, share, and discuss it.

State Intervention as Coproduction

The notion that state control, instead of ending online experiences, leads to "alter-production" is inspiring. It highlights how market and aesthetic principles conflict with state ideological goals, as well as their resilience even when facing a highly repressive state.[68] "Alter-production" as an analytical concept, however, focuses more on societal agency and impact, while discounting the role and influence of the state. I argue that the state-market-society interaction can be better framed as a process of "coproduction," which assigns more equal conceptual status to both the state and citizens. I use the concept of "coproduction," originally put forward by public administration scholars to capture citizenry participation in the design and delivery of public services, more to highlight state involvement in the production of digital experiences.[69] As already shown, the state has actively engaged in the production and consumption of internet literature by controlling and co-opting platforms and writers and by promoting works it favors. Therefore, the digital experiences are also coproduced by the state and mirror what it desires (as embodied in the works it promotes) and dislikes (manifested in what it marginalizes and censors).[70]

Through control and censorship, the state sets the baseline of what is acceptable, thereby defining what is safe (and profitable) for platforms and writers; this also determines what is available for readers to consume. Note that state control is not just about constraints. From the coproduction perspective, this control marks the limits while also allowing writers, platforms, and readers to probe what is permissible. For instance, many works on communism and modern or contemporary history are censored. This does not mean, however, that these topics are untouchable. Rather, state control reflects more the desire for such writings to reflect its preferences. This is why communism as an ideology keeps popping up in different genres, just in less threatening forms. Such limited tolerance is logical, because it allows the state to reap the benefits—the regime is still a communist one in name and continues to garner legitimacy from the ideology—without being harmed.

The state also engages in coproduction by promoting works that it likes. Although state promotion or endorsement may not necessarily translate into popularity, it signals the state's preferences, thus encouraging the production of sanctioned works; plus, resources that come with state promotion often help promulgate them. For instance, *Unparalleled Fireworks* (*Kuangshi Yanhuo* 旷世烟火) is a story about a woman's life trajectory and history of Wenzhou since 1949. The work was submitted to celebrate the seventieth anniversary of the PRC and won the 2019 China Writers Association's key works support grant, as well as the first prize of the 2019 National First Realistic Theme Fiction Contest. In her speech at the award ceremony, the writer proudly claimed the work was meant to present "the pluralized picture of how generations of people in Wenzhou grow together with the People's Republic," and the "safety of the topic" was its number one virtue.[71] She further elaborated, "I am a long-time Party member. . . . I used to work in Rui'an as deputy director of the Propaganda Department. I put a lot of effort into the political stance, the spirit of the era, and the ideology to ensure the topic is safe."[72] The speech is an open display of loyalty, which was a clear result of state co-optation and promotion.

State participation in coproduction is also reflected in the constant intervention by platforms in the writing process. Compared with other types of internet content providers, such as social media platforms, literature portals are much more deeply involved in content production, sometimes through micromanagement. Such intervention can be driven by market motives. But it often reflects state power, either as efforts to comply with or evade state constraints or as attempts to please the state by promoting what it prefers. Responding to state restrictions over historical dramas in 2019, Zhao Bin, vice president of the entertainment company Ciwen, commented, "It's not impossible to do it, the key is who is doing it and how."[73] Citing a successful example, he elaborated that the secret was to treat the fantasy genre as being realistic at its core and to imbue it with positive energy.

State intervention coproduces the digital experiences of readers (and audiences more broadly). When discussing the historical event of "burning books and burying Confucian scholars alive" (*fenshu kengru* 焚书坑儒), the writer of the Make China Great Again alt-history title *A Qin Bureaucrat* (*Qin Li* 秦吏) took the opportunity to opine: "All countries have their core values that the authorities try their best to promote. But if all other learnings are banned and everyone must recite the twenty-four-word mantra of prosperity, democracy, civility, and harmony, as well as the Party rules every day, who can bear it?"[74] The passage is a blatant critique of the state and of the Xi administration and thus was promptly censored on the WeChat Read App. Many readers, however, had already read and commented on the comment before it disappeared. These comments were generally critical toward state censorship. Two comments posted after the critical passage was removed defended the state: One mocked critical users, and the other argued that the author had "disregarded facts" for not recognizing how pluralized online voices had become in China.[75] In this scenario, we can see how state censorship coproduces readers' experiences, creating both the critical reaction of the earlier users and the defense of the state by later users as well as the conflict between the two groups. What makes this case even more interesting is that, despite this and many other instances of microcensorship, the fiction as a whole has survived and is even included in the NPPA's "Publication Project of Excellent Realistic and Historical Genre Internet Literature Works."[76] This again suggests that censorship is often not an end in itself, but rather a means for the state to coproduce digital cultural experiences.

CONCLUSION

In this chapter, I explored how the Chinese state, especially in the Xi era, coproduced internet literature experiences. Specifically, it imposed limits on topics and intervened frequently to keep portals and writers within the permissible zone of expression. In terms of the censorship targets, the state seems concerned with both political defiance and writings that were incompatible with its moral and aesthetic values. In addition, the state deployed cooptation and promotion measures to hold platforms and writers responsible for their works, incentivize self-censorship, and produce the state's preferred works. Although not all have willingly complied, as writers, readers, and platforms have resisted and complained, the state has established itself as an effective coproducer, setting the boundaries of the writings, diminishing and marginalizing works that it dislikes, and encouraging those it prefers.

Highlighting the state's involvement is not to discount the role and agency of other actors. As discussed earlier, platforms, writers, and readers have indeed resisted and complained. For my purpose, however, I focus less on the state-society struggle and more on the digital experiences, because for platforms, writers, and readers, coexistence with authoritarian rule has become part of daily life. In this sense, what I discuss resembles what Lisa Wedeen discovered in her award-winning book—that is, that citizens under authoritarianism can learn to live with, and become ambivalent toward, the repressive state.[77] In addition, although I acknowledge the state's coproduction role, I differentiate it from that of nonstate actors. The state primarily functions to set the bottom-line of what is acceptable and what is not acceptable, laying the groundwork for the construction of pop hegemony. Still, platforms, writers, and readers are the ones undertaking much of the actual creation, distribution, and consumption of these works of literature. Therefore, I will discuss in chapters 3 through 5 exactly how these market and societal actors shape the field and negotiate the power relations with the state, and the subsequent implications for authoritarian legitimation.

Chapter Three

MAKE CHINA GREAT AGAIN

Alt-History Fiction and the Chinese Dream

As early as the Tang dynasty (618–907 CE), fiction writer and scholar Shen Jiji wrote a short story titled *Record Within the Pillow*, in which a poor young scholar named Lu meets the Daoist priest Lü at a local inn. After hearing Lu's complaints about his life, Lü gives him a pillow to sleep on, promising that Lu will experience a desired life. While the inn owner begins preparing a meal of yellow millet, Lu takes a nap and has a wonderful dream in which he not only excels in the imperial examination and becomes prime minister but also marries a beautiful woman from a noble family. When Lu wakes up, the yellow millet meal is not yet ready. This tale then becomes the idiom of the "Yellow Millet Dream" (*Huangliang Yimeng* 黄粱一梦), which is widely used to describe unrealistic pipe dreams.

Many Chinese citizens are experiencing their "yellow millet dreams" through internet literature, which allows readers and writers to unleash their dreams and imagination in the literary world. Although scholars have studied online romance, poetry, game-based fiction, and fantasy literature, few have studied the popular genre of alt-history fiction, which is of particular interest because of its direct political implications.[1] This specific genre overlaps with but differs from historical novels that merely set their stories in a specific historical context. It includes all works that use history as the setup for the writers (and readers) to interrogate, reinterpret, and *hypothetically change* the course of history.[2] Often, these works involve main characters (whether physically or just souls, individually or as a group) traveling from the contemporary era to an earlier historical period.

The alt-history genre is highly popular. It is not a given category on literature portals, but we can gauge its popularity based on history and military genres, which overlap significantly with alt-history fiction. According to the most popular internet literature portal, Qidian, the history genre accounts for 12.3 percent of all genres (see table 2.1). Similarly, according to a 2018 survey, about 10 percent of writers have written a history or military title in the past, and 6.1 percent say history and military are their primary genres.[3] These numbers can be overestimations because not all history titles are alt-history (although my coding, as I explain in chapter 4, suggests that the overwhelming majority of history titles are in fact alt-history). These numbers can also be underestimations, because many alt-history works set in a more contemporary time, such as the reform era, are often categorized as "reality" or "metropolitan" genres. An alternative way to gauge the popularity of alt-history fiction is to examine it according to demand. My coding of the top 2,100 popular titles (out of 263,105) on the literature commentating portal, Yousuu (yousuu.com), reveals that at least 413 (about 20 percent) involve time travel or rebirth to change the past, thus fitting the category of alt-history in a broad sense.

More important, alt-history fiction titles are often political in nature. History and presentation of history entail multiple political attributes, especially in the Chinese context in which they have always functioned as important sources of political legitimacy. This legitimacy is reflected in the official history compilation tradition in China, through which the new dynasty is justified as a legally constituted authority by narrating the history of the previous dynasty.[4] Putting aside such direct legitimacy implications, the origin and spread of national identity and nationalism, as scholars in the field have long argued, depends on the shaping of history, especially in a banal setting through routine symbols and habits of language.[5] Studies on China have confirmed the impact of history on national identity and revealed how both state-sponsored and popular nationalism have tapped into history, especially sufferings in modern times.[6] Among the 413 alt-history works that I identified through coding, 238 belong to the Make China Great Again (MCGA) category, in that they focus at least partially on reviving or glorifying China rather than merely pursuing personal goals.[7] Because these works typically attempt to alter Chinese history from a twenty-first-century perspective, they provide a valuable opportunity to observe how citizens connect the nation's past, present, and future.[8]

How do the writers and readers of alt-history novels describe, evaluate, and attempt to change China's past? How do they imagine, or contest the imagination of, an ideal China in the process? What are the political implications, especially for the regime's legitimacy, ideology, and policies? I examine the politics of alt-history fiction by addressing these questions in the rest of the book. In this chapter, I introduce the MCGA theme in alt-history works as reflected in how narratives have repeatedly attempted to save China from historical crises or prepare the nation for challenges. Such a theme both represents the collective ethos of remedying the nation's past sorrows in the era of China's rise and echoes the state rhetoric of the "Chinese dream" under President Xi, which calls for national revival. Because MCGA works emerged earlier than the Chinese dream rhetoric, they are not simply responding to the state ideation, but instead are an omen and driving force of the latter. In this sense, they embody the conflation of societal and state ideations, manifesting how Chinese society, not just the state, perceives and responds to the "great changes unseen in a century."[9] Such state-society resonance provides a more direct and effective explanation of authoritarian legitimation than the "state control" and the "amusement to loyalty" arguments.

THE POLITICS OF WRITING HISTORY AND THE HISTORICITY OF WRITING

Literature, art, and other cultural consumerist experiences have significant political functions as vehicles of social mobilization, dissent, state control, and political indoctrination. Among all the cultural forms, presenting history holds particular political significance. Narratives of history and past experiences are in and by themselves political, especially in contemporary China.[10] For instance, the historical theater play *Hai Rui Dismissed from Office* (*Hai Rui Baguan* 海瑞罢官), by historian and politician Wu Han, which tells the story of the imprisonment of model Ming dynasty official Hai Rui for criticizing the emperor, is widely believed to have sparked the Cultural Revolution.[11] Although Mao praised the play when it first came out 1961, many interpreted the work as an indirect and subtle criticism of Mao. In 1965, Yao Wenyuan published "Criticizing the New Historical Drama *Hai Rui Dismissed from Office*," indicating a change in the wind.[12]

When Mao was finally convinced that the play was indeed a malicious allegory meant to attack him (as the intolerant emperor), Wu was criticized, and then imprisoned in 1968, where he died in 1969. This was not an idiosyncratic case of history serving as a political instrument under Mao. The *Liu Zhidan* novel, discussed in chapter 2, is another example. Directly related to the interpretation of the party's history and the historical roles of many senior cadres, including those of Mao and President Xi Jinping's father, Xi Zhongxun, *Liu Zhidan* became an alleged antiparty novel. It was accused of attempting to posthumously rehabilitate the purged Gao Gang, to plagiarize Chairman Mao's thought and misappropriate Mao's contribution, and to help Xi Zhongxun accumulate political capital for the purpose of usurping power.

In the reform era, history and its presentation still bear significant political functions in many ways. In particular, as Ian Johnson articulates eloquently, "history has become a battleground for the present" in China.[13] How to define and redefine the Communist Revolution, evaluate the Maoist and reform eras, and assess previous political leaders like Mao and Deng are critical issues for the regime to continuously justify its rule.[14] For instance, as Howard Choy finds, by way of historical fiction, writers in the Deng Xiaoping era were able to rewrite the past, thus undermining the grand narrative of official history.[15] To prevent controversies over these topics ripping the regime apart, the Communist Party of China (CCP) passed historical resolutions to set the official tone. For instance, in response to the ideological turmoil after Mao's death, the second historical resolution of 1981, despite disappointing many for failing to completely negate Mao, effectively confirmed Deng Xiaoping's leadership and prepared China politically for the reform without triggering a Khrushchev-style crisis. The third historical resolution, enacted in 2021, not only enshrined President Xi but also reiterated the CCP's narratives on critical historical events such as the Tiananmen movement. This continuity in official narratives on historical events shows how the party-state consciously instrumentalizes history to avoid political backlash and maintain its legitimacy. President Xi's concept of "two cannot negate" explicitly and blatantly reveals such intentions of the state. For him, "The period of history after Opening Up and Reform cannot be used to negate the period of history before Opening Up and Reform; and the period of history before Opening Up and Reform cannot be used to negate the period of history after Opening Up and Reform."[16]

In addition to pushing its historical agenda, the Chinese state in the reform era also attempts to censure and manage alternate memories and accounts of history, historical events, and historical figures.[17] Most notably, research and discussion on events such as the Great Leap Forward, the Cultural Revolution, and the Tiananmen movement are restricted, if not completely prohibited. Examples of censorship include the Chinese versions of Gao Hua's *How the Red Sun Rose*, which is about Mao, and Yang Jisheng's *Tombstone*, which is about the great famine following the Great Leap Forward. In recent years, under Xi, the state has renewed its criticism of "historical nihilism," writing that rejects or questions dominant frames of the past, which clearly targets accounts of history that deviate from official narratives.[18]

To the party-state today, history is not just a source of trouble and threat, but something it can tap into for legitimacy. Almost immediately after becoming general secretary of the CCP in November 2012, President Xi Jinping coined the concept of the Chinese dream, which is inherently a historical narrative of national revival. While reflecting the party's continuous effort to shift its legitimacy base from communism to nationalism since 1989, the Chinese dream can be understood as the official return of the main theme of Chinese modern history—national salvation and rejuvenation.[19] It is not simply an attempt by the party to reclaim legitimacy. Rather, the move resonates with popular nationalist sentiments and discourses, which have (re)emerged in the reform era and have gained momentum in the context of China's rise. Such resonance is historical because of the critical role history and historical narratives play in imagining the nation and shaping national identity, especially in contemporary China.[20]

The common past and the shared feelings for this past are important pillars of Chinese national identity and nationalism. According to Montserrat Guibernau, "Members of a nation tend to feel proud of their ancient roots and generally interpret them as a sign of resilience, strength and even superiority when compared with other nations unable to display a rich past during which the nation became prominent."[21] For states, "Control over the past is a fundamental cultural resource for building, maintaining, and legitimating nations and their polities."[22] In George Orwell's words from *1984*: "Who controls the past control the future; who controls the present controls the past."[23] Given China's long and glorious ancient history, and the humiliations it experienced in modern times, nationalist narratives, state sponsored or spontaneous, naturally focus on national survival and revival. The historical role of the party and the communist state enables the regime to present history in specific ways to harvest nationalist legitimacy.[24]

The intriguing relationships among history, nationalism, and regime legitimacy exemplify not only the politics of writing history but also the historicity of writing. Because the production and consumption of cultural experiences are embedded in the temporal and spatial socioeconomic and political setting of a society, such experiences together reflect the collective ethos of said society in the particular era, manifesting its shared awareness of reality, its general morality, and the common desire of societal members. Such "historicity" of cultural experiences explains why the European Renaissance is linked to specific styles of art and cultural genres.[25] Similarly, the Enlightenment corresponds to not only advancements in science, rationality, and industrialization but also distinct literature and art content and forms.[26] MCGA stories in this regard embody the features of the highly commodified and digitalized state-market-society dynamics in contemporary China.

The historicity of writing was also evident in late-Qing and Republican Era science fiction, which mirrored the shared experiences and perceptions of national humiliation among the Chinese people at that time and their desire for national revival. For literary critic and professor Mingwei Song, as a literary genre, Chinese sci-fi was from its inception "mainly a utopian narrative that projected the political desire for China's reform into an idealized, technologically more advanced world," with the central motif being "China will become a superpower."[27] But these works were more than nationalist utopian stories. They also functioned to propel China's modernization by encouraging the public to develop an interest in modern science and technologies and by probing the nation's potential development paths as well as its position in the modern world.[28] In fact, among early sci-fi writers was China's prominent modern thinker and reformer Liang Qichao, who authored *The Future of New China* (*Xin Zhongguo Weilai Ji* 新中国未来记) in 1902. This sci-fi novel outlined a blueprint of political reforms for the nation's self-strengthening and eventual ascendency to world power status.

Liang was not alone. He represented the collective ethos and efforts to pursue national revival at a time of national crisis, which could be identified in not only the cultural realm but also the broader socioeconomic and political trends of reforms and revolutionaries.[29] In this sense, those sci-fi works were one of the driving forces that led to the founding of the Republic of China in 1912 and the People's Republic of China (PRC) in 1949. Thus, what the CCP achieved in 1949 was as much the victory of a nationalist revolution as of a communist one.[30] This reasoning is nicely reflected in the epitaph on the Monument to the Heroes of the People by Mao:

> Eternal glory to the heroes of the people who laid down their lives in the people's war of liberation and the people's revolution in the past three years!
>
> Eternal glory to the heroes of the people who laid down their lives in the people's war of liberation and the people's revolution in the past thirty years!
>
> Eternal glory to the heroes of the people who from 1840 laid down their lives in the many struggles against domestic and foreign enemies and for national independence and the freedom and well-being of the people![31]

If late-Qing and early Republican Era sci-fi works and literature represent how the Chinese (especially the elite) longed for a bright future of modernity during a time when China was struggling in an abyss of internal decay and imperialist perpetration, MCGA titles display a similar yet qualitatively distinct collective ethos of national revival, which can also be identified in contemporary Chinese sci-fi works.[32] Flourishing in the age of the perceived imminent rise of China, these works are constructing dreams not to save the nation in an imagined future but to make up for the sorrows of the past. Although the collective ethos is nationalistic in nature, just like that of earlier sci-fi works, these contemporary works are inherently more proregime and pro–status quo. Instead of calling for or catalyzing a new wave of revolution, they function to affirm the historical trajectory as well as the party's rule that seemingly has rendered national revival foreseeable.

The quote from the epitaph on the Monument to the Heroes of the People also highlights another line of historical precedents of MCGA writing: the state-sponsored patriotic artistic production of earlier decades, including but not limited to main-melody dramas (a genre of television and film that promote proregime ideologies and narratives) and revolutionary or patriotic romances.[33] Evidently, such "patriotic artistic production" was (and largely still is) driven by the state; however, it represents more how the ideological state apparatus functions to socialize its subjects than how digitally enabled citizens participate in ideological governance, which is my focus.

MAKE CHINA GREAT AGAIN IN ALT-HISTORY

It is not just the Chinese who are obsessed with history or aspire to change it.[34] In the 1996 fiction *Making History* by Stephan Fry, a male contraceptive pill is sent back in time to prevent Adolf Hitler from being born. This change only makes things worse, however: Without Hitler, Germany, under another Nazi leader, manages to develop nuclear weapons, conquers Europe more successfully, and wipes out all Jews with a sterilizing water that is polluted by the very same contraceptive pill. Similarly, *The Butterfly Effect* is a 2004 US sci-fi film that depicts the unintended consequences of changing the past.

Chinese alt-history fiction stands out because of its popularity and direct political implications. It represents an important genre of internet literature that enjoys a huge market share and influence. As of today, literally thousands of alt-history titles have been published online, attracting millions of readers. Although many of them focus on personal desires of power, wealth, and romance (e.g., the popular *Searching for Qin* 寻秦记 by Huang Yi 黄易), they often task their protagonists with rescuing China from its historical humiliations or preventing the nation from slipping into crises, revealing a clear MCGA theme.[35] And by presenting, interpreting, and changing history, these titles bear important yet sometimes ambivalent political implications.

The MCGA theme is reflected in the historical time periods these titles tend to focus on and the major undertakings of the heroes. MCGA works cover historical periods as early as the Spring and Autumn period (771–476 BCE) to the twenty-first century, including all major historical junctures (see chapter 4, figure 4.1). Closer examination reveals a tendency to intervene at critical moments in history. For instance, novels situated during the Han and Three Kingdoms period (206 BCE–265 CE) tend to focus on the turmoil that followed the collapse of the Han when many historical figures shined and when history seemingly could have taken different paths. Fictions about the Song (North Song 960–1127 CE; South Song 960–1279 CE), Yuan (1271–1368 CE), and Ming (1368–1644 CE) dynasties often center on the reform era of North Song, the end of South Song, the end of Yuan (the beginning of Ming), and the end of Ming (the beginning of Qing). The failure of North Song reforms coincided with minority threats from Western Xia (Xixia 西夏), Liao 辽, and Jin 金; the South Song was then terminated by the Mongols; and the Ming (attracting more writers than any other dynasty) was the last Han Chinese dynasty, replacing the Mongol Yuan, which was then replaced by the Manchu Qing (1644–1912 CE). Thus, in MCGA fiction, writers rush to help North Song reform, to save South Song from the Mongols, or to facilitate the Ming ending the Yuan and then to prevent the Ming from demise. The late-Qing period attracts many writers because that was the time when the Han Chinese overthrew the Manchu, not to mention the fact that it was a critical moment for China to modernize and catch up with the West. Even works on Sui and Tang dynasties, often perceived as the peak of the ancient Chinese Empire, frequently try to make up for flaws—for example, to unify China earlier and remedy the wars of Sui and Tang with the ancient Korean states or Tang's defeat in the Battle of Talas.

Eight MCGA Tales

To give a better sense of what typical MCGA alt-history works look like, I introduce eight such works. I selected these cases not through random sampling but based on my reading experiences, with the purpose of covering different time periods. Although this approach prevents claims about representativeness, the selected works tend to be more popular and influential, and thus deserve more of our attention in such an explorative project. For a more systematic analysis of MCGA works, see chapter 4.

TANG CAVALIERS (*TANG QI* 唐骑)

This novel tells the story of a modern Chinese tourist named Zhang Mai, who travels to Central Asia after the demise of the Tang dynasty. Upon his arrival, ethnically Han migrants under the Protectorate of the Pacified West (*Anxi Duhufu* 安西都护府), who have lost contact with the central government for decades and are struggling with the expanding Arabic and Central Asian forces, mistakenly take Zhang for a special envoy from the Tang Court. Zhang revives this group and reestablishes a strong army, which he then leads to resurrect the great Tang.

Instead of equipping the hero with modern technologies (especially with weapons such as firearms), which is typical for alt-history works, *Tang Cavaliers* draws more heavily on nationalist spiritual inspirations.

As the writer contends in the concluding chapter: "Contemporary reality can always change the past. If the offsprings are successful, that will glorify the ancestors; if the offsprings fail, the historical evaluation of ancestors will be dragged down. What happened to the Greeks and Romans after the Renaissance is an example of the former; the Zhou, Qin, Han and Tang after the Sino-Japanese War is an example of the latter. In this [alternate] universe, maybe everything will be different."[36] The 3.5-million-character fiction includes 797 chapters, with its first chapter released in February 2010 and its last on December 30, 2014.[37] According to the Yousuu dataset, as of March 15, 2022, more than seven years after its completion, the work still ranks 476 out of 263,105 titles and is rated 7.7 out of 10 by 557 users. To put this rating into perspective, the average rating of all 23,958 titles that have received a score on the platform is 5.5.

RULING UNDER HEAVEN (ZAIZHI TIANXIA 宰执天下)

Quite a few alt-history titles focus on the North Song dynasty (960–1127 CE), among which is *Ruling Under the Heaven*, a popular fiction about a contemporary Chinese young man who, after a plane crash, travels back to North Song (1069 CE) when the dynasty was at a critical juncture of reform. Taking advantage of his modern knowledge and historical foresight, the main character, Han Gang, gradually outperforms his competitors and ascends to the top as the empire's prime minister. Throughout this process, Han initiates a range of military, economic, social, political, and ideational reforms, while promoting the development of science and technology. Consequently, North Song China is industrialized and modernized and ultimately turned into a capitalist parliamentary system. Not surprisingly, the neighboring minority states threatening North Song, such as Western Xia and Liao, are defeated. In this hypothetical time and universe, China manages to annex or extend its dominance to Mongolia, Vietnam, Korea, and Japan.

Started in 2010 and completed in early 2019 on Zongheng.com, this fiction has a total of more than 7.3 million characters published in 2,242 installments (i.e., chapters).[38] As of March 15, 2022, when I collected the data, it was the most popular alt-history fiction and the second most popular among all genres in the entire Yousuu dataset (263,105 titles in total), with a rating of 8.1 out of 10 by 4,854 users. This ranking is particularly impressive considering that Zongheng.com is a less popular platform than Qidian.com.

POINTING SOUTH (*ZHINAN LU* 指南录)

This work of fiction has an interesting setup: Unlike typical alt-history titles that involve contemporaries traveling back in time, this work centers on the historical figure Wen Tianxiang (1236–1283), who is a well-known national hero and martyr in China because of his loyalty to the South Song dynasty. After being captured by the Mongols, Wen refused to surrender and serve them, which led to his imprisonment and ultimate execution. In *Pointing South*, Wen is given another chance: Before being captured by the Mongols, he is injured and goes into a coma, during which he travels to and lives another life in the Republican Era, where he receives a modern education and gains rich military, organizational, and mobilization experiences as a CCP soldier fighting against the Japanese invasion. Equipped with newly gained knowledge, ideas, and experiences, Wen is now able to lead the resistance to successfully defeat the Mongols. In the process, he pushes for a series of reforms to transform and modernize South Song China economically, militarily, and politically.

Although nationalist in nature, as the story boils down to a defense of the Han Chinese dynasty against an enemy minority, this fictional account attempts to distance itself from Han chauvinism, which asserts the superiority of Han over other ethnic groups in China, by highlighting that all ethnic groups should be treated equally (except, perhaps, the Mongols). In addition, the title explores political reforms that indicate a liberal inclination, by introducing popular elections, a parliamentary system, and a constitution comparable to the English Magna Carta and the US Declaration of Independence. After defeating the Mongols, the fiction ends with a veteran asking whether Wen will keep his promises, suggesting a strong sense of a social contract between the state and its citizens.

This work of fiction, which has a total of 291 chapters and more than 1.5 million characters, was started in May 2006 and continued until July 2007.[39] As of March 15, 2022, almost fifteen years after its completion, the work ranked 2,545 in the Yousuu book list and was rated 7.8 out of 10 by 140 users. This record is notable considering the database of Yousuu (and its predecessor) date back only to 2011, and it relies on readers to recommend the works, thus disadvantaging older titles like *Pointing South* in ranking.

USURPING MING (*QIE MING* 窃明)

This novel tells a story of a young man, Huang Shi, who travels back to the late Ming period (1618 CE). Once there, he joins the army and uses his historical knowledge to maneuver between the declining Ming and rising Manchu forces, before setting up a base in North China where he trains an army with modern military discipline, tactics, and weapons. Huang embraces modern economic practices by developing industries and promoting trade. To expand revenue sources, he launches an expedition to Japan and defeats the pirates. To ensure the loyalty of his followers and support from Catholic missionaries, Huang instrumentalizes Catholicism. With all these efforts, he defeats the Manchu Qing dynasty.

This work of fiction expresses an explicit and blunt anti-Manchu sentiment, depicting the minority group as the enemy of Han and other minority groups living in China as well as the cause of China's sufferings in modern times. The fiction's anti-Manchu narrative reportedly prompted a reader to slap the Manchu history expert, Yan Chongnian, in the face two times at a book-signing event on October 5, 2008.[40]

The work of fiction also challenges the conventional perception of late-Ming Confucian scholars, especially figures such as Yuan Chonghuan. Traditionally, Yuan was regarded as a tragic hero—a Ming loyalist, who was wronged by the emperor and the people. Believing that he had betrayed the Ming dynasty, he was killed by slow slicing (凌迟), with his flesh eaten by angry Beijing residents. In *Usurping Ming*, however, Yuan is depicted as a real traitor. In general, the novel sees late-Ming Confucian scholar officials as corrupt, disloyal, and excelling at nothing but infighting. This perspective has sparked much discussion and influenced many readers.

The fiction, which was completed in 2008, has 330 chapters and 1.42 million characters. Because of its popularity, it was also published in print. As of March 15, 2022, it ranked 218 on Yousuu with a rating of 7.3 by 974 users.

MORNING STAR OF LINGAO (*LINGAO QIMING* 临高启明)

Typical alt-history titles involve one or a few time travelers. *Morning Star of Lingao*, however, tells the story of more than five hundred contemporary Chinese people, with various backgrounds and areas of expertise, traveling back to the late Ming dynasty (1628 CE) through a wormhole. These time travelers are highly prepared and organized, bringing with them large quantities of modern weapons, technologies, and industrial equipment. Upon arriving, they set up a base in Lingao County, Hainan Province. Unlike many alt-history titles that prioritize saving the nation from historical crises and unifying China as soon as possible, *Morning Star of Lingao* takes a slow approach. The time travelers have only occupied Hainan and part of Guangdong Province after more than 2,600 installments (more than eight million characters). The story spends a significant amount of time detailing how to build up various industries, establish a modern military force, and transform premodern China socially, economically, culturally, and politically. The work's collective production mode (discussed in chapter 5) and sociopolitical implications have attracted a huge audience, including users from the scholarly community. Many see the fiction as representing a thought experiment of the "industrial party," a largely proregime ideological group championing (further) industrialization as the blueprint for China's development.[41]

The first installment of *Morning Star of Lingao* appeared on Qidian.com in June 2009, and the work has been regularly updated. In March 2022, the fiction was ranked forty-seven on Yousuu, with an average rating score of six by 2,625 users. It ranks higher when measured by the comment counts (twenty-ninth) or by how many users have bookmarked it (372, ranking seventeenth).

F—K QING (CAO QING 草清)

As the title suggests, this work of fiction is about overthrowing the Qing dynasty. The writer does not intend to conceal his hatred toward the Manchu dynasty, as displayed in the introduction: "If you travel back to Qing but do not rebel, your ass should be fucked using an electric drill. If you travel back from 2012 to 1712, what is the only thing you can and should do? Rebel! Reason? None needed."[42]

Unlike many other anti-Qing alt-history titles that focus on the late Ming period to prevent the Manchus from taking over, or when the Qing dynasty was collapsing, this title starts in 1712, the heyday of Qing, to "break the myth of a prosperous [Qing] dynasty" and "cut off the visible and invisible pigtails [the Manchu symbol]."[43] Moreover, the writer claims that "it is not enough just to expel the barbarians and revive China. The aim is to resurrect the nation like the Han and Tang dynasties to surpass all European and Asian nations."[44] For this purpose, the author not only writes about the military aspect of the rebellion (or uprising) but also builds a new ideological construct close to capitalism to replace Confucianism, creates a religion, and even lets China join the Westphalian Society to expand its global influence. The work represents the expansionist fictions that are not satisfied with merely saving China, but that want to make China the "empire on which the sun never sets."

F—k Qing was first published in 2011 on Qidian.com. Wrapped up in 2013, it has 1,039 chapters and more than 3.95 million characters. On March 15, 2022, it ranked 270 on Yousuu with a rating of 6.9 by 963 users.

RED DAWN (*CHISE LIMING* 赤色黎明)

In this peculiar alt-history fiction, hero Chen Ke, who was born in 1980, travels back to 1905, six years before the fall of the Qing dynasty. Chen is depicted as a true believer of communism, who starts the Communist Revolution as soon as he arrives in the late Qing period, before the founding of the CCP in 1921. The fiction cuts short modern Chinese history in several senses. First, Chen brings with him scientific knowledge (he studied chemistry so he could start an alkali industry to raise funds, which also helps him win the Nobel Prize), the communist ideology (to indoctrinate followers and the masses), and organizational skills, tactics, and experiences derived from the Chinese Revolution.

Chen reads like a diehard follower of Maoism and copies what the CCP had done before 1949. Besides founding a People's Party and a red army as instruments for the revolution, he implements land reform, organizes production brigades, and even has rectification campaigns. Communism is repeatedly discussed as an ideology and a practice to the extent that it resembles preaching. Many readers, therefore, deem the work unreadable, whereas others love it. In the end, Chen retires and enables the People's Congress to pass power peacefully, through an election, to Mao Zedong and Zhou Enlai (named Li Runshi and Xiangyu in the fiction, respectively).

Red Dawn was published on Zongheng.com between 2011 and April 2014, with 968 chapters and nearly 4.6 million characters. Probably because it preaches communism, the title has been censored. Even its page on Yousuu was removed; however, the work was very popular. According to the

Internet Archive, it was rated 8.2 by 3,099 Yousuu users on April 2, 2019.[45] This score would still make the top ten list (out of 263,105 titles).[46] Moreover, it still appears on recommendation lists and frequently in online discussions, despite having been censored.

THE INDUSTRIAL TYCOON (GONGYE BAZHU 工业霸主*)*

The Industrial Tycoon represents alt-history titles that fall into the "metropolitan" (都市小说) rather than "history" category on literature portals. It is a story about a master student of mechanical engineering, Lin Zhenhua (a given name literally meaning "reviving China"), who travels back to 1979. Using his expertise and foresight (e.g., the collapse of the Soviet Union, which becomes an opportunity to seize resources and technologies from former Soviet Republics), Lin creates an industrial conglomerate, helping China develop much faster and win the economic and geopolitical competition against the United States. In the fiction, China completes its first nuclear-powered aircraft carrier in 2010, which pays a highly symbolic visit to New York on October 1, 2012 (the National Day of China). The writer contends: "This is the day when the Chinese aircraft carrier fleet visits New York. It is a normal visit, but one that shocks the world. Entering the New York port is a China-designed and China-built 100,000-ton nuclear-powered carrier representing the latest technologies on Earth. Its arrival indicates that China's blue-water navy is on par with the United States, the old hegemon of the seas. Its arrival announces to the world that China's rise, just like the red sun rising above the sea, is unstoppable."[47]

This title, which was first released on Qidian.com in September 2011 and concluded in January 2013, has 743 chapters and about 2.6 million characters. On March 15, 2022, it ranked 360 on Yousuu with a rating of 6.2 by 755 users. It has also been published in print and has won government awards, as noted in chapter 2. The title clearly echoes state propaganda in recent years, especially narratives on competition between the United States and China and the notion that "the East is Rising, the West is Declining."[48] For instance, in early 2018, state media promoted a ninety-minute documentary, *Amazing China*, showcasing achievements under Xi, especially megaprojects in realms of manufacturing, infrastructure, science and technology, and the military.[49] Although critics see it as overestimating China's strengths as well as adding to the "China threat" narrative, thus potentially further disadvantaging China amid its competition with the United States, the documentary was very popular among nationalists.[50]

Not all alt-history fiction works are the same. But as these surveyed titles reveal, they feature a salient MCGA theme. No matter which historical period they focus on—from the Tang dynasty to the contemporary era—these works attempt to save China from crises (e.g., *Tang Cavaliers*, *Pointing South, Usurping Ming, F—k Qing*, and *Red Dawn*), intervene at critical junctures to prevent the nation from falling into crises (e.g., *Ruling Under Heaven* and *Morning Star of Lingao*), or facilitate with national revival (e.g., *The Industrial Tycoon*). The specific MCGA plans these works have proposed vary significantly—from relying primarily on spiritual inspiration (*Tang Cavaliers*) to pursuing comprehensive reforms (*Ruling Under Heaven* and *Morning Star of Lingao*); from virtually having no political reforms (*Tang Cavaliers*) to advocating communist revolutions (*Red Dawn*) or experimenting with parliamentary politics (*Ruling Under Heaven* and *Pointing South*); and from trying to save China from minorities (*Pointing South, Usurping Ming*, and *F—k Qing*) to competing with the world's hegemon (*The Industrial Tycoon*). Such a variety of popular Chinese dreams, and their political implications, are discussed in more detail in the remaining chapters of the book. It is sufficient, however, to temporarily conclude that these titles represent popular imaginings of an ideal China, strong and prosperous.

MCGA as Popular, Market, and Official Narratives

Given that their MCGA theme clearly resonates with the official Chinese dream, these alt-history works arguably represent the convergence of popular sentiment and state ideology, which is both spontaneous and carefully curated by the state.[51] On the one hand, these works mirror and embody the collective ethos of Chinese society longing for national revival. On the other hand, their production and consumption are subject to heavy-handed state control and intervention. In this process, the state sets the bottom lines for, and citizens actively contribute to, the creation of social consent (the MCGA discourse in this case) that can be accommodated by the state ideology (e.g., the Chinese dream), which is then amplified and promulgated by techno-market factors, laying the foundation for China's future pop hegemony.

The core narrative of saving and reviving China has an origin that predates both the PRC and even the CCP. As mentioned earlier, sci-fi works of the late Qing and Republican Era reflect a similar theme of imagining a better China as a reaction to humiliations that the nation was experiencing. Alt-history titles similarly provide an outpost for the expression of this collective ethos, allowing average Chinese to learn about and reexperience what earlier generations have endured by joining the MCGA journey with their personal understanding, reasoning, and imagination. By remedying the past, these works connect the history and present and enable contemporary Chinese to speak to their ancestors spiritually: We are finally accomplishing the generational mission that you have passed on to us, and we are proud of that. We have even tried to make up the historical sorrows by rescuing you, although only in a hypothetical fashion.

One interesting example of this theme is found in *Pointing South*. The setup of the historical patriotic figure, Wen Tianxiang, traveling to the Republican Era, joining the CCP to fight the Japanese, and then going back in time links the sufferings of ancient China (the Mongol takeover) to the nation's modern crises (the Century of Humiliation and Japanese invasion), provoking compassion that connects all Chinese across time and space. The historical and societal roots explain why state and societal narratives of China's past, present, and future overlap significantly. Many Chinese, whether or not they identify with the regime, sincerely embrace the official Chinese dream, as it is built on China's history, especially its glories and humiliations. The fact that many MCGA titles, including the works discussed in this chapter, started to appear online before President Xi came to power, reflects the societal agency of the official Chinese dream as a state ideological construct.

The convergence of popular narratives and state ideology is also reflected in the fact that MCGA works frequently draw on the experiences of the Chinese Revolution, especially the ideations and practices of the CCP. For instance, both *Pointing South* and *Red Dawn* make explicit references to the Communist Revolution as a source of inspiration. Although this may reflect the influence of state patriotic education and indoctrination, drawing on actual historical experiences brings logical coherence and a sense of reality to alt-history works, which connects the citizenry and the party-state in a more organic fashion.[52] For many Chinese people, MCGA fiction writers included, the CCP is one of the major forces that have tried to save the nation, and its final "success" has provided a model to imagine the MCGA story. In fact, some Chinese netizens joke about Mao being a time traveler.[53] Therefore, when telling these stories, it is almost inevitable to "learn" from the history and the CCP, thus legitimizing the regime.

MCGA narratives, although popularly produced, are subject to state intervention. As detailed in chapter 2, the state engages in the coproduction of internet literature by combining censorship, co-optation, and promotional tactics. In particular, alt-history titles are heavily affected by topical control because of their direct political implications. With state censorship functioning as the "Time-Space Administration Bureau," writings on certain historical periods and events such as the Cultural Revolution, as well as those touching on communism and labor movements (e.g., the *Red Dawn*), or religious and minority topics, are carefully managed, if not outright banned. After all, despite their MCGA theme, such works may inspire sociopolitical mobilization, or produce historical memories, perceptions, and reactions that lead to the delegitimization of the regime. The state also affects the production and consumption of alt-history fiction at the microlevel, typically through service providers or self-censorship, just like for all other genres. For instance, it is best to skip the Tiananmen movement when writing about contemporary China (as in the case of *Industrial Tycoon*). To be compatible with state moral and aesthetic values, erotic content, which is attractive to readers, needs to be minimal. In addition, the state resorts to co-optation and promotion measures to incentivize literature portals, writers, and readers to promote what the state prefers. This explains why the *Great Power Heavy Industry* won multiple government awards.[54]

In sum, through reexperiencing, reinterpreting, and re-presenting history, alt-history MCGA fiction weaves together the societal collective ethos of national revival, the state effort to control and tap into nationalist legitimacy, and the techno-market rules of the attention economy. Although they allow writers and readers to express personal desires and reflect on China's past, present, and future (discussed in chapters 4 and 5), these works ostensibly resonate with the official Chinese dream, thus contributing to authoritarian legitimation. In fact, they further ensconce, flesh out, and give life to the latter, without which the official rhetoric would hollow out into a meaningless, colorless, and less relatable shell of propaganda.

CONCLUSION

Commentating on the phenomenally popular Chinese action film "Warrior Wolf 2," which set the box office record in China at USD 874 million, *New York Times* reporter Chris Buckley noted that even though the film differs from a typically straight patriotic film in China, it echoes state agenda in various ways: "The Chinese Communist Party is not mentioned. Instead, the film celebrates the prowess and hardware of the People's Liberation Army, including missiles launched from Chinese warships that unerringly destroy the bad guys while sparing the civilians hiding nearby. . . . But the story comes loaded with talk of China's rise and peaceful intentions—both standard Communist Party talking points—and the decline of the imperialist West."[55]

Alt-history titles play similar functions. Although their narratives resemble official rhetoric and are by no means free from state intervention—the state has promoted the Chinese dream narrative avidly—these works should not simply be dismissed as an extension of state propaganda.[56] Rather, they resonate with the official Chinese dream because of their shared historical roots and the common aspiration for national revival.[57] Such a resonance validates the state's ideological construct and enables it to recruit social and market actors to help mass manufacture and distribute proregime nationalist values, norms, and beliefs that are essential for authoritarian legitimation.

As commodified digital experiences, the writing and reading of alt-history MCGA fiction are mediated by market dynamics. Diverse market demands have led to a plethora of genres competing under the rules of the attention economy, which explains the simultaneous rise of the shared MCGA theme that taps the collective ethos of national revival to attract readers as well as the pluralization of MCGA ideas to meet readers' varying preferences. This mechanism is neither new nor distinct to China, as "patriotism" has long been commercialized around the globe.[58] In fact, while my research focuses on text-based web fiction titles, MCGA storytelling in recent years has become a transmedia phenomenon transcending the narrowly defined sphere of internet literature. A case in point is the plethora of comic-style MCGA videos, which have even made their way to YouTube, suggesting that their presence has grown only more pervasive with Chinese cyberspace. Figure 3.1 shows the playlist of one YouTuber, which alone offers 896 such titles, providing hours and even tens of hours of content. The featured title

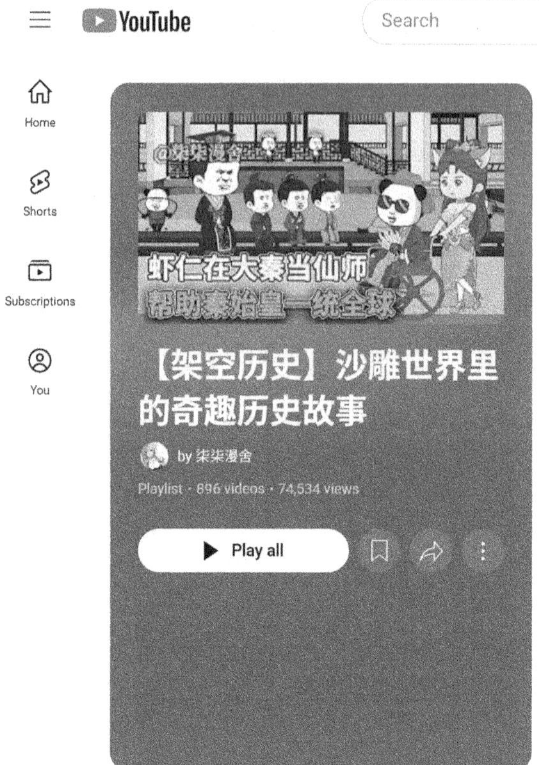

FIGURE 3.1. YouTube playlist of MCGA videos.

"Xia Ren Becomes Immortal Mentor of the Great Qin and Helps Qin Shi Huang Unify the World" is evidently a wild MCGA pipedream.

In chapter 4, I explore how MCGA works represent popular endeavors to explore, assess, and present history given techno-market dynamics and society agency. These works offer a rare opportunity to study nonofficial Chinese dreams and to compare such popular dreams with the official Chinese dream. By examining the variety of MCGA stories and the personal desires contained therein, I investigate how citizens engage in China's ideological contestation and how this process of state-market-society interaction constitutes a constructive destruction of regime legitimacy and a necessary step toward pop hegemony.

Chapter Four

THE VARIETY OF CHINESE DREAMS

MCGA and Ideological Interpellation

School children in China in the 1980s and 1990s were all taught "red songs," such as *Without the Communist Party There Would Be No New China*, whose lyrics follow:

> Without the Communist Party, there would be no New China.
> Without the Communist Party, there would be no New China.
> The Communist Party toils for the nation,
> With a single heart, it saves China.
> It points the path to the people's liberation,
> It leads China toward a bright future.
> It persevered through eight years of war against [Japanese] aggression,
> It improved the people's livelihood.
> It built base areas behind enemy lines,
> It brought the benefits of democracy.
> Without the Communist Party, there would be no New China.
> Without the Communist Party, there would be no New China.

This song reveals how the Communist Party of China (CCP) legitimizes itself by depicting itself as the sole savior of the nation. Ideally for the regime, there would be only one story of national revival with the party at the center of the narrative. In this regard, Make China Great Again

(MCGA) works, although they echo the official "Chinese dream" rhetoric of national revival, complicate regime legitimation in China: As commodified digital cultural experiences, these works enable writers and readers to present their interpretations, reflections, and aspirations of China's past, present, and future, which are not always compatible with state narratives, norms, and values. Therefore, like the market-based neoliberal nationalism that emerged in the 1990s in the cultural realm "simultaneously suggesting and subverting the state project of modernization," MCGA fictions bear more ambivalent implications for the state.[1]

In this chapter, I examine more closely how MCGA alt-history fiction, by popularly articulating and contesting various imaginations to achieve an ideal China as well as personal ambitions, enable societal consent negotiation of authoritarian rule. I find that although these works may deviate from state ideology, policies, and narratives, they are overall not quite threatening toward the regime. Rather, the production and consumption of MCGA works function as a process of "constructive destruction" that helps (1) validate, enrich, and popularize state-preferred norms, values, and beliefs; (2) promote pro–status quo tendencies; and (3) further weaken the role of cultural elites who tend to question, criticize, and rival the state. Therefore, I argue that while such popular participation allows citizens to contest the state in the ideational realm, it also activates ideological interpellation, a critical and necessary step of consent negotiation toward achieving pop hegemony.

CITIZEN PARTICIPATION AND POP HEGEMONY IN DIGITAL CHINA

According to Antonio Gramsci, "hegemony" is not just one-sided dominance but builds on the consent of citizens. An individual may "take part in a conception of the world mechanically imposed by the external environment" or "work out consciously and critically one's own conception of the world." He adds that a social group can have "its own conception of the world, even if only embryonic" while adopting a conception that is "not its own but is borrowed from another group."[2] The question then becomes, how does the ruling ideology achieve its status? To Gramsci, "Ruling groups do not maintain their hegemony merely by giving their domination an aura of moral authority through the creation and perpetuation of legitimating symbols; they must also seek to win the consent of subordinate groups to the existing social order." For a "historical bloc" to achieve cultural hegemony, it "must develop a world view that appeals to a wide range of other groups within the society" and "be able to claim with at least some plausibility that their particular interests are those of society at large." Moreover, it may "require selective accommodation to the desires of subordinate groups."[3]

Louis Althusser employed the concept of "ideological interpellation" to describe the process through which ideology "recruits" and "transforms the individuals into subjects."[4] The concept, though it assigns a passive role to subjects whose motives and agency are of little importance (with which I disagree), acknowledges that individuals need to be transformed into subjects. Such a process is subject to contradictions and struggle, albeit that the power relations between the ideology and individuals, or the state and citizens, are highly unequal. This reasoning suggests that the "popular consent" toward the ruling ideology can be contradictory and ambiguous in nature and that citizens can assume highly active roles in negotiating and sustaining it rather than simply being dominated or domesticated by it.

China in the reform era provides an excellent opportunity to apply, contextualize, and criticize the claims of Gramsci and Althusser, especially because of the coupled effects of economic reforms and the digital revolution. After all, according to Karl Marx, ideological transformation is linked closely to the material transformation of the economic conditions of production.[5] Evidently, economic reforms have brought about profound sociopolitical changes in China in the past few decades, including in state-society relations, with the state having retreated significantly from and loosening its control over society.[6] Chinese citizens now not only enjoy more socioeconomic freedoms and a bigger space to articulate and defend their interests but also have experienced an ideological liberation that has several interrelated aspects: (1) prior state ideology of Maoism and communism has lost its appeal among citizens (and party cadres), who became disillusioned through the Maoist era; (2) a state-initiated ideological evolution has been necessitated by the economic reforms to accommodate capitalism in a namely socialist country and the ease of ideational control (e.g., "emancipating the mind"); (3) the "ideological state apparatuses," such as mass communications, education, and cultural sectors, that were previously controlled tightly by the state, have been weakened; and (4) alternate ideations, homegrown or imported, which have contested the state's ideological hegemonic status (dubbed "spiritual pollution" by the state), have risen or resurfaced.[7]

The ideational liberation (or ideological confusion and chaos from the state's perspective) of the 1980s, less so in the 1990s, has abundant illustrations and embodiments, including the rise of "money worship" (an extreme form of materialism that pursues money as the primary measure of a person's worth, success, and happiness), the debate on "bourgeois liberalization" (ideational tendencies toward Western-style capitalism, liberal democracy, and individualistic values that were deemed as threatening the socialist system and the party's leadership), and the "high culture fever" (when Chinese intellectuals, scholars, writers, and artists eagerly engaged with new ideas to reevaluate Marxism, reassess tradition, and reengage Western thoughts after the Cultural Revolution).[8] The climax, evidently, was the 1989 Tiananmen movement, after which the CCP reiterated the Four Cardinal Principles to cement its leadership status ideologically and began to emphasize "stability triumphs all."[9] Although the CCP managed to stay in power, the crackdown, in the Gramscian sense, was far from a victory, as the party was able to reassert "domination" only with its coercive apparatus; it failed to reaffirm its ideological "hegemony," quite miserably, sending an explicit signal of the party betraying its ideological roots as well as the people.[10] Thus, instead of being the end of the hegemonic struggle, 1989 was only the beginning. Since then, the regime has needed to continuously relegitimize itself ideologically. This explains why the party-state has resorted to nationalism and performance as new sources of legitimacy, which is well reflected in the evolution of official ideologies, including Jiang Zenmin's Three Represents (which depicts the party as a catchall ruling party delivering performance instead of a class-based revolutionary party); Hu Jintao's scientific development (highlighting sustainable development rather than any political ideology), and Xi Jinping's Chinese dream of national revival.[11]

Additionally, the development of digital technologies has transformed China, materially and ideationally. Focusing just on state-society relations, the internet has empowered society, allowing citizens to better connect with each other, to mobilize and organize online and offline, to express their views, and to engage in governance through social media or e-government platforms.[12] Along with enhancing participation and pushing the state's boundaries, the brave new world of cyberspace has given Chinese society an edge as early pioneers in shaping this new *field* with, if not ahead of, the state, albeit only briefly. Online communities like forums articulated and formulated their norms and regulations in the late 1990s and early 2000s, when the state was still learning to control and manage the internet.[13] More recently, despite state intervention, social and market forces have deeply shaped popular digital cultural consumerist experiences, such as live streaming, gaming, and internet literature, as I highlight.[14] It is fair to argue that China has witnessed deeper, broader, and more pluralized participation than it had in the pre-internet age, challenging not only the state but also the cultural elites that previously dominated this realm.[15]

In short, China's ideological landscape has been transformed by both the reform era and the digital revolution. The reform has broken the state's monopoly over the ideological realm, with market and societal forces now playing an indispensable role in ideational production and promulgation. Access to the internet, by lowering the participation threshold for the masses, makes ideological contestation and expression more popular and less elitist. Although cultural elites are still influential in the ideational realm, their influence has declined in a relative sense.[16] It is within such a context that I study alt-history fiction as a window into ideological contestation in China and the process through which pop hegemony can be organically constructed. Thus, writers and readers are not just producers and consumers of everyday digital experiences but also active participants in "ideological interpellation."

CHANGING HISTORY, CHANGING CHINA

In addition to the MCGA theme that echoes the official Chinese dream, as revealed in the previous chapter, alt-history titles display an impressive level of diversity in many senses, especially regarding how they make China great. In this section, through systemic coding and analysis, I examine the specific reforms they propose to save and revive China, and the personal desires they pursue. In doing so, I reveal whether and how such digital consumerist experiences challenge or reaffirm authoritarian rule, as well as the implications for authoritarian legitimation.

Methods Notes

To study the variety of popular Chinese dreams in alt-history fiction and examine how they have attempted to make China great again, I collected the metadata on all the works listed on Yousuu, an internet literature commentary community platform, the most popular of its kind (N = 263,105). Then I coded the 2,100 most popular works from the list (less than 1 percent of the whole dataset), identifying 238 titles that fell into the MCGA category.[17] A student assistant and I coded the top two hundred MCGA titles by how history has been altered, giving special attention to the historical period each work focused on; whether it incurred reforms in military, economic, political, scientific and technological, or sociocultural realms; and how it dealt with minorities, or whether it involved territorial expansion.

In addition to these two hundred titles, I also drew on my personal reading experiences to supplement the analysis. The Yousuu dataset, while useful, is limited in a few ways. First, like other platforms in China, Yousuu is subject to state censorship, and thus some influential MCGA works, such as *Red Dawn*, which was removed from the website in 2019 (mentioned in chapter 3), are not included. Second, because Yousuu (and its predecessor, Dragon Sky's book recommendation channel) was set up only in 2011 and relies primarily on user-generated content, the platform has a slight bias against earlier works, because readers tend to consume and comment on more recent novels, as I acknowledged in chapter 3. Third, relying on user recommendations also means that Yousuu's collection is influenced by the preferences of its users, which certainly is not a representative sample of the Chinese population. For these reasons, I do not make any claim of representativeness about these findings, even though the sampled MCGA titles certainly are the more popular ones.

Reforming China in Alternate Universes

Figure 4.1 shows the distribution of the historical time periods featured in the two hundred coded MCGA titles. As discussed in chapter 3, these works cover periods as early as the Spring and Autumn period (771–476 BCE) to China's reform era. Although these titles demonstrate a strong attempt to intervene during critical historical junctures to save China from crises or continue its glories, the Ming dynasty stands out, with fifty-two of the two

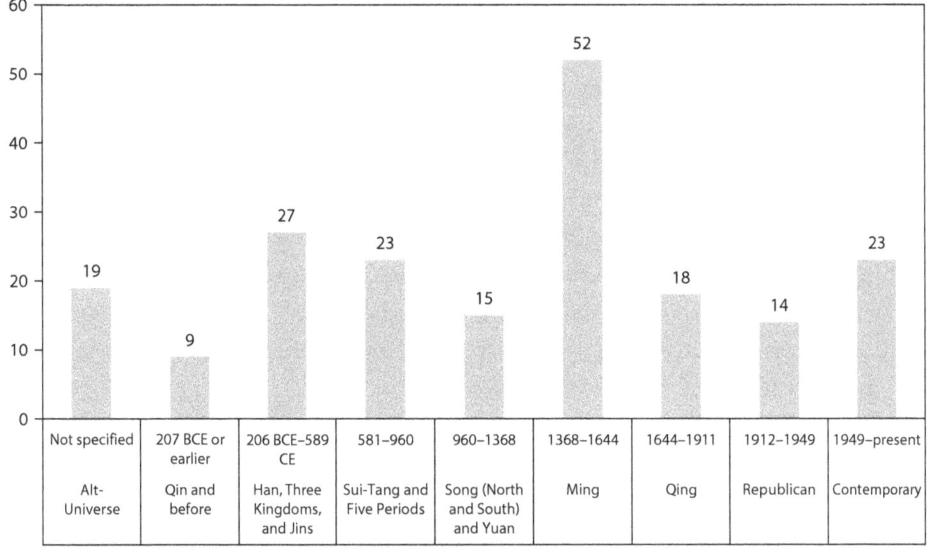

FIGURE 4.1. Historical periods of sampled MCGA fictions.

hundred MCGA titles focusing on this period. This "Ming fever," as Michael Szonyi termed it, demonstrates the eagerness to save the last dynasty by Han Chinese from the Manchu takeover and to prevent China from falling behind in the Age of Exploration and the Industrial Revolution.[18]

Table 4.1 provides an overview of the different types of reforms that MCGA fiction writers have proposed to revamp historical China. Overall, these works have attempted to modernize China in almost every aspect, including the military, science and technology, the economy, and politics, as well as sociocultural norms and practices. The majority of these titles have demonstrated an expansionist tendency.

TABLE 4.1
Proposed MCGA transformations

	Military	**Science and technology**	**Economic**	**Political**	**Sociocultural**	**Expansion**	**Minority**
Yes	123	133	172	93	150	129	142
No	77	67	28	107	50	71	56
Total	200	200	200	200	200	200	200

Of the two hundred MCGA fiction titles, 123 (61.5%) touch on military reforms, which include reforming military institutions covering the recruitment, organization, training, and command as well as bringing modern military technologies to premodern China. This focus on the military is logical, because an advanced military force is often deemed necessary to accomplish the MCGA goal—for many writers (and the Chinese in general), the crises the nation experienced in history were often caused by insufficient military capabilities in the face of "barbaric" minorities or "imperialists." Moreover, developing military capacity also helps the main characters of these titles pursue personal power ambitions, such as defeating competitors and conquering the world.

Nearly two-thirds (133) of the coded MCGA fiction works attempt to advance China's sciences and technologies to some degree. We include only scientific and technological advancements in the civilian realm (not military technologies). These advancements can be as "simple" as inventing soap, perfume, or glass to raising startup funds for the main characters, or pursing bigger adventures to induce broader industrial development and even full-scale industrial revolution. In some cases, modern academic and higher education institutions are installed to perpetuate this trend of scientific and technological progress.

About 86 percent (172) of the titles cover some form of economic reforms, including creating a market-based commercial economy, promoting domestic and international trade, and directly pushing for capitalism and industrialization. For such purposes, many writers introduce modern market institutions, the concept of property rights, intellectual property protection, and the modern banking system to ancient China.

Three-fourths (150) of the works touch on various sociocultural transformations, including reforming the education and ideological systems (e.g., shifting away from Confucius learnings; extending education opportunities to previously excluded social groups, such as women and the poor), improving gender equality (e.g., granting women economic, political, and social opportunities), and popularizing modern ideas (e.g., equality or civil, political, and social rights). Such reforms depict traditional China as a highly unequal patriarchal society that deprived many of its members, especially women and the poor, of opportunities and rights while stifling technological innovations. Some MCGA titles even attempt to transplant Christianity to China (see the discussion of *Usurping Ming* in chapter 3), believing that the religion and its missionaries could help modernize the nation, especially scientifically and technologically.

Compared with other reforms, MCGA fiction seems less likely to transform China politically, even in alt-universe settings. Out of the two hundred coded titles, only 93 (41.5 percent) include reforms of political ideologies or institutions in meaningful ways. Close reading shows that even when political reforms are included, they are often limited in nature, taking forms like adopting the imperial examination earlier or minorly restricting the power of the monarchy. Such observations suggest that writers are probably constrained. That said, some MCGA works, such as *Pointing South* (discussed in chapter 3), have seriously explored other possible paths of political development, such as institutionalizing meaningful checks and balances and introducing democratic systems like competitive elections and parliamentary politics.

The MCGA genre is nationalistic by definition. Therefore, it is intriguing to examine whether they display an expansionist inclination and attempt to annex territories beyond historical borders in the alt-universe. We coded the sampled titles using a conservative scheme: We did not include cases when dynasties defeated their minority enemies in history (such as the Han dynasty versus the Huns or the Song dynasties versus Jin, West Xia, or Liao) or reestablished dominance over the region without seizing or colonizing additional territory. Out of the two hundred works, almost two-thirds (129) display an expansionist tendency, although this varies significantly—some settle the boundaries beyond the specific historical periods the titles focus on, but within China's current territory; others take over neighboring states like Korea and Japan; still others feature a global expansion across all the inhabited continents. Most interesting, the global expansion is typically inspired by, and mimics, Western imperialist expansions.

China's history is rife with interactions between different ethnic groups, especially the Han and non-Han groups, which feeds contemporary Han chauvinism.[19] Although contemporary state policies emphasize ethnic harmony and depict all ethnicities as part of the Chinese family, Han Chinese often see minorities as a nuisance or even a threat, as reflected in the 142 MCGA fiction titles in our sample that discuss the Han-minority relations, almost all of which assume a Han-centric perspective. That said, these works have proposed different approaches to deal with minorities. Closer examination reveals that forty-four works see the relationship as primarily conflictual, thus adopting a suppressive minority policy; twenty-one works attempt to build more harmonious and equal Han-minority relations; and seventy-seven fall in between, depicting the relations as both conflictual and reconcilable. Of this last group, many identify one major minority enemy—the Huns during Han dynasties, the Mongols during Song and Ming, or the Manchus during Ming and Qing—while collaborating with other minorities; they may also employ a divide-and-conquer strategy to work with the soft-liners within the enemy ethnicity.

Note that this categorization does not do justice to the incredibly rich and nuanced reforms that MCGA works introduce. Significant variations exist within each of the categories in terms of both the specific reforms that are proposed and the extent to which the reform measures have been implemented. Moreover, the reforms play different roles in each of the works. For some, reforms are simply instruments to push forward the storylines; for others, reforms are central to the stories, with the writers providing lengthy justifications and operational details (e.g., in *Red Dawn*, which was seen as preaching by many readers for this reason; see chapter 3). The latter approach clearly suggests more serious reflections on Chinese history and the nation's present and future possibilities.

The Variety of Chinese Dreams

Although MCGA fiction reflects the convergence of the collective ethos and official ideation of China's revival, it is first and foremost a digital cultural consumerist phenomenon, which is spontaneous rather than state sponsored. Moreover, given the commodified nature of internet literature, MCGA fiction is digitally mediated and market driven. Therefore, although the works echo the state ideology of the official Chinese dream, the MCGA stories that they tell are far from being the same. Indeed, their production and consumption ultimately depend on the agency of writers (and readers) and the techno-market mechanisms, especially the competition for attention, which has pushed writers (and platforms) to come up with novel MCGA ideas. After all, readers are unlikely to be attracted to the same old cliché. To stand out (and make money), writers must differentiate their stories from others.

China's long history, the myriad of problems the nation has faced, and the imagination of writers (and readers) have all made MCGA differentiation possible. Although all about saving China, the types of crises and the historical settings in which such crises happen can vary. They can involve preventing the takeover of China by minorities—such as the Mongols or Manchus—or defeating imperialist powers in modern history—whether Britain, Russia, Japan, or a group. Moreover, saving China often requires a complex process, which involves various military, scientific and technological, economic, political, and sociocultural reforms. The different reforms project different Chinese dreams: Those centering on introducing modern military institutions and technologies imply the perception of China's past lacking military power. Works that push for breakthroughs in sciences and technologies often see ancient China's problem as being technologically stagnant. Those touching on the economic reforms attempt to break down China's natural economy and turn it into a commercial, ultimately capitalist, economy. Similarly, efforts such as religious reforms, universal education, and the emancipation of women to transform China's sociocultural characteristics indicate that the old practices and norms are no longer acceptable.

Political reforms, although often cautiously discussed and the specific measures significantly varied, reflect probes and imaginings about what is the best political system for China. Understanding how to set China's boundaries and its relations with the outside world portray MCGA writers' perceptions of and preferences for the historical and contemporary world order. Therefore, many works punish Japan in the alternate universe, make China a colonial power, or set up a more benevolent world order under Pax Sinica. Finally, the ways in which MCGA novels deal with minorities reveals the diverse and complex opinions toward ethnic relations and policies in contemporary China. The key question for the majority of the writers and readers who are Han Chinese is whether to be, or not to be, Han chauvinistic.

The historicity of MCGA stories reflects the continuous explorations of the Chinese people to revive the nation in modern history. Such explorations have created the shared experience and understanding of national humiliation for the entire society, and the CCP's victory seems to have affirmed the claim that "only the Communist Party of China can save China."[20] These attempts, failed or not, also suggest distinctive paths of national salvation, and thus different Chinese dreams. This means that the CCP, despite its dominance in sociopolitical life, especially its effort to shape historical narratives, does not have a monopoly on the interpretation of the Chinese dream. In fact, even the party acknowledges that the pursuit of national revival did not end with the founding of the People's Republic of China in 1949. The comparison and contrast of the Maoist and reform eras reveal the complexity of national revival, suggesting that a single path may not be sufficient to achieve the goal, because it took Mao to help China "stand up" (*zhan qilai* 站起来) and the reform era to make the nation "more prosperous" (*fu qilai* 富起来), and, ultimately, under Xi, "getting strong" (*qiang qilai* 强起来).[21]

Therefore, in addition to making up historical sorrows, the MCGA titles enable contemporary Chinese to probe other possibilities and to express dissatisfaction, albeit in a guarded and implicit fashion, toward the status quo. The hypothetical setup provides writers and readers with the convenience to imagine a different China. Thus, MCGA works are not simply nationalist pipedreams, but instead are thought experiments by the writers and readers to reflect on China's past, present, and future. Such historicity explains why, although these works are by definition unreal, writers and readers have emphasized that they should be realistic and logically coherent.

The agency of writers and readers, market incentives, and historicity may lead MCGA works to deviate from, or even contest, the state's ideological constructs and policies, including the official Chinese dream. For instance, some extremely popular MCGA titles institutionalize a parliamentary system or other forms of representative democracy (e.g., *Ruling Under Heaven* and *Pointing South*, introduced in chapter 3), constitutional rule, and checks and balances (e.g., *Pointing South*). These works represent serious contemplations of politics and quests for a better China, while also functioning as an indirect critique of contemporary China. A case in point is *Pointing South*, which introduces a series of "liberal" political reforms, including popular elections and a constitution modeling on the English Magna Carta and the US Declaration of Independence.[22] The writer justifies such reforms through Wen Tianxiang, whose rebirth name is Li Wenzhong:

> From Wenzhong's memory, he believed that the only way to address the ills of officialdom was to have popular elections. If people have the power to either appoint or remove the officials, local officials will not dare to be

> negligent. Even when an official acts recklessly because he is from a powerful noble clan, his opponents will quickly find his faults and expose him. Lack of public awareness or problems like vote-buying should not be cited as excuses for opposing elections at all. In Wenzhong's time, the ruling party [the KMT] used such excuses to justify its authoritarian rule, and the party to which Wenzhong belonged [the CCP] wrote many articles criticizing these excuses.[23]

Given what happened under communist rule after 1949, this passage seems intentionally sarcastic. As Wenzhong was inspired by his experiences in the communist base area, this is essentially "waving the Red Flag to knock down the Red Flag" (*dazhe hongqi fan hongqi* 打着红旗反红旗). The paragraph attracted readers' attention. In the WeChat reading app, one user remarks, "Not mentioning the Song dynasty, this is not achieved even today." Another user admits, "[election is a] universal value with which one has no choice but to agree." Such comments suggest that readers do take part in implicit criticism toward the current regime.

In addition, and quite ironically, alt-history fiction can upset the state more when it champions the official ideology of communism. As discussed earlier, *Red Dawn* is heavily censored; even works that advocate communism in a postapocalyptic world can be targeted (see chapter 2). Another work of fiction, *Qin Revolution* (*Ge Qin* 革秦), which learns from communism and Maoism to reform Qin during the Warring States era, was temporarily blocked, forcing the writer to change its title and storyline.[24] The state deems communism in MCGA titles threatening, probably because it can lead readers to question whether or not the party has changed. This does more than embarrass the regime. It also divides society—many Chinese citizens hope to hear "yes," whereas others prefer "no"; thus, the state cannot pacify all. Furthermore, communism nostalgia can threaten the regime by providing both ideological justification and mobilization tactics for popular contention.[25]

MCGA novels can also be disruptive in other ways besides discussing a different political system or the troubling ideology of communism. Many works are ostensibly Han chauvinistic (see anti-Manchu titles such as *Usurping Ming* and *F—k Qing* in chapter 3), thus directly challenging the state agenda of ethnic inclusivity and harmony, as reflected in the "Chinese nation" (*Zhonghua Minzu* 中华民族) notion, which transcends ethnic divisions.[26] In addition, many writers (and readers) aim to project China's influence or control beyond its current or historical territories. This expansionist tendency is against the official foreign policy, the rhetoric of "peaceful rise" under President Hu Jintao, and "the community of shared future for mankind" promoted by President Xi Jinping.[27]

Although many writers (and readers) see the subjugation of minorities (especially the "troubling" ones in history) and territorial expansion as necessities for a powerful China—to prevent another "barbarian" takeover or national humiliation, some writers have begun to reflect on the tensions in such choices. Take *Pointing South* again as an example. Although the fiction depicts Mongols as barbaric enemies, it promises an equal and inclusive China, stating that the government should protect everyone, including "minorities such as the Khitans and Jurchens, and even the Mongols and Semus who are willing to live on Chinese land."[28] The same fiction adopts an expansionist policy by sponsoring privateering (i.e., the practice of the state sponsoring privately owned ships to attack and rob enemy vessels) in Southeast Asia, mimicking the Europeans in the Age of Exploration. This begs the question of whether being a victim of foreign invasions and colonialism justifies China's exploitation of other nations. Acknowledging this tension, the author describes the inner struggle of a character: "In his mind, the new government is as clean as a newborn baby. One should not find in it deception, filthiness, or behaviors like robbery. But deep inside, a voice reminds him that the new government is neither good nor evil. . . . It is just the means . . . to make the nation rise faster and the people live more prosperously."[29]

Alt-History Fiction as Personal Fantasies

In addition to MCGA, alt-history titles typically also feature the adventures of writers and readers to achieve personal dreams. This is unsurprising given the popular consumerist nature of internet literature. To a large extent, writing and reading are highly personal experiences. In its early days, internet literature was more an act of individual expression with many writers aiming to achieve their personal dream of becoming professional writers.[30] As internet literature evolved into a commercialized industry that capitalizes on readers' attention, writers have become increasingly motivated to attract readers and entertain them. Even the MCGA theme is often instrumentalized for such a purpose. After all, there is no personal dream grander than saving the nation. Although such an individualistic inclination is hardly a signal of deviation in and of itself, because China has experienced more than four decades of socioeconomic reforms, it can conflict with the spirit of official ideology in two senses.

In the first sense, MCGA works often reflect personal desires for power, wealth, and women. Many essentially tell the story of how heroes "rise to the top" and become emperors, top officials, powerful generals, and the richest businessmen. Although this hunger for power can be justified by the argument that the main characters must grow powerful enough to influence the course of history, how these works treat women betrays the personal gratification nature of the pipedream (at least partially). Our coding results show that 126 of the 200 MCGA titles include stories of the male protagonists marrying more than one woman or having affairs with mistresses. In addition, as in other genres, readers can easily find erotic content in MCGA titles, which annoys female readers but functions to please the main target audience of male readers. Such strong urges for power and sex are not quite in line with the socialist core values. In this regard, MCGA tittles, like many other genres of internet literature, are essentially fantasies to entertain readers who are pursuing pleasure.[31]

In the second sense, the official Chinese dream is a collective one, in which individual citizens subordinate to and depend on the state. Although President Xi sees that dream as both the "dream of the Chinese nation" and "the dreams of every Chinese person," he also made it clear that "the future and destiny of each and every one of us are closely linked to those of our country and nation. One can do well only when one's country and nation do well."[32] For Xi and the CCP, "fulfillment of the dreams of individual citizens is bound to China's development as a nation, and that personal dreams will be realized only through the revival of the Chinese people as a whole."[33] In short, citizens' personal dreams not only are secondary to the collective Chinese dream but also are subject to state approval. Therefore, the highly individualistic and consumerist expressions in MCGA works, the many ways through which they make China great again, constitute a challenge toward the party-state, even when they do not explicitly intend to do so.

ALT-HISTORY FICTION AS IDEOLOGICAL INTERPELLATION

The thousands of alt-history MCGA titles tell a variety of Chinese dreams and reflect citizens' individualistic desires, which can be incompatible with state norms, values, or discourses. Yet such deviations, instead of posing deadly threats toward the regime, represent more popular participation in the ideological governance of contemporary China.[34] In fact, while MCGA fiction writing, reading, and reaction involve popular ideational contestation with the state, I argue that the entire process is constructive for the regime, functioning as the "ideological interpellation" necessary to achieve pop hegemony.

Nonthreatening Deviations

Although in alt-history MCGA titles, one can easily identify norms, values, beliefs, or practices that deviate from what the state prefers, such deviations are typically minor, nonsystemic, or guarded and implicit, and thus murky. For instance, *Pointing South* introduces democratic institutions like popular elections and even a Magna Carta–type constitution, which is a sarcastic move given none such institutions exist in modern China. The nationalistic MCGA theme might explain why the work has not been censored, but it also might not have been censored because of how these democratic institutions and ideas are introduced. Rather than advocating democracy fervently, the writer depicts it as an exploration, as reflected in the inner struggle of the main character:

> Of course, Wen Tianxiang does not know that the problem plaguing him at that moment in fact has confused generations of Chinese in another time and space. . . . Of course, he cannot find the correct answer. To be sure, the answer in Wenzhong's memory is also fragmented, with many inconsistent parts. Wenzhong demanded the central [KMT] government at the time for democracy. But the party he belonged to [the CCP] and the ideas that he pursued [communism] need absolute obedience. . . . He firmly believes in the system granting people the right to vote and elect officials from below, but has to face the many disappointments in reality. . . . He is plagued by erratic thoughts, beyond what he can bear. So much so that he . . . forgets one very important thing: it is too early to consider how to govern the country

right now, as he is not even sure that the Song will survive the attacks of Northern Yuan.[35]

Being uncertain, ambivalent, and struggling can be a strategy to criticize without triggering censorship, as it softens the tone significantly, which in turn renders such criticism nonthreatening.[36] The writing suggests that, in the end, democracy is not the ultimate answer, but a means to achieve more important goals such as national salvation. In doing so, the writer creates enough cushion space and signals enough loyalty to the state that the fiction does not become subversive. If democracy is only optional, all other explorations, including that of the Chinese party-state, can be equally legitimate. Moreover, the fact that the protagonist was an anti-Japanese communist soldier, and that the idea of popular elections was inspired by the CCP's practice, while ironic, makes the subtle criticism "rightful," thus affirming the regime's historical legitimacy as both a vanguard democratic force (before 1949) and a nationalist force (resisting Japanese invasion).[37] Although the CCP has failed to deliver on its democratic promises, which it is aware of (as reflected in President Xi's "two cannot negates"—one should not use the Maoist era to negate the reform era and vice versa—a clear attempt to prevent citizens from exploiting the incongruity), such historical legitimacy is still useful for the regime.[38] At least, the party can argue that it has experienced institutional reforms, ideological adaptations, and policy changes, through which it can correct itself in the long run (and thus, even if it makes mistakes, one should not overthrow it but wait for its self-correction).

Even MCGA stories of communism, which have been diligently censored by the state, may not be that threatening. While asking tough questions regarding the nature of the regime that may facilitate collective mobilization, these works reaffirm the regime's communist legitimacy. The reform-era state might have shifted to nationalism and performance for legitimacy.[39] The ideology, however, can still be beneficial to the regime, especially since Maoism and communism are now regaining popularity.[40] Considering that the party has yet to officially renounce communism (the opposite is likely true in recent years as witnessed by Bo Xilai's popularity and President Xi's influence), discussing saving China with communism in a fiction may help pass on the "red genes."[41] Although these works may inspire popular contention, they are not subversive in nature and instead represent the loyalists signaling popular dissatisfaction to the party and demanding it return to the right path.

Moreover, as shown in chapter 2, state involvement in internet literature coproduction keeps the destruction of regime legitimacy under control. Given the state's coercive power, it can effectively set the bottom line for what is (not) acceptable. State influence is further amplified as platforms, writers, and readers consciously avoid or actively comply with state intervention to maintain the limited space of expression or for the sake of profit. In this sense, however, the commodified and expressive nature of internet literature allows and even encourages critical writing to a certain extent, and it also limits the criticalness to a nonthreatening level, similar to what Maria Repnikova has described as "guarded improvisation."[42]

Constructive Destruction

In addition to posing only limited threats, deviations, and criticisms, alt-history works also function as "constructive destruction," which is more than mere amusement to death or loyalty.[43] Rather, alt-history indicates a set of mechanisms that transform ideational contestation in Chinese cyberspace into a process of ideological interpellation. As this analysis shows, in addition to reinvigorating support for the state by invoking proregime nationalism, as reflected in the MCGA theme, these writings actively legitimize and strengthen the regime by enabling the public to participate in the negotiation and making of the social consent of authoritarian rule.

First, both "ideological interpellation" and "cultural hegemony" imply social participation in consent construction. Allowing ordinary citizens to make China great again, even in ways that differ from the official narratives, these MCGA works make "China's rise" and "national revival" more relevant to everyone, thus strengthening the nationalist collective ethos that glues state and citizens together. The variety of popular dreams also makes the official ideology more embracive (even if the state does not intend to do this), thus endorsing the state's overall agenda in the ideational realm. If the Chinese dream is for everyone in China, average citizens ought to be part of imagining it. By enabling individual citizens to directly engage in the making of an ideal China and the negotiation of its shared norms, values, and beliefs, alt-history fiction practices the inclusivity that the state seemingly promises.

Second, MCGA fiction facilitates ideological interpellation by popularizing official narratives about history and the regime, especially given the overall ineffectiveness of state propaganda and indoctrination.[44] Writing about and discussing history and politics used to be a restricted domain reserved for the state (in the Maoist era) or elite intellectuals (in the 1980s) who produce and distribute narratives that are deemed authoritative. Such authorized and official narratives, while being dominant, often are out of touch with ordinary citizens, who prove to be nonreceptive to them and therefore may keep their own unauthorized versions of history.[45] Popular MCGA fiction helps the state address this problem, especially as it has become an important source through which the average Chinese person can "learn history."[46] The face-slapping incident of historian Yan Chongnian, inspired by *Usurping Ming*, illustrates how influential online fiction can be to readers' understanding of history (see chapter 3). By telling stories of learning from and repeating what the party has preached and done, these works reproduce, validate, and legitimize official history as a reasonable, if not the sole, pathway of development for China. After all, imitation is the sincerest form of flattery. Moreover, wrapping state ideological constructs and official discourses in cyber-consumerist experiences fits what Johan Lagerkvist has called "internet ideotainment."[47]

Even when MCGA stories deviate from what the state prefers, they can still support the regime. By questioning and criticizing official narratives in a nonsubversive fashion, MCGA titles may make the regime and its norms, values, and practices more relatable and even appealing. Although these works of fiction explore multiple possible paths of development as well as alternative political ideologies and systems, these works generally fit the state's ideological agenda and socialize citizens with beliefs, norms, and values that are pro–status quo, if not outright regime-legitimizing. For instance, the expansionist tendency of MCGA fiction, while seemingly inconsistent with official rhetoric and policy in foreign relations, echoes the realist power politics reasoning underlying Chinese foreign policy, as reflected in official slogans such as "those who fall behind will be beaten."[48]

Moreover, many MCGA titles directly draw inspiration from the party's revolutionary history. Some, such as *Red Dawn*, nearly copy the CCP's ideology and strategies verbatim. Others, like *Pointing South*, which include Western liberal democratic elements, also borrow heavily from what the party did before 1949, including land reform and the introduction of grassroots elections. All such works echo the narratives found in official history textbooks and state propaganda. Although the fact that the party has betrayed its promises makes such works ironic, they nonetheless legitimize the Communist Revolution, an integral part of the regime's legitimacy.

MCGA works do not have to parrot official narratives, norms, or beliefs to be constructive for the state. Because they involve saving China from historical crises, merely describing the bloodshed, violence, and sufferings in troubled times can help readers recall the bitterness of the past and remind them of the comparatively happy life they live today. For instance, the author of *Morning Star of Lingao* (discussed in chapter 3) writes of how the protagonists have transformed the Tanka community, which owned no land and thus had to live on boats until settled by the CCP. The fiction details the miserable life experiences of the Tanka families, their poverty, and the discrimination they suffered before measures are taken to improve their conditions, which are similar to those the party introduced after 1949. In this way, "the recalling of bitterness of the old society and contrasting it to the happiness of new" functions as what Jeffrey Javed calls "moral mobilization" that bolsters the regime's legitimacy.[49]

Because remembering the bitterness of the past functions to shape one's political expectations, two critical questions can be asked: (1) What are the types of past bitterness that are remembered; and (2) given all the hardships in history, what is cherished today? MCGA works, because of their focus on historical crises, suggest that peace, social equality, and freedom from "barbaric" or foreign invasions are the prioritized goals. Liberty and democracy, although not completely absent, are less prominent and typically are presented as means rather than an end, which is understandable because of both state censorship and the limits of historical context (it would read as quite unrealistic to introduce full democracy in the twelfth or thirteenth centuries).

Some MCGA titles promote cynical and extremely utilitarian attitudes, which are advantageous to the party-state. Self-proclaimed righteousness and purity of the regime, as state propaganda often projects, can be a burden for the autocracy because these claims raise citizens' expectations and political efficacy, rendering any governance grievance a cause for popular dissatisfaction and contention. This reasoning explains the rightful resistance and constructive noncompliance phenomena in China—citizens protest because they still believe in the regime.[50] MCGA titles often feature cruelty, violence, and deception, thus lowering readers' expectations about politics and the quality of daily life, which is again beneficial for the regime. Moreover, some MCGA titles typically advocate for extreme utilitarianism, implying that to make China great, any action, whether cruelty, violence, or deception, is acceptable. In fact, going back in time to change history is in and of itself cheating, regardless of how persuasive the story is. Whether readers deem the conceit justified or reasonable, such plots demoralize and instrumentalize politics. If politics is dirty and self-interested, with all the negatives being its indispensable parts; if the end justifies the means; if equality is hard to come by; if freedom and democracy are flawed and not without a price; and if force is a justified means to gain and maintain power, what shall and can one expect of the current regime? In this sense, these MCGA works may socialize readers into cynicism and utilitarianism, thus accepting, and even agreeing with, the status quo.

Finally, MCGA titles, and internet literature overall, function to dilute the power and influence of traditional intellectuals and cultural elites, thus working to the advantage of the regime. Despite increased state control and co-optation since 1989, intellectuals and cultural elites such as writers, journalists, and lawyers remain critical toward the regime. Their influence in the discursive and ideational realm has been challenged in the digital age. Although some elites have adapted well, as exemplified in the emergence of the public intellectuals online as opinion leaders, they are now relatively marginalized overall. Since the middle-2010s, public intellectuals as a group have been defamed among the public.[51] Some have even argued that the elitist "serious" literature has such a limited audience that even the state now shows a lack of interest in repressing the field.[52] Indeed, by enabling a rising cacophony, the internet and social media distract the audience from and offset the impact of these critical intellectuals, with their more critical and threatening ideas and narratives, even when they are not censored by the state, being flooded, outpaced, and deconstructed in the digital space.[53] Popular consumerist experiences such as internet literature, albeit at times critical and thought-provoking, are much less threatening. As vanguard writer Chen Cun has lamented, the freedom of the internet has led literature nowhere: "I thought that we could do a lot of things with the [internet-enabled] freedom. Now that we have freedom, and the cage is wide open for you to fly. Yet, you failed once again."[54] Shao Yanjun, Peking University professor and internet literature scholar, explicitly argues that popular literature in China is more conservative, thus more politically safe, compared with "elite literature."[55]

Such an anti-elite and anti-intellectual inclination is apparent in some MCGA works. *Usurping Ming* disrupts the conventional positive depiction of late-Ming Confucian scholars. This work as well as many others also rectifies the names of notorious eunuchs, such as Wei Zhongxian, praising them for being more competent and more loyal. Such writings, while deviating from official narratives of history and seemingly irrelevant to contemporary politics, fuel popular defamation of public intellectuals, who are likened to the Confucian scholars in these works: self-righteous dilettantes full of empty talk and little else. A more direct example is *Ruling Under Heaven*. In a chapter published on November 10, 2013, the writer used a popular meme "Shut up, we're discussing democracy and you do not have a say" (*Bizui, women zai taolun minzhu, mei ni shuohua de fen* 闭嘴, 我们在讨论民主, 没你说话的份), which was widely used by netizens to mock public intellectuals as being self-entitled and ideologically intolerant, thus not truly standing for liberal democratic values, as they claimed.[56]

CONCLUSION

Through state intervention and the collective ethos of national revival, alt-history titles feature a shared MCGA theme that echoes the official Chinese dream. They also project a variety of popular dreams and personal desires that reflect different perceptions of history, reality, and the future of the nation from those of the state. The discrepancies and deviations about how to make China great and the proper relations between state and citizens, however, can be critical for the state, functioning more as a form of "constructive destruction" that is, overall, inherently nonsubversive, rather helping to validate, popularize, and enrich state or pro-regime norms, values, and beliefs.

Such "constructive destruction" contributes to ideological interpellation, which is crucial for pop hegemony, because the latter cannot be achieved single-handedly by the state. Popular resonance of state ideology, as reflected in MCGA writings, can be helpful but is still insufficient because the notion of pop hegemony requires individual citizens to actively participate in negotiation, contestation, and production of consent. Therefore, for the state, pursuing absolute control over the ideational realm may be undesirable. Aldous Huxley worries less about *1984* than the *Brave New World* because the former would predictably provoke resistance.[57] Tight control, rigid propaganda, and forced ideological indoctrination only alienate citizens. Controlled deviations and tolerance can paradoxically benefit authoritarian rule because they make the regime look less bad, while also giving citizens a chance to negotiate with the state, without disrupting the regime and the common ground of accepted norms, values, and beliefs.[58] In this sense, ideological interpellation entails a different governing philosophy, with the state no longer pursuing full control but rather accommodating and embracing social participation in exchange for consent of its rule. The reasoning for social participation in pop hegemony extends to readers of internet literature, whose role in the coproduction of digital cultural experiences I examine in chapter 5.

Chapter Five

MORE THAN AUDIENCE

Reader Participation in MCGA

In Chinese, the expression "people who read" (*dushu ren* 读书人) is often used to refer to the educated elite class of gentry scholars, which implies not only the ability to receive information through reading but also an active social, political, and intellectual role. In other words, to some extent, it is equivalent to the Western idea of the intellectual. In modern and contemporary China, those who read—that is, university professors, college students, and writers—have been pioneers in exploring the paths of national development, ideationally and politically, as witnessed in major sociopolitical events such as the May Fourth Movement and the Tiananmen Student Protest.

Writers and readers of online novels are typically not regarded as part of the elite intellectual class. Yet, thanks to improved education and the expansion of digital media, they have gained the ability and opportunity to engage in the production and consumption of cultural experiences, a realm previously reserved almost exclusively for elite intellectuals. Therefore, they have become what Sebastian Veg calls unofficial or grassroots "*minjian*" intellectuals.[1] In this sense, I examine the political implications of this enormous new intellectual group—writers in the millions and readers in the hundreds of millions, joining as a major force in the cultural and ideational contestation of twenty-first-century China.

In the previous chapters, I explored how writers, along with online platforms, and the state have shaped the production of alt-history fiction.

Although I have acknowledged the critical role of readers, I have yet to investigate them in an in-depth and systematic fashion. In this chapter, I do just that, discussing how readers serve not only as an audience and as consumers but also as prosumers engaging in the coproduction of digital experiences. I argue that their participation, mediated by the attention economy rules, is part of an "ideological interpellation" process that both challenges and strengthens the state in the ideational realm, thus bearing crucial implications for authoritarian legitimation and China's future pop hegemony.

READERS IN THE AGE OF PROSUMPTION

The digital age is one of "prosumption." First coined by the futurist Alvin Toffler, this term captures the long-existing and increasingly trending phenomenon of people producing their own goods and services in the digital age, thus serving both the roles of producer and consumer.[2] The idea, which is in itself not new, has attracted scholarly attention and inspired many similar concepts as digital technologies have developed, especially since the Web 2.0 era, as user-generated and shared content has become the dominant mode of digital experience production, distribution, and consumption.[3] According to George Ritzer and colleagues, platforms such as wikis, blogs, and social networking sites have become "ultimate social factories," allowing capitalist systems to "extract value from the unpaid material labor of the prosumers" and "earn even greater profits than they would from the exploitation of workers."[4]

I do not intend to theorize how prosumption in the digital age affects capitalism or the economic model. Instead, I focus on how readers as prosumers coproduce the digital cultural experiences of internet literature. As discussed in chapter 1, the internet and social media have thoroughly transformed the relationships among readers (or broadly the audience or users), writers (content creators), and publishers (platforms)—indeed, since its beginnings, internet literature in China has been a literary enthusiasts' hobby that has helped transform many readers into writers. As a result, the boundaries between producers, consumers, and distributors are not as clear-cut as they used to be. In particular, readers now play a much more active role throughout the process.

First, the writer-reader boundary is an easy one to cross. There is virtually no hurdle to jump to become a writer for anyone who has received a modest level of education. A 2016 survey of online fiction writers finds that the top three reasons they started writing were (1) having a dream of becoming an author since youth (50.9 percent of the respondents); (2) having read many titles, and therefore believing they could also write (42.5 percent); and (3) having read a lot, and thus growing dissatisfied with others' writings (20.8 percent).[5] Although the survey is not based on a representative sample, the results are indicative of trends.

Moreover, the prosumption of internet literature is often community-based.[6] In such cases, community members can simultaneously be readers and writers; they engage in the process not only as readers who provide feedback and inspiration for writers but also as writers. Take *Morning Star of Lingao* as an example. This fiction was collectively conceived on the now-defunct Sonicbbs platform, where one user posted this question in 2006: "How can we survive and change history should we be able to travel back to the late Ming period with a large amount of modern knowledge and products?" This question sparked lively discussions among fellow community members who shared their ideas in a series of follow-up postings. Then, in 2008, Sonicbbs users were again mobilized to imagine traveling to the late Ming, and this enthusiastic participation led to three interrelated collaborative writing projects, with *Morning Star of Lingao* being the most successful. Even though, since it started on Qidian.com in 2009, one user, Xiao Feng 萧峰 (aka *Chuiniuzhe* 吹牛者 Boaster), has assumed the role of chief writer, this work of fiction still relies on a collective role-playing production approach. This approach works with hundreds of contributors adopting the more than five hundred named characters, developing their roles and drafting relevant stories, which are then selected, edited, revised, and sometimes rewritten before being integrated into the main storyline. Moreover, thousands of netizens actively participate by providing historical, technological, and other useful reference materials or ideas for the work.[7] Although most other works do not adopt this approach, this collective production mode has proven to be successful, attracting a huge readership.

Second, internet literature, like other digital consumerist experiences, is an attention economy, which gives readers significant power to influence the production and consumption process.[8] The tremendous and ever-growing number of works made available, and the ability of readers to instantaneously vote with their attention, force writers and platforms to compete with one another, which in turn, according to Alexander Lugg, ensures literary production and its continued improvement to be strongly dictated by readers' values and preferences.[9] The need to better attract, maintain, and capitalize on readers' attention explains why long novels have become the dominant form of writing in Chinese internet literature and why certain genres flourish more than others do. Accordingly, the plethora of MCGA titles is not just the result of writers' preferences (or state promotion) but instead reflects a huge and consistent market demand from the readers, which is often reflected in clicks, subscriptions, rankings, and comments. In addition, the inclination to keep readers' attention for as long as possible has rendered writing a constant social process for authors to bond with their readers to cultivate their affinity and loyalty, which is mediated digitally through the online platforms. Therefore, writers must be more responsive and accommodating to a more active readership (and audience) in their writing and beyond—as part of pop culture and the pan-entertainment industries, internet literature has become a transmedia "fan economy" with readers idolizing both the works and the writers—or they may be punished by the rules of attention economy.[10]

The third way readers play a more active role is through activities such as commenting, recommending, and other types of interactions with writers and fellow readers. In doing so, readers engage with internet literature works while also creating and consuming digital experiences that derive from and move beyond these works. Thanks to digital technologies, commenting on or voting for a novel, communicating with the writer, and creating fan works are now all indispensable parts of the internet literature experience. Such experiences can take place on dedicated reading apps, literature portals, and social media platforms, such as forums, blogs, microblogs, QQ groups, and WeChat friend circles. These digital experiences can be as casual as a click, a like, or a short comment or as involved as more serious commitments, such as writing longer and more thorough critical or referral pieces, producing full-blown derivative stories, translating the works into other languages, or converting these works into comics and videos.[11] Such experiences often move beyond the original works and expand to include interactions with writers and other readers, significantly enriching the digital experiences of internet literature.

READER-WRITER INTERACTION IN INTERNET LITERATURE

Readers play an indispensable role in the production and consumption of internet literature. In particular, they interact with writers daily as prosumers, shaping the creation activities of the latter. For instance, imagine for some reason—having read too many titles or to pursue your literary dream—you intend to transform yourself from a reader into a writer. One of the first decisions you make is picking a genre and a platform. Given the rules of the attention economy, reader preferences, and other considerations such as your own expertise, certain genres and platforms will seem more likely than others to ensure success.

Once you start writing, you will constantly engage readers, often trying to appeal to them because you want to attract and retain their attention. You will need to publish regularly and frequently, because readers will not follow a new writer who fails to do so. Literature portals like Qidian provide many functions to facilitate writer-reader interaction, especially reader engagements, which you should take advantage of. Such functions include voting for preferred titles (which affects ranking and promotion opportunities), tipping (which increases your income and ranking), and providing annotated comments (which can provide useful feedback to improve writing and also allows readers to interact with each other). They often categorize readers based on their reading, consumption, and interaction activities, and grant higher-level readers more privileges.[12] In doing so, they encourage reader engagement and spending, which also benefit you. Take *My Heroic Husband* on Qidian.com as an example. Among its readers, at least two have tipped more than CNY100,000, sixteen have tipped more than CNY10,000, and hundreds have tipped more than CNY1,000 (CNY1 is about USD0.137).[13] Although writers must share the tipping income with the platform, this equates to a significant amount of revenue.[14] As a writer (especially a newbie), you closely monitor indicators, such as clicks, subscriptions, and tips. Although you may insist on writing what you like, you are incentivized to please readers (at least those on your platform). Some common practices include answering the call for more frequent updates, revising the plots (e.g., replacing a sad ending with a happy one), absorbing good suggestions, and even naming characters after readers. You also want to acknowledge your generous tippers, or publish extra installments dedicated to them. In addition, you can connect to readers by publishing sideline stories of the work, including derivative writings in your work, or sharing details of your personal life, reflections on writing, and comments on public affairs (as the author of *My Heroic Husband* often does).

Writers interact with readers not just to please them. Writing is hardly sustainable without enough readers who follow, pay, tip, and vote for as well as accompany you through comments, encouragement, and sometimes even criticism.[15] Although you may focus on the portal where you publish, it is a good idea to check other platforms as you constantly try to attract more readers and improve your writing. In fact, many writers were or are still members of literature forums and other online communities where they interact with readers and other writers. You may also engage with works by other writers for social purposes (such as later promoting each other's works), to get inspired, or simply because you enjoy reading. When you finish writing one title, you hope to carry readers over to your new novel or even to a different platform that offers a better contract.

Although I have highlighted how readers affect writers, this is not a one-way street. In internet literature, readers and writers are mutually attracted, and all interactions start at this point of attraction. After all, readers will not engage with a title unless they are interested in some way (like it or hate it). This gives writers an opportunity to influence readers (who in turn affect writing) intentionally or unintentionally. Given the political nature of MCGA works, this process often functions to socialize readers (and writers) politically. For instance, as mentioned in earlier chapters, *Red Dawn* is widely perceived as preaching communism, sparking discussion and debate among readers (even the state acknowledges this in the sense that it censored the work). The author of *My Heroic Husband* wrote a long essay admitting his intention to socialize readers politically: "I never write about [my positions] directly. The right way is to allure people with YY [*yiyin*, lust of the mind or literally mental masturbation] fantasies and then convert them subtly. When writing *Hidden Kill*, I wanted to convey the youth and warmth I long for. . . . In *My Heroic Husband*, what I truly want to write about is patriotism. . . . Such topics sound very profound, maybe too profound. But at least I wrap them in fantasies in my books [to make them more accessible]."[16] It is beyond the scope of this book to discuss whether writers can affect readers' behavior and attitudes, and vice versa, especially when politics is woven into fantasies, but existing studies suggest they do.[17] Sporadic evidence also shows some observable influences. For instance,

Usurping Ming has not only fueled a change in perception toward gentry scholars in the late Ming (from more favorable to more negative) but also emboldened a reader to slap a Qing history scholar in the face.[18] It is important to at least acknowledge the roles of both writers and readers in creating, maintaining, and negotiating the MCGA discourse, which bears critical implications for ideational governance in China.

COMMENTING AS IDEOLOGICAL INTERPELLATION

Their pervasive and profound involvement has evidently made readers indispensable prosumers coproducing the digital experiences of internet literature, including the experience of MCGA fiction. Given my purpose, this raises an obvious question: How do readers engage in and shape the ideational contestation? In this and the following sections, I conduct a comparative analysis of reader comments to investigate how readers have engaged with MCGA works and how, in the process, they interact with the state, writers, and fellow readers. I argue that, through commenting, readers partake in the creation, spread, and negotiation of the MCGA discourse, which in turn bears implications for ideological interpellation.

Methods Notes

Because it is virtually impossible to provide a thorough panoramic study of all participatory activities of readers—they can interact with the works on many different platforms in various ways ranging from simply clicking to creating fan works—I focus on reader comments given my interest in discourse and discursive practices. I use comments on popular titles from the vibrant literature community, Yousuu, rather than annotated comments on literature portals to make the research more manageable.[19] Specifically, I collected the top twenty comments for each of the top 2,100 titles from the site, among which 238 are MCGA. Separating MCGA works from the rest, I created two datasets with 4,760 and 37,006 comments by 2,112 and 8,950 users, respectively, with a time span from 2011 to 2022.[20]

To analyze the data, I employ a quantitatively informed content analysis approach that combines manual reading and automated text analysis. Automated analysis techniques can process large quantities of data with ease and provide a big-picture view of the discursive patterns. My close reading of the texts ensures a more accurate understanding and interpretation of the data, allowing for the discovery of nuanced discursive practices and dynamics typically missing in automated text analysis.

In the remaining sections, I follow Norman Fairclough's three-dimensional critical discourse analysis that focuses on text, discursive, and social practices.[21] I start from the text level by first identifying the keywords and their distribution using automated text analysis techniques. I then move to the discursive level to map the thematic patterns and dynamics associated with comments on MCGA and non-MCGA works comparatively. By interpreting the discursive practices at the social level, I reveal how readers, through commenting activities, interact with the writers, each other, and the state, thus highlighting how they, instead of being a passive audience, are active contributors and contestants of authoritarian legitimation and pop hegemony.

Automated Analyses and the Results

As a first step, I conducted topic analysis using latent Dirichlet allocation (LDA) modeling to provide a big-picture view of how readers comment on MCGA works. As one of the most popular natural language processing techniques, LDA modeling is an unsupervised algorithm that extracts topics from a text corpus under the assumption that similar topics share similar keywords.[22] Table 5.1 presents the results of a fitted LDA topic model, which is based not solely on the frequency but also on the relevance of a term under a specific topic.

The results show that topic 1 primarily includes terms about the literary and aesthetic quality of the works, such as "figure/character," "plot," and "writing style." Terms associated with topic 2 are mainly about storylines and the plots, as well as social life and personal desires, such as "women," "emperor," and "affection." Both topics indicate the digital consumerist nature of internet literature, thus are likely not distinct to MCGA comments. In comparison, topics 3 and 4 reflect the alt-history and political nature of MCGA works as indicated by keywords, such as "time traveler," "end of the Ming," "nation/state," "politics," "rebellion," and "revolution." Although these two topics share some keywords, such as "development" and "science & technology," topic 3 features terms like "emperor" and "contest for supremacy," which reflect more personal desires to pursue power.

TABLE 5.1
LDA topic modeling of MCGA comments

Topic 1 (34.2% of tokens)	**Topic 2 (22.3% of tokens)**	**Topic 3 (21.8% of tokens)**	**Topic 4 (21.7% of tokens)**
人物 (figure/character)	女人 (women)	皇帝 (emperor)	中国 (China)
情节 (plot)	恶心 (disgusting)	穿越者 (time traveler)	国家 (nation/state)
文笔 (writing style)	智商 (intelligence)	明末 (end of the Ming)	工业 (industry)
剧情 (storyline)	皇帝 (emperor)	天下 (under the heaven)	屁股 (butt)
描写 (description)	太监 (eunuch)	金手指 (golden finger)	政治 (politics)
后宫 (concubines)	剧情 (storyline)	种田 (farming)	世界 (world)
三国 (Three Kingdoms)	东西 (things)	三国 (Three Kingdoms)	思想 (thought)
刻画 (portrayal)	感情 (affection)	发展 (development)	革命 (revolution)
时代 (era)	老婆 (wife)	明朝 (Ming dynasty)	民族 (nation/ethnicity)
风格 (style)	设定 (setting)	科技 (science and technology)	日本 (Japan)
塑造 (shape)	脑子 (brain)	土著 (aboriginal people)	社会 (society)
感情 (affection)	后宫 (concubines)	争霸 (contest for supremacy)	发展 (development)
后期 (later stage)	儿子 (son)	势力 (clout/power)	时代 (era)
缺点 (shortcoming)	抄袭 (plagiarism)	大明 (Great Ming)	推演 (deduction)
月关 (Yueguan [pen name])	毒草 (poisonous weed)	乱世 (turbulent times)	造反 (rebellion)
前期 (early stage)	文青 (arty youth)	时期 (period)	满清 (Manchu/Qing)
题材 (genre)	垃圾 (garbage)	现代人 (contemporary person)	美国 (United States)
配角 (supporting role)	情节 (plot)	造反 (rebellion)	征服 (subdue)
太监 (eunuch)	公主 (princess)	时代 (era)	tg (yokel communists)
文字 (words)	毒点 (toxic point)	路线 (route)	科技 (science and technology)
考据 (textual research)	弱智 (half-witted)	斗争 (struggle)	技术 (technology)
爽文 (pleasure fiction)	古代 (ancient time)	身份 (identity)	汉人 (Han [ethnicity] people)
细节 (detail)	角色 (role)	那种 (that kind)	建立 (establish)
资料 (material)	龙空 (Dragon Sky forum)	敌人 (enemy)	经济 (economy)
精彩 (wonderful)	事情 (matter)	描写 (description)	民国 (Republic of China)
种田 (farming)	孩子 (child)	崇祯 (Chongzhen emperor)	文化 (culture)
优点 (merit)	智障 (mentally retarded)	无双 (unmatched)	垃圾 (garbage)
爽点 (pleasure point)	无脑 (brainless)	毒点 (toxic point)	精神 (spirit)
角色 (role)	生活 (life/livelihood)	太子 (crown prince)	清朝 (Qing dynasty)
印象 (impression)	三观 (value orientations)	古代 (ancient time)	满遗 (Manchu sympathizers)

Such desires, according to Heather Inwood, imply a hedonistic impulse of YY (*yiyin*, lust of the mind).[23] Their frequent appearances indicate personal gratification is an important driver of MCGA dreams.

To better understand readers comments on MCGA as compared with non-MCGA works, I conducted a frequent word analysis. Appendix tables A.2 and A.3 show the top three hundred frequently used words from non-MCGA and MCGA comments, respectively.[24] These results echo our topic analysis findings in that readers of both MCGA and non-MCGA titles discuss the literary and aesthetic quality of the works as well as their storylines and plots; terms like "society," "women," and "female" that reveal societal aspect and personal desires also appear in both keyword lists. Furthermore, comparing these two frequent word lists and removing all those that appear in both from the MCGA list, the remaining keywords, as shown in table A.4, clearly reveal the political features of the MCGA genre. These keywords include "rebellion," "revolution," "democracy," and "capitalism," as well as those of national identity, such as "nation/ethnicity," "Manchu/Qing," and "Han ethnicity." In addition, terms such as "Great Ming" and "Republic of China" reflect the historical periods the genre focuses on, and keywords such as "industry," "technology," "institution," "reform," and "construction" embody these MCGA plots well, as discussed in chapter 4. Overall, the keyword analysis reveals active reader participation in deliberating MCGA dreams.

Terms like "nation/state" and "politics" are among the most frequently used words in non-MCGA comments, indicating that although these titles are comparatively less political, their writers and readers may engage with political topics as well.

Beyond the Keywords: Analyzing the MCGA Discourse

The automated analysis reveals that, in addition to assessing the literary and aesthetic values of the works, readers critically engage in MCGA explorations in their comments. Building on these findings, I examine the discourse that emerges from the MCGA comments through a close reading of the text and "click language," like upvoting.[25] Doing so provides an excellent opportunity to further map the state-society interaction in the ideational realm, especially how state narratives resonate or conflict with the popular discourse.

MCGA titles explore various political, economic, and social reforms to build an ideal China. Readers, by commenting and other coproducing activities, also actively participate in such explorations, often by debating with the writer and other readers why a certain developmental path may or may not work. Given their role as prosumers, it is not surprising that reader comments often echo MCGA works in terms of political orientations. First, not quite surprisingly, both automated text analysis and close reading of the comments find nationalism to be a highly salient theme, reflecting the societal resonance of the official "Chinese dream" ideology. In addition to the content of specific comments, nationalist sentiments are directly manifested in readers' rating of works, with the worst-performing titles almost all being criticized for nationalist reasons. For example, 86 percent of the comments assigned one star (the lowest on Yousuu) to the fiction *Jing Chu Empire* (*Jingchu Diguo* 荆楚帝国), because readers believed the writer is whitewashing Japanese atrocity during World War II. The most upvoted comment under this title called the writer a "bastard Japanese-hybrid" (*Ri Za* 日杂).[26]

This is not the only writer who has been accused of being a foreign "bastard" or a spy. For instance, the highly popular non-MCGA fiction *Joy of Life* (*Qing Yunian* 庆余年), which has been adapted to television, was flooded by one-star raters because its author defended the K-pop idol Kim Taeyeon during the Sino-Korean dispute, in which China reacted strongly against the US–South Korea initiative to deploy a Terminal High-Altitude Area Defense (THAAD) antimissile system.[27] Kim posted a picture of a Lotte brand candy on her Instagram, an action perceived by many Chinese as supporting the company Lotte, which had provided land for the deployment of THAAD. The controversy resulted in a 38 percent one-star rating on *Joy of Life*. In particular, fifteen out of twenty of the top-rated comments were one star. The writer had to issue an apology on Weibo to appease the angry readers.[28] Such cases demonstrate the power of nationalism to shape online discourse (and perhaps that of readers to affect writing). The fact that these titles continue to be widely read and enjoyed by many, however, suggests that room exists for alternative norms, values, and beliefs, or at least the chance to opt out the controversy.

Second, like MCGA titles, comments on MCGA works demonstrate a proregime ideological tendency. This tendency is reflected in the popularity among readers of one subcategory of MCGA fiction commonly dubbed as "aiding-communist" works (*yuangong wen* 援共文). The typical storyline involves protagonists, often time travelers, who go back in time to assist the Communist Party of China (CCP) and the regime in various ways. A case in point is *Never Declassify* (*Yongbu Jiemi* 永不解密), which is about a young man who goes back to the 1980s to help the CCP "predict" the major domestic and international trends. The fiction is the third most bookmarked title among the 238 MCGA titles (667 times). One reader comments:

> The plot twists and turns, and it's truly fascinating. Something off topic: no matter what, no Communist Party, no new China. Somehow, I suddenly thought of the phrase from *Lady Bird*, "What if this is the best version?" . . . In cyberspace, there are so-called public intellectuals, "big Vs" [opinion leaders] or shouting beasts [derogatory term for professors] constantly attacking the Party. But what if this is the best China that could be achieved at this stage? Other than criticizing and insulting, we'd better try our best to repay and build the motherland, not act like keyboard warriors, let alone the lackeys of imperialists![29]

For another example, commenting on the fiction *Rescuing the Great Ming* (*Qiangjiu Da Mingchao* 抢救大明朝), readers disagreed with each other about whether capitalism or communism would save China. Trying to conclude the debate, one reader argues: "I read many comments, and they are all bullshit! Let me spill the truth: (1) Communism cannot save China. (2) Communism with Mao at the core can save China. (3) Communist theory of our country is completely different from the original one. (4) What saved China was not any ism, but Mao and his colleagues and all heroes who strived for the ideal. . . . Some may ask: could capitalism have saved China? My answer: Absolutely not."[30]

Although several more popular comments on this work of fiction, as indicated by the number of upvotes, complain that communism does not fit in the historical context, the fact that many readers expect to transform late-Ming China by introducing communism, even before the Industrial Revolution, is quite indicative. Moreover, even those who argue that the given historical context is not fitting for communism have in fact embraced the Marxist analytical framework of "the base versus the superstructure." In this sense, such contestation still affirms the ideological legitimacy of the party and the regime. Moreover, this comment is in fact explicitly proregime by arguing that it is not communism, but instead Chinese-style communism, with Mao at the core, that can save China.

Other than the ideological and nationalist components, even seemingly less political elements of the comments have political implications. One salient theme in the comments is the pursuit of power. Although this is about personal fantasies, it is related to MCGA: To effectively transform China, it is convenient (if not necessary) for the protagonists to accumulate power, even though MCGA serves merely as the means or justification of power grabs. The pursuit of power is also related to MCGA in a more intriguing way. For writers and readers of alt-history fiction, an important question to ask is whether it is reasonable to strive for certain reformative goals given the historical context. Does industrialization and proletarian revolution make sense before modern times? Can one time traveler singlehandedly transform a premodern society? If not, the pursuit of power becomes both an end in itself (providing personal gratification for writers and readers) and a justified means to achieve the MCGA goals (i.e., to fend off "barbaric" invasions or end a period of turmoil). Indeed, readers frequently debate writers and each other on whether certain MCGA reforms are "reasonable" or too YY (pipe dreaming). Related, writers are often accused by critical readers of being the "golden finger," because they grant unreasonable advantages to the main characters.[31] Writers are expected to do enough research to situate the stories properly in the historical context.[32] Moreover, the pursuit of power is often related to seeking dominance for China. China's ancient glory, especially its regional dominance, has been a key spiritual source of Chinese nationalism. Inversely, its humiliations in modern history are often perceived as the consequences of a powerless nation.

MCGA comments, echoing MCGA fiction, also reveal a morally problematic social discourse. Like other online fiction genres that cater primarily to male readers, MCGA works often sexualize women, as reflected in terms like "concubines," "women," and "wife" (see table 5.1).[33] Commenting on the popular alt-Song dynasty fiction *Ruling Under Heaven*, one user stated: "[T]he plot that I care about most is always when the [the main character] slept overnight in the emperor's bed, and when the adorable queen displayed her jade body. Wake up, [the writer]! Instead of pushing for parliamentary democracy, it is better to push down the adorable queen!"[34] This comment received 535 upvotes, more than twice the second most upvoted comment on this title, which revealed a sexist inclination among the primarily male readership. Moreover, several other comments praised the erotic component. The popularity of such content poses a challenge to mainstream morality, although such "moral corruption" is widely observed in the reform era with the expansion of citizens' socioeconomic autonomy and the state's retreat from the realm. To be fair, not all readers like such sexist elements. At least three out of the top twenty comments on the fiction criticized the protagonist's relationship with his underage maid. Considering the rising feminist movement as well as the popularity of female-oriented fiction genres, this observation reveals a divided, contested, and gendered socio-moral order rather than a homogenous one in contemporary China.[35]

Commenting as Sociopolitical Practices

In addition to creating a discourse that echoes that of MCGA titles, as the previous section reveals, commenting is also social practice, through which readers actively construct their relationship with the writers, each other, and the state.[36] In doing so, they function to socialize writers and fellow readers.

First, through commenting, readers voice their views and preferences, thus incentivizing writers to behave in certain ways. As far as MCGA works are concerned, the widespread comments that advocate nationalism and reaffirm communism not only signal to writers a market preference of such content but also may help the state discipline the writers when they deviate.[37] Such a disciplinary function is particularly evident when readers are directly in conflict with the writers, forcing them to admit their faults and apologize, as in the case of *Joy of Life*, whose author was attacked for picking the Korean idol over his motherland.

Sometimes writers are criticized for reasons other than appearing to be traitors. It can simply be that they have not tried hard enough to save the motherland from its hardships. For instance, the fiction *The Rise of a Great Writer in Republic Era* (*Mingguo Zhi Wenhao Jueqi* 民国之文豪崛起) tells the story of a young man who time travels to 1926 and becomes a prominent writer but fails to save China from the Japanese invasion and other sufferings sooner. Readers are deeply disappointed in the lack of action. As one user put it: "That era was a deep-to-the-bone wound. It hurts so much that it is compulsory for people to do something. . . . This novel, however, more or less prescribed half an ounce of opium, and took out a straw to suck the juice from the wound."[38] Another user made a similar point: "The scumbag main character was laying on a woman's body, but suddenly remembered that the nation was suffering, tens and thousands of people were in dire situations. He felt guilty and slapped himself in the face. He blamed himself, 'How can you be distracted when fucking a woman?' "[39] These are the two most upvoted comments in the entire dataset of comments on MCGA titles (986 and 854 times, respectively), showing that this sentiment resonated with the readers.

Second, commenting is inherently an interactive and dynamic process through which readers speak to and debate with each other, typically by replying to or voting on the comments. For instance, it is common for readers to share, deliberate, and debate on the plots, characters, or any other elements of the works. Some salient themes include whether or not the stories are original and the plots are realistic. Interactions between readers can be political, too. For instance, commenting on *Hello Japanese Devils, We Are Game Players* (*Guizi Nihao Women Shi Youxi Wanjia* 鬼子你好我们是游戏玩家), one user asks: "Is it appropriate to joke about your ancestors' blood-bathing fight [against the Japanese]? Having fun and it's over?" This comment sparked a fierce debate, receiving 279 upvotes and 208 replies. For many readers, the Japanese invasion is a painful topic not to be taken lightly. Thus, the excessive entertaining tone of the fiction is not acceptable for them. For others, this is just another YY (pipedream or lust of the mind) fantasy, which is no big deal, and one should just enjoy it. Some readers even consider the work laudable because they perceive killing the Japanese invaders to be a patriotic act. The debate echoes that of the notorious anti-Japanese dramas that still enjoy a huge audience despite being widely criticized for their ridiculous plots.[40]

Another example is *Spy Stories* (*Dieying Fengyun* 谍影风云), a fiction about a young time traveler going back to 1936 and joining the CCP's underground network to fight against Japanese spies. Some readers question why the hero would join the CCP, given the historical context. One reader responds to the criticism by providing three reasons why the plot is logical, citing the main character's CCP membership before traveling back, the incompetence of the ruling nationalist party (the Kuomingtang or KMT), and the instrumental calculation of siding with the winner.[41] This comment recorded 322 upvotes and 117 responses, indicating its popularity and the active involvement of other readers.

Third, through commenting, readers can directly interact with the state. They are fully aware of and may react to state intervention in their digital experiences. Plenty of the comments mention terms such as "404" or "harmony," both referring to state censorship. Readers mostly do not show an overly critical attitude (maybe because of censorship) but do see state control as an inconvenience. When a title gets censored, many readers often share links or clues that direct fellow readers to locations where the work can still be found, rather than voicing complaints. For example, one author of several time-traveling titles to the Soviet Union has even developed a reputation for being constantly censored. Yousuu users nonetheless talk about his works and tell each other where his works can be found.

In some cases, readers have complained about censorship. Such complaints are not about supporting free speech, but rather express dissatisfaction that the state has targeted the wrong types of content. As one reader put it: "Those writing about smoking, drinking, messing with women, advocating capitalism, and fawning over the West are not blocked. But works supporting the Communist Party are all blocked. Sure enough, the enemy is in the Central Propaganda Department."[42]

THE BUTTS, IDEOLOGICAL INTERPELLATION, AND POP HEGEMONY

For many readers, reading and commenting are personal experiences of a consumerist nature. For others, reading is inherently political, and so is commenting, through which they engage in the political process of "ideological interpellation" consciously or subconsciously. According to one reader:

> Some naïve inexperienced readers may . . . think that we are just reading a novel, how come it is related to ideology? But sorry, while you can try to avoid politics, politics won't let you go. In this world with increasingly intense contradictions, any de-politicization and de-ideologicalization attempts and

> the petite bourgeois sentiment about a quiet and pleasant life and personal experiences will be crushed by the giant wheel of time.
>
> . . .
>
> [Was] it ten years ago, when [. . .] "reverse nationalism" was rampant, writing such a fiction might not getting him into trouble. . . . Yet, the time of ideological chaos and disorder is finally over. With China growing ever stronger and the conflicts with the West increasingly intensified, and in reaction to "reverse nationalism," China has witnessed an unprecedented rebound of nationalist sentiment in recent years. . . . We know that with the inevitable split between China and the West, even if the state knows that nationalism and statism are double-edge swords . . . it has no choice [but to resort to them]. . . . Such a trend is destined.[43]

The reader clearly sees internet literature as a field of ideological contestation and shows a strong distaste for "reverse nationalism"—the inclination to reject one's own national identity in favor of foreign cultures. In his comment, the reader also mentioned *The Last Transfer of Western Tang Empire* as an exemplary work that rides the nationalist trend well. This 2019 short ad film by China's state-owned payment network, UnionPay, tells a story that took place in 790 CE, when the once great Tang dynasty was already in decline and its control over the frontier Western Regions was severely weakened. A small Tang troop transferring military expenses to one of the last frontline fortresses was ambushed by enemies. The last surviving soldier and an army deserter who was subdued by the soldier when trying to steal the money continue the journey. In the end, the soldier dies in a battle protecting the money, and the army deserter carries on and accomplishes the mission.

This quoted reader, who sees internet literature as a field of ideological confrontation, is not alone. The perception is broadly embodied in the debate about one's "butt" (or stance), a term that appears 159 times and is the most frequent term that is distinct to MCGA comments (table A.4; the term ranks third in topic 4 in table 5.1). A close reading of the comments shows that use of the expression "butt" has two dimensions: nationalism and class. The nationalism dimension, evident in the previous quote, is straightforward, requiring one to stick to the Chinese (versus foreign) or Han identity (versus other ethnic groups). Thus, if one goes back to the Qing dynasty, the only "butt correct" (in a sense similar to "politically correct") option is to rebel against the Manchu rulers (and to defend China against imperialists, whenever relevant). When traveling to the Ming dynasty, however, one can either overthrow the empire or save it because it is a dynasty by Han Chinese.

By being an extremely salient factor conditioning the ideological contestation, and with a proregime tendency, nationalism is a "double-edge sword" for the state, as the previous quote rightly points out.[44] Reader comments, like MCGA works, generally affirm regime legitimacy, yet they can be troubling as they often embody Han chauvinism, showing blatant hostility toward minority groups, such as the Manchus and Mongols. One reader, who gave a five-star rating to the fiction *Late Ming* (*Wan Ming* 晚明), reasons: "The work does . . . not quite belong to the 'fairy grass' category. But, since it is a story of killing barbaric Manchus, it gets a bonus point from me personally. So 'fairy grass,' and recommend!"[45] The comment uses an unofficial "grass" rating system that is popular among readers. This system includes four rankings: (1) "poisonous weed" (not recommended); (2) "dry grass" (recommended if starving); (3) "edible grass" (recommended); and (4) "fairy grass" (the best one can get). The fiction is among the highest rated, with only 4 percent of the readers giving it a one-star review, the lowest percentage of all MCGA titles. In contrast, *Hunting Great Qing* (*Soulie Daqing* 狩猎大清), which was accused of siding with the Manchus against the Han, was rated one star by 92 percent of the readers.

The class dimension of the "butt" issue is, generally, about whether or not someone is on the people's side. Although not without contestation, MCGA comments have displayed a left-leaning inclination, or communism nostalgia, as reflected in keywords, such as "revolution," "struggle," "yokel communists" (a nickname for the CCP that highlights its perceived down-to-earth quality), and "Taizu Emperor" (e.g., the first emperor of a dynasty, often referring to Mao) (table A.4; also topic 4 in table 5.1).[46] Thus, it is "butt correct" to side with the communists, especially in modern history that predates the People's Republic of China (PRC), as the "aiding-communist" titles have demonstrated. Such butt-correctness, however, bears more ambivalent implications for the party in the contemporary context: Although it is largely proregime, it also raises questions about whether the party-state has betrayed its ideological roots, and thus the people it has claimed to represent.

Indeed, readers display dissatisfaction with the regime for deviating from its communist origins. An example is *Great Power Heavy Industry* (see chapter 2). This novel earned several government awards, but it was less well received on Yousuu: 48 percent of readers gave the work one star, criticizing it for advocating a private economy and defaming state-owned enterprises.[47] In the words of one reader: "Although [the writer] has become a joke [among Yousuu readers], he must do very well in real life, because what he advocates is essentially enlightened despotism, which is in line with what those in power prefer. For fartizens [referring to powerless citizens, like a fart], you need no brain, you just wait to be arranged. As a fartizen, I will let my butt govern my head and express my strong opposition. Thus, I must rate it as 'poisonous weed.'"[48]

As noted earlier, "poisonous weed" is the lowest rank in the "grass" rating system. Although this criticism often targets writers and other readers, it ultimately points to the party-state that allows, if not directly causes, the disempowerment of citizens to happen. In this sense, the "butt" issue creates a predicament for the regime by affirming its legitimacy based on historical and ideological legacies, while simultaneously indicating popular awareness of and discontent with the fact that the regime has not adhered to its ideological roots. This runs counter to President Xi's "two cannot negates" spirit, which states that one cannot use the first thirty years of the PRC under Mao to negate the reform era and vice versa.[49] This is ironic, because it is the party that has tirelessly indoctrinated the materialist class-struggle perspective into the minds of the citizens.

Given that the regime has used nationalism as an alternative source of legitimacy, can nationalism help the regime overcome this predicament? Existing studies suggest that this strategy seems to have worked thus far.[50] Upon closer examination, however, the MCGA comments suggest this may not always be the case. As one reader put it:

> Nationalism played a progressive role in the modern history of revolution and resistance against imperialism. However, after the establishment of a socialist country, particularly in the more recent restoration of capitalism, playing the nationalism card is undoubtedly self-dividing for the proletariat class. Will capitalists stop exploiting you because of the shared imagined community? "The aristocracy, in order to rally the people to them, waved the proletarian alms-bag in front for a banner. But the people, so often as it joined them, saw on their hindquarters the old feudal coats of arms, and deserted with loud and irreverent laughter." —*Manifesto of the Communist Party*[51]

This comment, while falling short of directly attacking the regime, clearly pits nationalism against communism in the context of China, indicating no easy way out of the ideological predicament.

CONCLUSION

Through commenting and other prosumption activities, readers coproduce MCGA experiences and engage in ideational interpellation, which confirms rather than disrupts regime legitimacy. Could the readers—and especially their nationalist expression—be creations of state trolling? Although this is a valid concern, existing studies suggest that state trolling focuses primarily on social media sites for crisis management, glorifying top leaders, and promoting government policies.[52] Previous studies have also identified traits of state trolling, which are absent from my dataset.[53] Furthermore, it is unfair to simply argue that the prosumption of readers produces only a rally-around-the-flag effect. As this analysis reveals, many readers consciously partake in ideological contestation and, in the process, sometimes challenge the regime. For the Chinese party-state, although nationalism can harness popular support, it may well become extreme or degenerate into Han chauvinism, thereby hurting the state's foreign relations or ethnic policies, if not sparking outright pushback from the public. Communism as an ideology and the party's revolutionary legacy similarly bear intriguing implications for the regime, which has arguably betrayed its roots. Some citizens still allow the party to claim ideological legitimacy, but others have started to question its right to rule, although not quite as explicitly, thus revealing how such a source of legitimacy is a historical legacy that must be carefully maintained. This predicament explains why the state has suppressed some procommunism titles and the young Marxists (especially when they try to join labor or feminist movements), while at the same time emphasizing its "red genes" and trying to "make China Marxist again" (maybe just rhetorically) as a strategy of ideological governance.[54]

The ideological contestation is not restricted to the political realm. Seemingly nonpolitical but morally controversial elements such as sexist content challenge the party-state because it still sees itself as having the mandate to supervise and guide citizens, and moral performance is an important part of its cultural governance and source of legitimacy.[55] Such content, however, as reader comments show, is highly popular and may function to amuse readers to loyalty, thus benefiting authoritarian rule.[56]

Admittedly, despite its popularity, Yousuu may not provide a representative sample of online fiction readers. Because of its connection to the literature forum Dragon Sky, which is known for male-oriented military and alt-history genres, Yousuu users tend to be pickier regarding historical accuracy and more ideologically motivated than readers on other platforms. In addition, reader comments (or other interactions) on many other platforms, such as literature portals and reading apps, can display different dynamics than those on Yousuu. Such differences complicate the picture, but they do not invalidate the argument, given that commenting (regardless of the specific forms it takes) remains a critical way for readers to engage in the prosumption of the digital experiences of internet literature. Therefore, no matter where they are consumed, the ideological interpellation function of MCGA titles (as analyzed in chapters 3 and 4), especially in regard to its implications for authoritarian legitimation, remains similar. That said, if stronger nationalist inclinations and communist nostalgia (as in the case of Yousuu) buy the state more historical and ideological legitimacy, then they also pose a more serious challenge to the regime. An audience that less critically embraces MCGA stories may constitute less of a threat but perhaps also provides the regime with less communist and nationalist legitimacy.

CONCLUSION

Pop Hegemony in the Making

On August 29, 2023, during US Secretary of Commerce Gina Raimondo's visit to China, China's tech giant Huawei released Mate 60 Pro, a flagship phone packed with powerful upgrades that included the mysterious 5G-capable Kirin 9000s chip, which is reportedly manufactured at the seven-nanometer level. This was not an ordinary product release, given the extremely harsh sanctions the United States has imposed on Huawei. In fact, it reportedly raised concerns in Washington that "U.S. sanctions have failed to prevent China from making a key technological advance."[1] As the phone was originally set to launch on September 12, the decision to release it on August 29, with no prior notice, was likely a deliberate response to Raimondo's visit.

In China, the new phone was not just an instant market success, triggering a "buying spree" among consumers.[2] It also sparked a national frenzy celebrating Huawei's breakthrough as a major victory against the United States in their prolonged technological war. The timing of the release was widely interpreted as "slapping the U.S. in the face," with many mocking Raimondo as Huawei's brand ambassador and sharing memes picturing her holding a Mate 60 Pro.[3] The popular sentiment reflected in the Huawei case, combining a consumerist tide and deep-running aspiration of national revival, resonates perfectly with the make China great again (MCGA) theme. After all, the story is legendary, with one company singlehandedly defeating the world's only superpower, as many Chinese see it. In a sense, the story echoes the MCGA fiction *Industrial Tycoon*, discussed in chapter 3, which concluded with a Chinese aircraft carrier visiting New York to declare China's victory over the United States in the economic and technological competition.

By examining the production, distribution, and consumption of internet literature, especially MCGA fiction, I have explored how the Chinese state, market, and social forces have interacted with one another and coproduced the digital consumerist experiences that shape the ideational landscape in contemporary China. This process has taken place against the background of the significant structural changes China has experienced in the past few decades, including socioeconomic liberalization, the information revolution, the rise of China as a global power, and the state's continuous effort to seek new sources of legitimacy, especially since 1989.

By seeing internet literature as a commodified political field in which state, market, and societal actors interact to shape power relations and meanings, I have embraced the state-society paradigm and highlighted the "mutual transformative accommodation" of state and society, which, according to Richard Baum and Alexei Shevchenko, "lies at the very heart of China's post-reform political experience."[4] Unlike studies on Chinese cyberpolitics that take an activism-oriented perspective and focus on hot-button issues on selected social media sites, I have examined the politics of everyday digital experiences. Such experiences serve the critical yet understudied functions of socializing citizens in authoritarian politics and negotiating state-society relations, especially in the ideational realm.[5]

The state's role in coproducing digital experiences is evident through a series of censorship, management, and cooptation efforts. The state sets ground rules, preventing the commodified field from becoming a major source of ideational threats. Instead of strategizing the state's behavior and depicting (or assuming) it as an omnipotent actor that takes every move after careful calculation, however, I assign a relatively passive role to the state in regard to the market and citizens.[6] I adopt this perspective for two specific reasons. First, given its power and resources, the state plays a decisive role in authoritarian political processes, but it is far from omnipotent.[7] In contemporary China, social, economic, technological, and cultural changes are so drastic and rapid that the state often is not the initiator, but the follower and respondent, and in some cases, it is like a firefighter reacting to a fire alarm. Although it may control, manipulate, and take advantage of these changes, the state can hardly preempt or avoid surprises and shocks. In numerous realms in which the state has yet to notice, reach, or control, social and market forces flourish. Second, the conceptions of both cultural hegemony and ideological interpellation imply deep and active involvement of nonstate actors, such as citizens and the market.[8] This involvement is especially true in China, where a reforming communist regime is trying to regain social consent and where it is the social and market forces that really drive the nation's development. Therefore, when it comes to ideological governance, the state has no choice regarding whether it *intends to* engage in the process; instead, the state is challenged by social and market forces and is offered the opportunity to coproduce such experiences. Its choices—to resist and control or to accommodate and exploit—condition the outcome of consent negotiation as well as the resilience of the regime in the ideational realm.

My analysis suggests that digital experiences of MCGA fiction may contribute to pop hegemony, but there are two caveats. First, as discussed in previous chapters, the platforms, writers, and readers are not completely in line with the state in terms of both interests and ideational orientations. As a cultural consumerist phenomenon, internet literature is first and foremost market- and society-driven, with platforms, writers, and readers undertaking business, literary, ideational, and entertainment explorations. Although MCGA titles share the state's goal of national revival, they reveal a variety of "Chinese dreams" that differ from the state politically, economically, socially, and ethnically and in terms of its foreign relations. The consumerist nature of MCGA works is also reflected in the pursuit of personal desires, such as sex and power, which are not quite in line with the "core socialist values" the state advocates.[9]

Second, negotiating social consent for authoritarian rule is an ongoing process and pop hegemony is still in the making. The state has not yet (re)gained ideational dominance. The status quo, although conducive to regime resilience, is an uneasy equilibrium between the state, society, and market.[10] The state needs to continuously convince the citizenry to accept and even facilitate its rule, which is a daunting task given the myriad challenges involved in governing China. Riding the MCGA trend seems to be a convenient choice because national revival is the common denominator between the state and its citizens. China's ever-pluralizing society, however, has made it increasingly difficult for the state to satisfy the diverse needs of its citizens, to convince everyone that it is on the right path, and to justify the sacrifices and compromises needed along the way. The COVID-19 pandemic, for instance, while initially allowed the state to show its competence and validate its promises to represent the best interests of the people, and thus to earn performance legitimacy, eventually evolved into a political debacle as citizens could no longer bear the draconian lockdown.[11] It is equally challenging for the state to prevent nationalism from becoming too extreme and hurting its other policy goals. For instance, many hardcore nationalists expressed disappointment when the state failed to respond more aggressively to Nancy Pelosi's visit to Taiwan in August 2022, which was deemed as a violation of China's national sovereignty.

In addition, even if sailing under the MCGA banner helps the state achieve ideational dominance, this is likely only a tentative and partial solution. What if China's rise is interrupted, or even experiences a temporary setback, such as with the mishandling of the COVID-19 pandemic or the subsequent economic recovery? And what happens after China achieves national revival, or what if its rise leads to counterbalancing efforts by other powers like the United States or India? Questions like these mean that the state must constantly renegotiate pop hegemony with its citizens.

Situated at the intersection of cyberpolitics and cultural studies in the context of China, I contemplate existing studies and advance the scholarly enterprises in several ways. First, I add to existing studies on the coexistence of an empowering internet and enduring authoritarianism. Building on works highlighting more nuanced mechanisms of state adaptation and digital participation, I extend our attention to digital cultural consumerist experiences like internet literature and reveal how citizens and the market, through such experiences, play important roles in legitimizing China's authoritarian regime. This finding challenges the conventional wisdom about authoritarian rule being imposed, and thus costly to maintain. It also supports a much bolder argument than that of the state successfully co-opting social participation, or that of citizens defending the regime because they dislike regime critics.[12]

Second, focusing on internet literature and the relevance of history in contemporary politics, I engage with and contribute to the burgeoning scholarly enterprise on cultural politics as well as the politics of history and memory in China.[13] As the first book to systematically examine MCGA fiction and its political implications, this research organically connects literature, history, and politics, revealing the micromechanisms of cultural politics and implications for authoritarian rule. Moreover, unlike other books that focus on the state, especially its role in producing proregime patriotic arts and literature, or traditional types of intellectuals, I examined digitally empowered ordinary citizens and how their everyday practices not only challenge the state in the cultural realm and contest its legitimacy but also contribute to authoritarian legitimation.[14]

Third, I speak to works on how digital media affect authoritarian and democratic politics beyond China. Although earlier books have examined how digital media may challenge authoritarian rule, many have noted the rise of digital authoritarianism, discussing how autocracies may utilize digital technologies to their advantage.[15] Scholars have also recognized that digital media can be detrimental to democratic politics, especially because of popular participation in disinformation or misinformation.[16] By highlighting popular participation in authoritarian legitimation, I not only add to the literature on digital authoritarianism but also connect it to studies of digital challenges to democracy.

Fourth, I also speak to the literature on democratic backsliding in the digital age as the MCGA trend discussed in this book resembles that of MAGA and populist movements in many democracies. Digitally mediated popular sentiment can provide support for authoritarian rule (as in the case of China) and be utilized to weaken democracy. More specifically, like MCGA in China, MAGA rhetoric as well as populist narratives in other cases exploit the popular nostalgia for glories past and disappointment with the present, creating a sense of urgency to save the nation, which in turn is used to justify abrupt or subtle subversion of democratic rules, norms, and values.[17]

PAST, PRESENT, AND FUTURE IN AND BEYOND MCGA FICTION

In *The Japanese and the War*, Michael Lucken details the Japanese cultural memory of World War II, which has three layers: the population's early expectations, the war trauma, and the postwar politics of memory. Lucken perceptively notes, "Every culture tends to develop rationales that are consistent with its own representations and interests."[18] Chinese MCGA fiction, internet literature, and contemporary culture writ large similarly reflect the nation's memories of the past, perceptions of the present, and explorations of the future, as well as the interactions among the three.

MCGA fiction, just like many contemporary cultural consumerist forms, has deep historical roots. The genre exploits China's extensive historical experiences and memories, glories and humiliations alike, as political cultural resources. On the one hand, these works embody the collective effort to trace, learn, and reflect on history, which, despite the consumerist motives, resonates with the ancient intellectual and political tradition of historiography and history research that links history learning to the rise and fall of dynasties.[19] On the other hand, by (re)narrating, (re)interpreting, and (re)forming history, MCGA works engage with the imagination and reimagination of China as a community and the Chinese identity.

The historicity in MCGA fiction represents a dialogue between contemporary Chinese and their ancestors. The trend of China rising increases the self-confidence of Chinese people in the twenty-first century and triggers their memories of past glories and regrets that must be remembered and remedied. MCGA works, therefore, stand for and bridge the history and present. By way of reading, exploring, and (re)imagining history, writers and readers relive the joys and sorrows of their forefathers. And with the prescience and expertise, ideas, and knowledge that they bring from the contemporary era, they attempt to tackle the challenges and dilemmas the ancient Chinese faced. In this way, the present listens and responds to the past through a digital-mediated literary imagination.

Such communication is certainly not a one-way street. Although ancient Chinese people could not appraise their descendants' accomplishments, they shaped the ideas and behavior of the latter through recorded actions and words. For contemporary Chinese people, their forefathers have passed on memories and expectations that they must live up to. Many examples embody such an ancestral MCGA legacy. The Han dynasty slogan, "Those who dare to attack the Mighty Han will be executed no matter how far they are" (*mingfan qiang Han zhe, suiyuan bizhu* 明犯强汉者，虽远必诛), can be readily found in MCGA works. It also appears in the blockbuster movie *Wolf Warrior 2*, only with "the Mighty Han" replaced by "China."[20] The last poem by the South Song poet Lu You 陆游 on his death bed, which all elementary school students must recite, dictates to his son that "the day when the [Song] emperor's troops sweep the North, you must not forget to tell me at my tomb." Such legacies have influenced Chinese society far and deep, setting the basic tone for MCGA fiction.

This "historical nationalism" is not found only in MCGA titles. For instance, one can find nationalist sentiment at points in the popular mythical fantasies, such as the serial *Crazy Stories from Hmong Frontiers* (*Miaojiang gushi* 苗疆蛊事). In the epilogue of its fourth sequel, the writer explains why the protagonist is set as a successor of the South Sea Sect (*Nanhai pai* 南海派, or South China Sea Sect):

> From the bottom of my heart, I have always favored the South Sea Sect.
>
> In fact, when I drafted the setup for the fiction, I put Tian Shan Shenchi Palace, East Sea Penglai Island, Miao Frontier All Poison Cave, and South Sea Xiankong Island together [as the fourth sacred lands]. Because the South Sea is far away from the heartland of our nation and is barely heard of, people only talk about three sacred lands . . . instead of four.
>
> But without the slightest doubt, the South Sea belongs to China forever.
>
> This will never change no matter how upset the Philippines or Vietnam are about it.[21]

This passage links the territorial dispute in this time and space to the fictional world, which readers in turn consume and internalize, perhaps willingly. In doing so, it helps confirm China's claim on the South China Sea.

What is particularly interesting about this serial is that some of its main characters are part of the ethnic minority of the Hmong, but they show a strong Chinese identity. In one of its sequels, the protagonist is set to have both Han and Hmong bloodlines.[22] Through poisonous magic, he inherits the memories of his Hmong ancestors, one of which was a special envoy sent by the ancient Hmong state Yelang to warn the Han dynasty about the invasion of a mythical devil force. Instead of sending help, the Han dynasty tortured and killed him before ultimately wiping out Yelang. Although the betrayal and conflicts between Han and Hmong are mentioned more than once, the work still embraces ethnic harmony. In fact, the writer likens the Yelang envoy to Su Wu, a Han diplomat who was captured and detained for nineteen years during his mission, but who nevertheless made his way back home. Inspired by both heroic ancestors—one Hmong and one Han—the protagonist learns about courage, integrity, and faithfulness to one's mission. The ethnic tensions seem to have never existed. Whether the writer in these cases is expressing nationalistic sentiment out of sincerity or just to please the readers or the state, this sentiment functions to help imagine the shared community of China.[23] By mixing ethnic historical stories and juxtaposing ancestral heroes from Hmong and Han, the writer embraces the notion that all minorities belong to the same "big Chinese family" that the state promotes.[24]

Such "historical nationalism" found in MCGA fiction, internet literature, and beyond evidently reflects the social reality of contemporary China. For this reason, the genre is not simply digital cultural consumerism. Rather, as discussed in the introduction, it is closely interrelated to other popular cyber-phenomena, such as the "voluntary fifty-cent army," the "little pink," the "industrial party," and "Ruguanism," which together constitute a nationalist proregime discursive cluster that competes with other forces, especially regime critics and proliberal voices. Such thoughts and their competition with other discourses bear critical implications for where China is headed in the future.

MCGA works of fiction connect the past and present, and they ultimately point to China's collective outlook into the future, especially what an ideal China should look like, the most pressing task it needs to address, the grand goal to pursue, and the proper path to take. Like other societies, China is complicated and diverse. The pervasiveness of the MCGA discourse in and beyond internet literature reveals its shared outlook of national revival, which can be understood as a response from the Chinese people to its ancient civilization, its sufferings in the modern time, and its rise in the contemporary world. Such an outlook builds on a nationalist core and has a collectivistic orientation, because it emphasizes the salvation of the nation more than the empowering of individual citizens. It also implies a clash-of-civilizations perspective, which focuses on the confrontation between China and external threats instead of domestic tensions between the repressive state and its citizens.[25] Therefore, this outlook aligns well with the state ideation of the Chinese dream.

Such past-present-future resonance is pervasive in China's cultural consumerist realm, and it is being capitalized on by the state. For example, to celebrate the seventieth anniversary of the People's Republic of China (PRC) in 2019 and the centennial anniversary of the party in 2021, the state rolled out a series of "patriotic" movies. Among them is *My Country, My Parents*.[26] The film highlights the bloodline and spiritual inheritance across generations with four segments covering the anti-Japanese War (before the PRC era), China launching its first satellite (the Maoist era), the making of China's first television commercial (the reform era), and a humanoid from 2050 time traveling to 2021 (the future and the present). The popular movie, which ranked fourth in box revenue in 2021, beating *Fast and Furious 9* in the Chinese market, evidently aims to invoke a narrative of past, present, and future to affirm the regime's legitimacy. This intention is also revealed in its viral promotional song, *As You Wish* [translated by the author]:

> Since you have suffered for the sweet life that I enjoy now,
> I will live your dream to the fullest.
> May I not let you down, may I march courageously,
> every single day in this golden age.
> . . .
> You are where I come from,
> and where I will return to.
> All roads in the world will lead me to you.
> And I'll love the world that you loved,
> wish for the smiling faces that you desired.
> I'll hobble along, holding your hand.
> Please take me to the future.
> . . .
> Now the nation is safe, and life is peaceful.
> Is this what you ever wished for?
> Oh, children, rest in their dreams,
> Rest the way you loved so much.
> . . .
> And I'll meet the world you were never able to see,
> write the poems you were never able to finish.
> [You are] the moon on the horizon, the thought in my mind.
> You are always by my side.[27]

The song is a confession that Chinese today ("I") make to their forefathers ("you"), who have sacrificed for national revival. It is also a promise about the future, as terms such as "tomorrow," "children," and "the world you were never able to see" indicate. This sense of "inheritance" and connection among past, present, and future echo what is found in MCGA fiction.

POP HEGEMONY IN THE MAKING

Seeing MCGA fiction as part of ongoing ideological contestation helps us probe into China's pop hegemony in the making. Specifically, by exploring history and the quest for an ideal China, these works have together proposed a preferred version of social consent for the state and other social groups to respond to. What should China look like—in particular, politically? I have identified three major components of the political system MCGA writers and readers envision.

The first component is nationalism. The very MCGA theme indicates a strong desire for national revival, which is the common denominator between the state and its citizens. Whether China will replace and replicate the United States as the imperialist hegemon or become a communist power that aims to end inequality, exploitation, and oppression both domestically and across the world, the minimal requirement for the party-state is to deliver China's global rise. This is not an easy task given the many obstacles China now faces, including the economic slowdown, population crisis, staggering inequality, intensified conflicts with foreign powers, and internal political struggles.[28] Moreover, the state must balance between exploiting nationalism for legitimacy and preventing it from getting out of control, thus hurting its foreign policy goals or intensifying domestic ethnical tensions, both of which can hinder national revival.

The second component is improved governance. Writers and readers of MCGA fiction expect the state to deliver economic growth, better living standards, and government efficiency as well as to defend China's national interests and improve its international status. As economic growth slows down and problems like inequality, social mobility, and corruption become more salient, citizens naturally expect the government to address all these issues, too. Many have turned to communism and its Chinese variant, Maoism, for solutions, thanks to the state's long-term indoctrination. Such ideology is regaining popularity both within society, as reflected in the neo-Maoist movement, and among elites, as Bo Xilai's Chongqing model embodies.[29] In this sense, communism and revolutionary history provide the regime with much needed ideological legitimacy but are also haunting it and will continue to do so for the foreseeable feature.

The third component is limited participation. Instead of actively seeking political rights or overthrowing authoritarian rule (maybe due to state censorship), MCGA works have shown considerable tolerance for "meritocracy."[30] So long as the regime can deliver on national revival and improved governance, whether or not power is democratically accessed is of less concern. Writers and readers of MCGA fiction, however, often expect the state to be accountable and responsive to the people, either through institutionalized channels like petitioning or through mechanisms such as media supervision. In other words, if we distinguish between the procedural and substantive definitions of democracy, and see "access to power" and "exercise of power" as two separate processes, we can argue that writers and readers care more about substantive democracy and how the state exercises its power.[31] That said, quite a few MCGA titles have explored alternative paths of political development, such as the parliamentary system, constitutional rule, and popular elections. Reflected in the widespread pursuit of personal desires, they have demonstrated an unwillingness to give up on the socioeconomic freedoms of the reform era. Even works that reveal a communist nostalgia often do not endorse totalitarian control over society, in that they rarely return China to the Maoist era.

Such political aspirations echo the "Three Principles of the People" that Sun Yat-sen advanced as the foundation of the Republic of China, namely nationalism (*minzu* 民族, opposing imperialism and the Manchu rule), people's livelihood (*minsheng* 民生, social welfare, also referred to as socialism), and people's rights (*minquan* 民权, or democracy). Although Sun envisioned a full set of political rights that people should enjoy, he made compromises in this regard, seeing a tutelage period necessary to educate people about democracy.[32] The fact that the Communist Party of China also claims to have inherited Sun's legacy implies that the regime may be willing to, and capable of, adapting its ideology to embrace these principles as the basis of social consent and pop hegemony.

Admittedly, the sociopolitical reality of contemporary China is much different from that of Sun's time. China has transformed dramatically, with its citizens now living more affluently, enjoying more socioeconomic freedoms and rights, and being much better educated and informed about the world than their counterparts in the late Qing and early Republican Era. The Chinese state has evolved over time. The current regime features much stronger capacity to control and govern the population as well as considerable resilience and adaptability to challenges than its predecessors. Meanwhile, despite state control, twenty-first-century Chinese society is overall far more vibrant, pluralized, and politically active. The interaction between a more vibrant society and a stronger state in the digital environment shapes the future of China.

MCGA fiction presents a highly popular vision of an ideal China, but other social actors (and the state) also partake in the curation of history and the envisioning of the nation's future. Since 1989, some Chinese liberal intellectuals have turned to the Confucian tradition and history to "justify an institutional restraint on the authoritarian regime and engage in dialogue with different civilizations and refine, rather than replace, the existing liberal world order."[33] Proliberal regime critics also constantly push the boundaries, trying to negotiate consent toward a more liberal-democratic direction.[34]

Compared with MCGA and proliberal citizens, the state has its own preferences regarding where China will head. Whether out of its authoritarian nature, the ideological urge to transform the society, or to prevent anything from disrupting the Chinese dream, the party-state has demonstrated a procontrol tendency. I have revealed *how* the state attempts to control, manage, and utilize digital experiences to its advantage, suggesting that the state has thus far captured internet literature and appropriated it for the purpose of authoritarian legitimation.

The "state capture" argument leads to a quite pessimistic outlook for China's democratization and liberalization. Yet, there are other possibilities. On the one hand, state capture may not be the worst-case scenario, with pop hegemony promising a far more dystopian future. This future can be described as the *Brave New World of 1984*, in which the state, equipped with digital technologies, imposes total surveillance over society, and citizens not only amuse themselves to loyalty or death but also willingly embrace state control. The plethora of MCGA fiction by no means suggests that pop hegemony is inevitable, but it suggests the possibility by revealing that voluntary support for authoritarian rule can be achieved through consent negotiation.

On the other hand, we are far from doomsday. The theoretical root of my qualified optimism is the dyadic relationship between the despotic and infrastructural power of the state, with the former referring to the state's ability to impose its will over society (often through coercion), and the latter its ability to penetrate society and implement its policies. According to Michael Mann and others, modern states often face constraints when exercising despotic power, because they cannot change the fundamental rules of society at will without risking intense opposition.[35] Sociologist and China expert Dingxin Zhao explicitly argues that the two are clearly negatively correlated, and if the state pursues excessive power concentration to enhance despotic power, its ability to coordinate and penetrate society will decline.[36] As discussed earlier, China features a highly pluralized cyberspace and society. State control, especially blatant censorship and repressive measures, can easily trigger resistance.

Because social consent for authoritarian rule must be negotiated to be effective, pop hegemony requires the state to tolerate, carefully manage, and encourage social participation. Ironically, the party-state does not always recognize this, but instead relies more on its coercive apparatus and demonstrates an overly controlling and suppressive tendency.[37] In the realm of internet literature, as I have shown, the state has censored many works, even proregime titles. In particular, its efforts to purify history and fight "historical nihilism" betray the state's deep sense of insecurity about a citizen-driven consent negotiation. As an article on the state-run *Guangming Daily* website puts it: "Historical nihilism gained more channels to spread in the internet age, distorting history and even fabricating out of thin air materials that travel across time and space, blocking and weakening the halo of national heroes through 'black sunglasses,' spoofing and dwarfing national spirit using a 'distorting mirror,' and ridiculing and vilifying national culture via a 'tinted mirror.'"[38] Evidently, the state prefers to single-handedly define the field and control the process.[39] This approach, however, is often counterproductive and self-defeating. After all, pop hegemony is as much about the state adapting and justifying its rule as about citizens making sense of, reconciling with, and actively participating in the system they live in.

It is somewhat unimaginable that China will slip completely back into totalitarianism, despite some observers arguing so.[40] Chinese citizens, proregime or not, have tasted the socioeconomic freedoms and the more prosperous life that builds on such freedoms. Moreover, China has opened its door and can hardly shut itself off. The digital media, while controlled and manipulated, allows for the "symbolic representations of an expanding array of social actors" and provides them with the window to peek into the outside world.[41] Many social actors, ranging from writers, artists, and critical journalists to workers and peasants, are contesting the regime's legitimacy and its account of history.[42] Even MCGA works demand improved governance and participation. In this sense, they reflect China's unfinished endeavor into modernization, which is more about Westernization than re-sinicization—returning to tradition and making China more "China"—just like the "Three Principles of the People" and the communist movement.

CHINA IN THE WORLD

Given its distinct nature, putting China into a comparative perspective is often challenging, but it can also be empirically and theoretically rewarding. Indeed, when studying the MCGA phenomenon, I could not help but compare it to the Make America Great Again (MAGA) trend in the United States and ponder the global implications of China's pop hegemony.

MCGA, MAGA, and Populism

Although it was the hallmark of Donald Trump's 2016 and 2024 presidential campaigns and his two terms as president, MAGA as a concept arose separately from Trump. US politicians had used the slogan before, including Ronald Reagan when running for president in 1980, as well as Bill Clinton in his 1992 campaign.[43] Even for Trump, 2016 was not the first time he had invoked the slogan. His 2011 book, *Time to Get Tough: Making America #1 Again*, already outlined his later political agenda. All this suggests that, just like MCGA, MAGA is not merely the result of some politicians' personal whims, but an ideological token with profound sociohistorical roots, thus explaining its continued influence among the US public and the Republican Party, even after Trump's defeat in 2020.

The US case reflects and is part of a modern global surge of populism. Although fundamentally an ideology (or a movement or a syndrome) that distinguishes between "the people" and "the elite," believing politics should represent the will of the people, populism can be easily combined with other different ideologies.[44] Besides being anti-elitist and antiestablishment, populism often displays strong xenophobic, anti-immigration, and racist inclinations, especially in Europe and the United States.[45] For instance, like MAGA in the United States, the Sweden Democrats, a far-right party with neo-Nazi roots, not only campaigned on issues such as immigration, religion, and crime, but also called for "Sverige ska bli bra igen" (Sweden Will Be Great Again) during the 2022 Swedish general election; the party ended up winning 20.5 percent of the popular vote, becoming the second-largest party in Parliament.[46] This is not an exception. Populist parties in other European countries have gained traction and often won big in elections. Brothers of Italy, for instance, won the 2022 Italian general election with its MAGA-like slogan, "Pronti a risollevare l'Italia" (Ready to Revive Italy).[47] In short, populism has become mainstream in Western democracies, with a demand side that explains the success of such far-right parties.[48]

It is beyond the scope of this book to systematically compare MCGA with MAGA, and certainly a stretch to categorize MCGA as a populist movement in China. Despite falling short of explicitly vowing itself to be an anti-elitist agenda, however, the discussion on "butt-correctness" in chapter 5 reveals the strong urge for readers and writers to sit on the people's side.[49] Although not subject to electoral pressure, the Chinese state, especially under President Xi, has attempted to garner populist support by way of policies and narratives, such as anticorruption and "common prosperity." To some extent, it is not surprising that observers see China as an example of populist authoritarianism and Xi as a populist president.[50] In addition, like MAGA in the United States and European populism, MCGA has significant nationalist and chauvinistic components, advocating for Chinese and Han supremacy.[51] Although MCGA works of fiction are generally less about racism and anti-immigration, one can easily smell traces of xenophobia wafting from them. Moreover, both Western populism and MCGA aspire to restore the glories of the past, as their slogans have blatantly displayed.[52]

In addition to ideational similarities, MCGA, MAGA, and European populism characteristically share the structural background of globalization and the changes of the digital revolution that have drastically transformed the world, which might have affected the West and China differently, but are producing similar fruits. In this sense, MCGA and populism in the West can be understood as two sides of the same coin.[53]

Looking at the European cases, Helen Milner finds that globalization (in the form of trade), technological change (in the form of automation), and the financial crisis have all contributed to the popularity of populist right-wing parties.[54] Similarly, MAGA supporters see themselves as victims of globalization, blaming emerging economies such as China for stealing their jobs and technologies.[55] Digital technologies, while benefiting democratic politics in multiple ways, help unleash anti-elitist and antiestablishment sentiments, which are exploited by politicians who now directly appeal to the public. Such dynamics have promoted populism, explaining phenomena such as the "Twitter Presidency" of Trump, who capitalized on both digital media and white rage.[56] Moreover, digital-mediated cross-boundary communications, instead of promoting understanding, often heighten identity conflicts, making it difficult to scale the empathy wall domestically while also provoking animosity or even a "clash of civilizations" sentiment across national boundaries, especially in the context of geopolitical competition.[57]

Like the US and other Western democracies, China has been transformed by globalization, but more as a beneficiary than a victim. Its economic reforms (opening up and joining international trade) have enabled China to grow from a poor, largely agrarian society, based on a planned economy, to the world's largest manufacturing power. This economic success is a primary condition for the MCGA narrative—China is so close to a national revival that it is time to remedy history. In addition, digital media has affected and transformed Chinese politics in complicated ways, with observers debating on whether and how it has challenged or enhanced authoritarian rule. Yet, like in the West, it has expanded popular participation and intensified identity politics, as the variety of digitally empowered social activism and intense competition in discourse reveal. MCGA, although deeply rooted in the collective ethos of national revival, could not have been possible but for the fact that millions of Chinese citizens are now able to engage in online expression and digital consumerism.

Evidently, the influences of globalization and the digital revolution have shaped domestic sociopolitical and international power dynamics, which in turn have conditioned MCGA in China and populism in the West synchronically but in different ways. This structural perspective suggests that, just like Trump did not create MAGA but instead exploited the idea, the Chinese state did not create MCGA, or the Chinese dream, but has taken advantage of it. In other words, MCGA fiction, like the sci-fi works that emerged in the late Qing and early Republican Era, are answering the call of, and reflect, the great transformation of its time. This echoes James Leibold, who likens contemporary Chinese Han identity to the phenomenon of whiteness in the United States, arguing that both are historically contingent and can be mobilized for personal, political, and economic purposes.[58] Because China and the West have experienced globalization and the digital revolution in vastly different ways, they both aspire to national revival and are for this purpose willing to support more assertive leaders. Yet, they still have very different outlooks. MCGA Chinese people generally see the goal of national revival as imminent under the party's leadership. Thus, this view is less about dissatisfaction with the regime. In contrast, MAGA (and populism in the West in general) reflects more a sense of discontent and insecurity, and thus this view is often highly detrimental to democratic politics. In addition, such different outlooks also feed into the US–China rivalry and global power politics, especially how the United States and its allies have perceived China and its rise in the post–COVID world.[59]

Global Implications of China's Pop Hegemony

Comparisons with MAGA and populism in the West help place MCGA within a broader global trend. One natural question then becomes: What are the potential implications for the international community if China's pop hegemony becomes the reality? This discussion is necessarily speculative, but nevertheless it is important given China's economic might, political influence, and increasingly assertive foreign policy under President Xi, whichever path the nation takes matters.

The global implications are multifold. Above all, China's pop hegemony, should it become the reality, implies a geopolitical power reshuffle. Although the Chinese state has reiterated, sincerely or instrumentally, that the PRC does not seek to challenge the international order or replace the United States, MCGA stories explicitly or implicitly assume China's regional and even global primacy (see chapter 4).[60] Certainly, popular imaginations regarding what Pax Sinica would look like vary significantly: whether they depict a US-style hegemonic system or a more equal community of the shared future for humankind.[61] These imaginations are not directly translatable into official foreign policy, either.[62] They all necessitate, however, defeating the world's current hegemon, because that would be the symbolic moment that China achieves national rejuvenation (regardless of whether China intends to become the world's new hegemon or not) and the result of realpolitik calculations, given the current US–China rivalry (the United

States wants to stop China's rise, and thus has to be defeated). In this regard, MCGA narratives echo well other popular ideations, such as Ruguanism and Wolf Warrior diplomacy, which, from the Chinese nationalist's perspective, are justified strategies for resisting the US hegemon.

Besides ousting the US hegemon, another important implication relates to how China may export its norms, values, and ideas, as well as its governing capacity globally.[63] In fact, while it is debatable whether China has consciously promoted its model of governance, it has started to project its digital influence.[64] For instance, China is the major exporter of digital surveillance technologies across the globe, especially to Africa, Asia, and Latin America.[65] Moreover, like Russia, China has long been a champion of "cybersovereignty" and argues for extending national sovereignty in cyberspace, a notion that resonates with many countries in the Global South.[66] Worried about foreign interference and other cyberthreats, even democracies such as the United States have effectively enhanced regulation over digital media.[67]

Notably, China can project its influence in a passive way. Merely being a "successful" authoritarian regime can inspire and encourage other autocracies—"if China can do it, so we can"—not to mention they can actively learn from China. In a sense, China's pop hegemony model may rival the surveillance capitalism model grown in the capitalist soil of the United States, although both project gloomy futures for humankind.[68] It may be overly pessimistic to predict that we are doomed, either in the Chinese way (pop hegemony) or in a more Western fashion (e.g., surveillance capitalism), but at this stage, it is critical to caution against constructing our own "road to digital serfdom."[69]

APPENDIX

For a discussion of table A.1, see chapter 2.

TABLE A.1
Top fifty words used to introduce SAPPRFT-recommended works

Words	Counts	Words	Counts
故事 (story)	52	读者 (reader)	10
人物 (figure)	27	不同 (difference)	9
生活 (life)	23	充满 (full of)	9
描写 (description)	22	积极 (positive)	9
主人公 (main character)	21	家庭 (family)	9
情节 (plot)	20	经历 (experience)	9
历史 (history)	19	鲜明 (distinct)	9
语言 (language)	17	背景 (background)	8
主角 (main character)	17	宏大 (grandiose)	8
爱情 (love)	14	矛盾 (contradiction)	8
成长 (growth)	14	曲折 (complicated)	8
命运 (fate)	14	文化 (culture)	8
人生 (life trajectory)	14	现实 (reality)	8
世界 (world)	14	叙事 (narrative)	8
生动 (vividly)	13	部落 (bribe)	7
题材 (genre)	13	架构 (setup)	7
展现 (demonstrate)	13	角色 (role)	7
情感 (affection)	12	抗战 (anti-Japanese war)	7
时代 (time)	12	可读性 (readability)	7
塑造 (shape)	12	青年 (youth)	7
形象 (image)	12	人性 (human nature)	7
穿越 (time travel)	11	体现 (manifest)	7
精神 (spirit)	11	细节 (detail)	7
性格 (temperament/ character)	11	细腻 (exquisite)	7
真实 (truthful)	11	想象 (imagination)	7

For a discussion of tables A.2–A.4, see chapter 5.

TABLE A.2
Top frequently used words in non-MCGA comments

Terms	Freq.	Terms	Freq.	Terms	Freq.	Terms	Freq.
世界 world	3341	打脸 face-slapping	353	容易 easy	245	幻想 fantasy	185
剧情 storyline	3150	影响 influence	347	巅峰 peak	242	样子 appearance	185
文笔 writing style	1775	脑子 brain	343	普通 common	240	npc nonplayer character	184
人物 figure/character	1665	妹妹 sister	339	看来 it seems	238	动漫 anime	184
后宫 concubines	1265	文青 arty youth	338	优秀 excellence	238	脑残 brain-damaged	184
游戏 game	1068	恐怖 horror	337	看起来 seemingly	236	情怀 feeling/devotion/affection	184
无限 infinity	989	垃圾 garbage	332	宇宙 universe	236	势力 clout/force	183
太监 eunuch	979	原因 reason/cause	332	改变 change	234	文明 civilization	183
感情 affection	921	原著 original work	328	质量 quality	234	拥有 own/possess	183
现实 reality	921	玩家 player	327	空间 space	232	战争 war	183
智商 intelligence	905	教主 hierarch	322	神作 masterpiece	232	追求 pursuit	183
恶心 disgusting	842	细节 detail	318	对话 dialogue	230	爱情 love	182
副本 instance dungeon (game)	827	关系 relation	316	主神 supreme deity	230	女儿 daughter	182
金手指 golden finger	789	味道 taste	316	安排 arrangement	229	压抑 depress	180
套路 routine	763	吸引 attract	316	知识 knowledge	229	不足 shortage/shortcoming	179
系统 system	740	适合 suitable	314	充满 full of	228	凡人 mortal/ordinary person	179
性格 character	688	大神 great god/guru	312	描述 description	228	加入 join	179
女人 women	685	异界 alien world	309	热血 righteous ardor	228	绿帽 cuckold/green hat	179

Terms	Freq.	Terms	Freq.	Terms	Freq.	Terms	Freq.
好看 interesting/good-looking	643	印象 impression	309	坚持 insist/persist	227	bug bug	178
生活 life	632	创意 creativity	308	心理 mentality	227	冲突 conflict	178
发展 develop(ment)	622	代入 substitute	307	异能 superpower/ultra-ability	227	大纲 outline	178
配角 supporting role	609	文风 style of writing	307	后续 follow-up	225	纠结 tangled	178
能力 ability	597	欢乐 joy/joyful	305	身份 identity	225	元素 element	178
社会 society	570	期待 expectations	303	建议 suggestion	223	地图 map	177
力量 power	561	圣母 Virgin Mary/ self-righteous	302	气运 fate/destiny/luck	221	兴趣 interest	177
有趣 interesting/fun	561	经历 experience	300	选择 choice	220	官场 officialdom	176
脑洞 imagination	558	实力 might/strength	300	粉丝 fan	219	文抄公 plagiarist	176
题材 genre	550	种田 farming	298	惊艳 stunning	219	冒险 adventure	175
强行 done by force	547	重要 important	296	文章 article	218	情感 emotion	175
时间 time	547	美女 beauty	290	变身 (body) transformation	216	可爱 cute/cuteness	173
同人 fan fiction	537	玄幻 mythical fantasy	289	想法 idea	214	纯粹 pure/purity	172
修仙 cultivate to immortality	536	战斗 battle	289	boss boss	212	看书 reading	172
逻辑 logic	532	任务 mission	288	人性 human nature	212	全书 whole book	172
三观 value orientations	528	小白 noob	285	普通人 ordinary people	211	想起 think of	172
升级 upgrade	528	娱乐 entertainment	285	原创 original	211	语言 language	172
体系 system/setup	521	科幻 sci-fi	276	符合 conform to	210	找到 find	172
毒点 toxic point	517	类型 type	276	公司 company	210	感受 feel(ing)	171
爽点 pleasure point	513	末世 apocalypse	274	身上 body/on one's body	209	西幻 Western fantasy	171

(*continued*)

TABLE A.2
(*continued*)

Terms	Freq.	Terms	Freq.	Terms	Freq.	Terms	Freq.
缺点 shortcoming	501	尴尬 awkward	273	学习 study/learn	209	想象 imagination/imagine	171
爽文 pleasure fiction	501	私货 personal view	273	技能 skills	207	大佬 big boss	169
妹子 girls	484	男人 men	272	方式 manner	206	视角 perspective	169
仙侠 fairy fantasy	482	事情 matter	271	暧昧 ambiguous	205	高潮 climax	168
希望 hope	474	无聊 boring	271	笔力 writing skill	205	回来 return	167
时代 era	467	人生 life	270	光环 halo	202	警察 police	167
网游 online game	467	老婆 wife	269	孩子 child	201	位面 planes	167
名字 name	465	强大 powerful	269	精神 spirit	200	传统 tradition	166
电影 film	461	轻松 relaxed/easy	269	奇幻 magic fantasy	200	疯狂 crazy	165
文字 words	456	灵异 supernatural	268	天下 under the heaven	199	结合 combine	165
人类 humanity	447	完美 perfect	268	皇帝 emperor	198	桥段 trope	165
合理 reasonable	439	无脑 brainless	266	思想 thought	198	组织 organization	165
精彩 wonderful	433	解释 explain	265	平淡 insipid	196	格局 setup	164
干粮 field rations	421	修炼 practice	265	体验 experience	195	能量 energy	164
烂尾 unfinished	419	简单 simple	264	意义 significance	195	时期 period	163
节奏 beat/tempo	409	表现 performance	261	屌丝 diaosi/loser	194	心态 mindset	163
地球 earth	407	努力 effort	261	杀伐 kill/massacre	194	成绩 achievement	162
毒草 poisonous weed	407	成长 grow/growth	260	差不多 similar/more or less	193	狗血 cliché/cheesy	162
装逼 show off/poser	406	形象 image	260	出彩 outstanding	193	和谐 harmony	162
武侠 martial arts	403	水准 level	258	杀人 killing people	193	鲜明 distinct	162

Terms	Freq.	Terms	Freq.	Terms	Freq.	Terms	Freq.
反派 villain	399	吐槽 complain/ridicule	258	设计 design	193	认真 earnest	161
女性 female	396	严重 grave	258	说实话 honestly speaking	192	特点 characteristic	161
国家 nation/state	395	弱智 half-witted	257	相信 believe	192	合理性 rationality	160
存在 existence	392	新意 novelty	257	理由 reason/motive	191	身体 body	160
白文 noob fiction	391	超级 super	254	dnd Dungeons & Dragons (game)	190	司机 driver/chauffeur	160
朋友 friend	379	敌人 enemy	254	怀疑 suspect	190	女主角 heroine	159
黑暗 dark	377	亮点 highlights	253	种马 stallion/stud man	190	生命 life	159
世界观 world view	377	魔法 magic	253	混乱 chaos	189	舒服 comfortable	159
接受 accept	375	智障 mentally retarded	253	事件 event/incident	189	父母 parents	158
主线 main theme	371	意思 meaning	252	幽默 humor	189	商业 commerce	158
莫名其妙 baffling	369	yy lust of the mind	250	修真 cultivation	188	土著 aboriginal people	158
搞笑 funny	366	导致 lead to	250	发生 happen	187	细腻 exquisite	158
优点 merit	365	姐姐 big sister/sister	249	火影 Naruto (Manga)	187	法师 mage	157
有意思 interesting	360	厉害 sharp/intense	249	看见 see	187	cp coupling (pairing)	156
经典 classic	357	流畅 smooth	248	典型 typical	186	天才 genius	156
科技 science and technology	357	温馨 warmth/coziness	247	讨厌 hate/abominable	186	文化 culture	156
无敌 invincible	357	龙空 Dragon Sky (a forum)	246	政治 politics	186	拯救 save	156
看不下去 cannot finish	354	人设 persona	245	准备 preparation	186	职业 profession	156

TABLE A.3
Top frequently used words in MCGA comments

Terms	Freq.	Terms	Freq.	Terms	Freq.	Terms	Freq.
人物 figure/character	465	土著 aboriginal people	79	抗日 anti-Japanese	56	推动 promote	43
剧情 storyline	429	希望 hope	79	男人 men	56	相比 in comparison	43
文笔 writing style	414	斗争 struggle	78	手段 means	56	相信 believe	43
皇帝 emperor	360	儿子 son	78	主线 main theme	56	成长 grow/growth	42
后宫 concubines	317	印象 impression	78	白文 noob fictions	55	大神 great god/guru	42
时代 era	270	选择 choice	77	布局 layout	55	道路 road	42
发展 develop(ment)	233	帝国 empire	75	格局 setup	55	科普 popular(ization of) science	42
政治 politics	224	技术 technology	75	军阀 war lord	55	心理 mentality	42
金手指 golden finger	212	老婆 wife	75	商业 commerce	55	大清 Great Qing	41
智商 intelligence	207	私货 personal view	75	视角 perspective	55	崛起 rise	41
国家 nation/state	205	接受 accept	74	严谨 rigorous	55	母亲 mother	41
感情 affection	196	形象 image	74	观点 opinion	54	女儿 daughter	41
太监 eunuch	196	打脸 face-slapping	73	亮点 highlights	54	权谋 tactics	41
世界 world	188	大唐 Great Tang	73	优秀 excellence	54	小人 the petty man/scumbag	41
种田 farming	188	经典 classic	72	代入 substitute	53	兄弟 brother	41
合理 reasonable	184	看不下去 cannot finish reading	72	狗血 cliché/cheesy	53	不知 don't know	40
科技 science and technology	179	名字 name	72	奴才 minion	53	出色 outstanding	40
天下 under the heaven	177	水准 level	72	文人 literati	53	代表 representing	40
屁股 butt	159	轻松 relaxed/easy	71	想法 idea	53	典型 typical	40
恶心 disgusting	157	文风 style of writing	71	战国 Warring States period	53	电视剧 TV drama	40

Terms	Freq.	Terms	Freq.	Terms	Freq.	Terms	Freq.
社会 society	156	鞑子 barbarian	70	表现 performance	52	疯狂 crazy	40
工业 industry	153	文化 culture	70	封建 feudal	52	国内 domestic	40
女人 women	152	小白 noob	70	认真 earnest	52	黑暗 dark	40
争霸 contest for supremacy	146	月关 Yueguan (pen name)	70	关系 relation	51	角度 angle	40
缺点 shortcoming	137	制度 institution/regime	70	加入 join	51	纠结 tangled	40
思想 thought	136	改革 reform	69	决定 decide	51	立场 position	40
造反 rebellion	134	军队 army	69	身上 body/on one's body	51	起家 make one's fortune	40
爽文 pleasure fiction	133	乱世 turbulent times	69	吸引 attract	51	无聊 boring	40
大明 Great Ming	132	事情 matter	69	二战 World War II	50	研究 research	40
军事 military	132	龙空 Dragon Sky (a forum)	68	解释 explain	50	语言 language	40
毒点 toxic point	125	汉人 Han (ethnicity) people	67	民主 democracy	50	处理 handle	39
逻辑 logic	125	合理性 rationality	67	幽默 humor	50	导致 lead to	39
民国 Republic of China	125	存在 existence	66	准备 preparation	50	反派 villain	39
推演 deduction	125	流畅 smooth	66	崇祯 Chongzhen emperor	49	尴尬 awkward	39
生活 life/livelihood	124	大腿 thigh (powerful figure)	65	回来 return	49	功力 skill	39
时期 period	123	智障 mentally retarded	65	全书 whole book	49	人性 human nature	39
路线 route	116	功底 basic skills	64	统一 unification	49	认识 recognize/understanding	39
知识 knowledge	116	人民 the people	64	文章 article	49	失望 disappointment	39
配角 supporting role	115	征服 subdue	64	笔力 writing skill	48	文明 civilization	39

(*continued*)

TABLE A.3
(continued)

Terms	Freq.	Terms	Freq.	Terms	Freq.	Terms	Freq.
套路 routine	115	tg yokel communists	63	建设 construction	48	无敌 invincible	39
细节 detail	115	对话 dialogue	63	理由 reason/motive	48	无语 speechless	39
资料 material	115	方式 manner	63	美女 beauty	48	意思 meaning	39
性格 character	113	风流 romance	63	百姓 the masses	47	支持 support	39
题材 genre	111	经历 experience	63	不合理 unreasonable	47	父亲 father	38
爽点 pleasure point	110	精神 spirit	63	公公 eunuch	47	感受 feel(ing)	38
战争 war	106	期待 expectation	63	厉害 sharp/intense	47	结合 combine	38
改变 change	105	弱智 half-witted	63	妹子 girls	47	类型 type	38
革命 revolution	105	重要 important	63	说实话 honestly speaking	47	勉强 reluctant	38
垃圾 garbage	105	装逼 show off/poser	63	嘴炮 lip service/verbal attack	47	太祖 Taizu emperor (Mao)	38
三观 value orientations	103	敌人 enemy	62	孩子 child	46	特点 characteristic	38
好看 interesting/good-looking	102	烂尾 unfinished	62	科举 imperial examination	46	特色 feature	38
民族 Nation/ethnicity	102	利益 interest/benefit	62	莫名其妙 baffling	46	玩意 stuff	38
强行 done by force	101	符合 conform to	61	农民 peasant	46	武力 force	38
时间 time	99	水浒 Water Margin (novel)	61	圣母 Virgin Mary/self-righteous	46	重新 again	38
文字 words	99	太子 crown prince	61	吐槽 complain/ridicule	46	操作 operation	37
能力 ability	97	味道 taste	61	西方 the West	46	到位 in place	37
现代人 contemporary person	97	严重 grave	61	新意 novelty	46	汉族 Han (ethnicity)	37
优点 merit	95	游戏 game	61	资本主义 capitalism	46	坚持 Insist/persist	37
毒草 poisonous weed	94	安排 arrangement	60	曹操 Cao Chao (historical figure)	45	看书 reading	37

Terms	Freq.	Terms	Freq.	Terms	Freq.	Terms	Freq.
官场 officialdom	94	历史小说 history fictions	60	充满 full of	45	民族主义 nationalism	37
有趣 interesting/fun	94	脑洞 imagination	60	光环 halo	45	脑袋 head	37
考据 textual research	91	公主 princess	59	汉奸 Han (ethnicity) traitor	45	盛世 prosperous age	37
热血 righteous ardor	91	贵族 noble	59	碾压 crush	45	思考 reflection	37
脑子 brain	90	救国 save the nation	59	朋友 friend	45	听说 heard about	37
身份 identity	90	描述 description	59	生产力 productivity	45	出彩 outstanding	36
势力 clout/force	89	适合 suitable	59	实力 might/strength	45	地位 status	36
女性 female	88	系统 system	59	手下 subordinate	45	巅峰 peak	36
现实 reality	88	细腻 exquisite	59	想当然 wishful thinking	45	缺乏 lack/shortage	36
原因 reason/cause	88	有意思 interesting	59	质量 quality	45	生动 vivid	36
建立 establish	85	抄袭 plagiarism	58	出身 origin	44	世纪 century	36
精彩 wonderful	85	容易 easy	58	传统 tradition	44	体现 embody	36
节奏 beat/tempo	83	幼稚 naive	58	集团 group	44	体制 system/regime	36
文青 arty youth	83	经济 economy	57	理论 theory	44	屠杀 massacre	36
满清 Manchu/Qing	82	展现 display	57	世家 aristocratic family	44	阴谋 conspiracy	36
无脑 brainless	82	搞笑 funny	56	压抑 depress	44	正确 correct	36
影响 influence	81	简单 simple	56	不足 shortage/shortcoming	43	政权 regime	36
yy lust of the mind	80	建议 suggestion	56	古人 the ancients	43		
干粮 field rations	80	看来 it seems	56	杀人 killing people	43		

TABLE A.4
Most distinctive frequently used words in MCGA comments

Terms	Freq.	Terms	Freq.	Terms	Freq.	Terms	Freq.
屁股 butt	159	风流 romance	63	农民 peasant	46	处理 handle	39
工业 industry	153	利益 interest/benefit	62	西方 the West	46	功力 skill	39
争霸 contest for supremacy	146	水浒 Water Margin (novel)	61	资本主义 capitalism	46	认识 recognize/understanding	39
造反 rebellion	134	太子 crown prince	61	曹操 Cao Chao	45	失望 disappointment	39
大明 Great Ming	132	历史小说 history fiction	60	汉奸 Han (ethnicity) traitor	45	无语 speechless	39
军事 military	132	公主 princess	59	碾压 crush	45	支持 support	39
民国 Republic of China	125	贵族 noble	59	生产力 productivity	45	父亲 father	38
推演 deduction	125	救国 save the nation	59	手下 subordinate	45	勉强 reluctant	38
路线 route	116	抄袭 plagiarism	58	想当然 wishful thinking	45	太祖 Taizu emperor (Mao)	38
资料 material	115	幼稚 naive	58	出身 origin	44	特色 feature	38
革命 revolution	105	经济 economy	57	集团 group	44	玩意 stuff	38
民族 nation/ethnicity	102	展现 display	57	理论 theory	44	武力 force	38
现代人 contemporary person	97	抗日 anti-Japanese	56	世家 aristocratic family	44	重新 again	38
考据 textual research	91	手段 means	56	古人 the ancients	43	操作 operation	37
建立 establish	85	布局 layout	55	推动 promote	43	到位 in place	37
满清 Manchu/Qing	82	军阀 war lord	55	相比 in comparison	43	汉族 Han (ethnicity)	37
斗争 struggle	78	严谨 rigorous	55	道路 road	42	民族主义 nationalism	37
儿子 son	78	观点 opinion	54	科普 popular science	42	脑袋 head	37
帝国 empire	75	奴才 minion	53	大清 Great Qing	41	盛世 prosperous age	37
技术 technology	75	文人 literati	53	崛起 rise	41	思考 reflection	37

Terms	Freq.	Terms	Freq.	Terms	Freq.	Terms	Freq.
大唐 Great Tang	73	战国 Warring States period	53	母亲 mother	41	听说 heard about	37
鞑子 barbarian	70	封建 feudal	52	权谋 tactics	41	地位 status	36
月关 Yueguan (pen name)	70	决定 decide	51	小人 petty man/scumbag	41	缺乏 lack/shortage	36
制度 institution/regime	70	二战 World War II	50	兄弟 brother	41	生动 vivid	36
改革 reform	69	民主 democracy	50	不知 don't know	40	世纪 century	36
军队 army	69	崇祯 Chongzhen emperor	49	出色 outstanding	40	体现 embody	36
乱世 turbulent times	69	统一 unification	49	代表 representing	40	体制 system/regime	36
汉人 Han (ethnicity) people	67	建设 construction	48	电视剧 TV drama	40	屠杀 massacre	36
大腿 thigh (powerful figure)	65	百姓 the masses	47	国内 domestic	40	阴谋 conspiracy	36
功底 basic skills	64	不合理 unreasonable	47	角度 angle	40	正确 correct	36
人民 the people	64	公公 eunuch	47	立场 position	40	政权 regime	36
征服 subdue	64	嘴炮 lip service/verbal attack	47	起家 make one's fortune	40		
tg yokel communists	63	科举 imperial examination	46	研究 research	40		

NOTES

INTRODUCTION

1. Andrew J. Nathan, "The Alternate History of China: Could Beijing Have Taken a Different Path?," *Foreign Affairs* 101, no. 5 (2022): 234–40.
2. China Internet Network Information Center, *Di 52 Ci Zhogguo Hulian Wangluo Fazhan Zhuangkuang Tongji Baogao* [The 52nd China Statistical Report on Internet Development], CNNIC, August 28, 2023, https://www.cnnic.cn/n4/2023/0828/c88-10829.html.
3. Jun Liu, *Shifting Dynamics of Contention in the Digital Age: Mobile Communication and Politics in China* (Oxford University Press, 2020), 63–65.
4. Antonio Gramsci, *Selections from the Prison Notebooks of Antonio Gramsci*, ed. Quintin Hoare and Geoffrey Nowell Smith (International Publishers, 1971); and T. J. Jackson Lears, "The Concept of Cultural Hegemony: Problems and Possibilities," *American Historical Review* 90, no. 3 (1985): 567–93.
5. For instance, see Daniela Stockmann and Ting Luo, *Governing Digital China* (Cambridge University Press, 2025); and Lizhi Liu, *From Click to Boom: The Political Economy of E-Commerce in China* (Princeton University Press, 2024).
6. Ian Johnson, *Sparks: China's Underground Historians and Their Battle for the Future* (Oxford University Press, 2023); Perry Link and Dazhi Wu, *I Have No Enemies: The Life and Legacy of Liu Xiaobo* (Columbia University Press, 2023); and Ban Wang, *Illuminations from the Past: Trauma, Memory, and History in Modern China* (Stanford University Press, 2004).
7. Sebastian Veg, *Minjian: The Rise of China's Grassroots Intellectuals* (Columbia University Press, 2019).
8. Michel de Certeau and Steven Rendall, *The Practice of Everyday Life* (University of California Press, 1984).

9. Elizabeth Economy, *The World According to China* (Polity, 2022).
10. Jiwei Ci, *Democracy in China: The Coming Crisis* (Harvard University Press, 2019); Minxin Pei, *China's Trapped Transition: The Limits of Developmental Autocracy* (Harvard University Press, 2009); and Minxin Pei, "China: Totalitarianism's Long Shadow," *Journal of Democracy* 32, no. 2 (2021): 5–21.
11. Andrew J. Nathan, "China's Changing of the Guard: Authoritarian Resilience," *Journal of Democracy* 14, no. 1 (2003): 6–17; Heike Holbig and Bruce Gilley, "Reclaiming Legitimacy in China," *Politics and Policy* 38, no. 3 (2010): 395–422; Hongxing Yang and Dingxin Zhao, "Performance Legitimacy, State Autonomy and China's Economic Miracle," *Journal of Contemporary China* 24, no. 91 (2015): 64–82; and Iza Yue Ding, *The Performative State: Public Scrutiny and Environmental Governance in China* (Cornell University Press, 2022).
12. Aleksandra Kubat, "Morality as Legitimacy Under Xi Jinping: The Political Functionality of Traditional Culture for the Chinese Communist Party," *Journal of Current Chinese Affairs* 47, no. 3 (2018): 47–86; Elizabeth J. Perry, "Cultural Governance in Contemporary China: 'Re-Orienting' Party Propaganda," in *To Govern China: Evolving Practices of Power*, ed. Vivienne Shue and Patricia M. Thornton (Cambridge University Press, 2017); Christian P. Sorace, "The Chinese Communist Party's Nervous System: Affective Governance from Mao to Xi," *China Quarterly* 248, no. 1 (2021): 29–51; and Bin Xu, "Moral Performance and Cultural Governance in China: The Compassionate Politics of Disasters," *China Quarterly* 226 (2016): 407–30.
13. Scholars debate on whether "legitimacy" or "legitimation" better explains enduring authoritarianism in China. See Thomas Heberer and Gunter Schubert, eds., *Regime Legitimacy in Contemporary China: Institutional Change and Stability* (Routledge, 2008); and Gunter Schubert, "Political Legitimacy in Contemporary China Revisited: Theoretical Refinement and Empirical Operationalization," *Journal of Contemporary China* 23, no. 88 (2014): 593–611. According to Sandby-Thomas, legitimacy captures the durability of the Communist Party of China but legitimation entails the active and contested political process of legitimacy creation, modification, innovation, and transformation. See Peter Sandby-Thomas, "How Do You Solve a Problem Like Legitimacy? Contributing to a New Research Agenda," *Journal of Contemporary China* 23, no. 88 (2014): 579.
14. Gadi Wolfsfeld et al., "Social Media and the Arab Spring," *International Journal of Press/Politics* 18, no. 2 (2013): 115–37.
15. For instance, see Guobin Yang, *The Power of the Internet in China: Citizen Activism Online* (Columbia University Press, 2009); Liu, *Shifting Dynamics of Contention in the Digital Age*; and Andreĭ Soldatov and Irina Borogan, *The Red Web: The Struggle between Russia's Digital Dictators and the New Online Revolutionaries* (PublicAffairs, 2015).
16. Ronald Deibert et al., eds., *Access Denied: The Practice and Policy of Global Internet Filtering* (MIT Press, 2008); Ronald Deibert et al., eds., *Access Controlled: The Shaping of Power, Rights, and Rule in Cyberspace* (MIT Press, 2010); and Ronald Deibert et al., eds., *Access Contested: Security, Identity, and Resistance in Asian Cyberspace* (MIT Press, 2011).
17. Rongbin Han, *Contesting Cyberspace in China: Online Expression and Authoritarian Resilience* (Columbia University Press, 2018); Rebecca MacKinnon, "China's Censorship 2.0: How Companies Censor Bloggers," *First Monday* 14, no. 2 (2009),

https://firstmonday.org/article/view/2378/2089; and Margaret E. Roberts, *Censored: Distraction and Diversion Inside China's Great Firewall* (Princeton University Press, 2018).

18. Mary Gallagher and Blake Miller, "Who Not What: The Logic of China's Information Control Strategy," *China Quarterly* 248, no. 1 (2021): 1011–36; Rongbin Han and Li Shao, "Scaling Authoritarian Information Control: How China Adjusts the Level of Online Censorship," *Political Research Quarterly* 75, no. 4 (2022): 1345–59; Gary King et al., "How Censorship in China Allows Government Criticism but Silences Collective Expression," *American Political Science Review* 107, no. 2 (2013): 326–43; Peter Lorentzen, "China's Strategic Censorship," *American Journal of Political Science* 58, no. 2 (2014): 402–14; and Yun Tai and King-wa Fu, "Specificity, Conflict, and Focal Point: A Systematic Investigation into Social Media Censorship in China," *Journal of Communication* 70, no. 6 (2020): 842–67.
19. Ronald Deibert, "Cyberspace Under Siege," *Journal of Democracy* 26, no. 3 (2015): 64–78; Aleksandr Fisher, "Demonizing the Enemy: The Influence of Russian State-Sponsored Media on American Audiences," *Post-Soviet Affairs* 36, no. 4 (2020): 281–96; Deen Freelon et al., "Black Trolls Matter: Racial and Ideological Asymmetries in Social Media Disinformation," *Social Science Computer Review*, 2020; Marcel H. Van Herpen, *Putin's Propaganda Machine: Soft Power and Russian Foreign Policy* (Rowman and Littlefield, 2016); Gary King et al., "How the Chinese Government Fabricates Social Media Posts for Strategic Distraction, Not Engaged Argument," *American Political Science Review* 111, no. 3 (2017): 484–501; Johan Lagerkvist, "Internet Ideotainment in the PRC: National Responses to Cultural Globalization," *Journal of Contemporary China* 17, no. 54 (2008): 121–40; and Roberts, *Censored*.
20. On digital monitoring and tracking practices, see Xu Xu et al., "Information Control and Public Support for Social Credit Systems in China," *Journal of Politics* 84, no. 4 (2022): 2230–45. On "total surveillance," see Kai Deng et al., "Xi Jinping's Surveillance State: Merging Digital Technology and Grassroots Organizations," in *The Xi Jinping Effect*, ed. Ashley Esarey and Rongbin Han (University of Washington Press, 2024).
21. Ashley Esarey and Qiang Xiao, "Political Expression in the Chinese Blogosphere: Below the Radar," *Asian Survey* 48, no. 5 (2008): 752–72; Han, *Contesting Cyberspace in China*; and Yang, *Power of the Internet in China*.
22. Yanqi Tong and Shaohua Lei, "War of Position and Microblogging in China," *Journal of Contemporary China* 22, no. 80 (2013): 292–311; and Johan Lagerkvist, *After the Internet, Before Democracy: Competing Norms in Chinese Media and Society* (Peter Lang, 2010).
23. Han, *Contesting Cyberspace in China*; Kecheng Fang and Maria Repnikova, "Demystifying 'Little Pink:' The Creation and Evolution of a Gendered Label for Nationalistic Activists in China," *New Media and Society* 20, no. 6 (2017): 2162–85.
24. On nationalism serving as the source of proregime discourse, see Rongbin Han, "Cyber Nationalism and Regime Support Under Xi Jinping: The Effects of the 2018 Constitutional Revision," *Journal of Contemporary China* 30, no. 131 (2021): 717–33; Ying Jiang, *Cyber-Nationalism in China: Challenging Western Media Portrayals of Internet Censorship in China* (University of Adelaide Press, 2012); and Hailong Liu, ed., *From Cyber-Nationalism to Fandom Nationalism: The Case of Diba Expedition in China* (Routledge, 2019). On disliking the opposition force, see Han, *Contesting Cyberspace in China*.

25. Cara Wallis, "New Media Practices in China: Youth Patterns, Processes, and Politics," *International Journal of Communication* 5 (2011): 406.
26. Fang and Repnikova, "Demystifying 'Little Pink'"; and Han, *Contesting Cyberspace in China.*
27. The *Dongfang Journal* launched in August 2018 by the China Institute at Fudan University to promote Chinese discursive power in the social sciences published a series of articles on the phenomenon. For instance, see Nanfeng Lu and Jing Wu, "Lishi Zhuanzhe zhong de Hongda Xushi: Gongyedang Wangluo Sichao de Zhengzhi Fenxi" [Grand Narrative at History's Turning Point: Political Analysis of the Internet Ideology of China's Industrial Party], *Dongfang Journal,* no. 1 (2018): 49–60 and 118–119; and Peng Yan, "'Gongyedang:' Yige Wenhua Jingguan de Suxie" [The "Industrial Party": A Sketch of Cultural Landscape], *Dongfang Journal,* no. 4 (2019): 31–40. Also see Kristin Shi-Kupfer et al., "Ideas and Ideologies Competing for China's Political Future," *Merics Papers on China,* no. 5 (2017): 1–90.
28. Again, the *Dongfang Journal* featured a special issue on "Ruguanism" in September 2020. See, for instance, Yifan Ma, "'Ruguanxue' de Huayu Shengcheng Jiegou jiqi Chulu" [The Discourse-Generating Structure of "Ruguanism" and Its Way Out]), *Dongfang Journal,* no. 9 (2020): 53–63; and Yuan Kong, "'Ruguan' yu 'Fazhou:' Guanyu Zhongguo Jueqi de Liangzhong Zhishilun Tujing" ["Ruguan" and "Crusade Against King Zhou": Two Epistemological Approaches of China Rise], *Dongfang Journal,* no. 9 (2020): 25–31.
29. Leigh Sarty, "'East Rising, West Falling': Not So Fast, History Suggests." *Washington Quarterly* 44, no. 3 (2021): 91–106.
30. Elaine J. Yuan, *The Web of Meaning: The Internet in a Changing Chinese Society* (University of Toronto Press, 2021).
31. Guobin Yang, *The Wuhan Lockdown* (Columbia University Press, 2022), 184–85.
32. Raymond Williams, *Marxism and Literature* (Oxford University Press, 1977).
33. Stuart Hall, "Popular Culture, Politics and History," *Cultural Studies* 32, no. 6 (2018): 929–52; Jonathan Dean, "Left Politics and Popular Culture in Britain: From Left-Wing Populism to 'Popular Leftism,'" *Politics* 43, no. 1 (2023): 3–17; Gabriel A. Almond and Sidney Verba, *The Civic Culture: Political Attitudes and Democracy in Five Nations* (Princeton University Press, 1963); and Ronald Inglehart, "The Renaissance of Political Culture," *American Political Science Review* 82, no. 4 (1988): 1203–30.
34. In this regard, the book echoes some earlier studies, such as Bingchun Meng, *The Politics of Chinese Media: Consensus and Contestation* (Palgrave Macmillan, 2018); Yuan, *Web of Meaning*; and Shaohua Guo, *The Evolution of the Chinese Internet: Creative Visibility in the Digital Public* (Stanford University Press, 2020).
35. Yang, *Power of the Internet in China.*
36. Peter Dahlgren, "The Internet, Public Spheres, and Political Communication: Dispersion and Deliberation," *Political Communication* 22, no. 2 (2005): 147–62; and Jens Damm, "The Internet and the Fragmentation of Chinese Society," *Critical Asian Studies* 39, no. 2 (2007): 273–94.
37. Guobin Yang, "Technology and Its Contents: Issues in the Study of the Chinese Internet," *Journal of Asian Studies* 70, no. 4 (2011): 1044.
38. On the lively and dynamic internet culture, see Paola Voci, *China on Video: Smaller-Screen Realities* (Routledge, 2010); David Kurt Herold and Peter Marolt, eds., *Online Society in China: Creating, Celebrating, and Instrumentalising the Online Carnival*

(Routledge, 2011); and Luzhou Li, *Zoning China: Online Video, Popular Culture, and the State* (MIT Press, 2019). On the politics of popular culture, see Dan Chen, "Seeing Politics Through Popular Culture," *Journal of Chinese Political Science* 29, no. 1 (2024): 185–205; and Karl Gerth, *Unending Capitalism: How Consumerism Negated China's Communist Revolution* (Cambridge University Press, 2020).

39. Nan Enstad, *Ladies of Labor, Girls of Adventure: Working Women, Popular Culture, and Labor Politics at the Turn of the Twentieth Century* (Columbia University Press, 1999); Todd Gitlin, *How the Torrent of Images and Sounds Overwhelms Our Lives* (Macmillan, 2007); Rob Rosenthal and Richard Flacks, *Playing for Change: Music and Musicians in the Service of Social Movements* (Routledge, 2015); Sidney Tarrow, *Power in Movement: Social Movements and Contentious Politics* (New York: Cambridge University Press, 1998); Jeffrey N. Wasserstrom and Elizabeth J. Perry, eds., *Popular Protest and Political Culture in Modern China* (Westview, 1994); and Liesbet Van Zoonen, *Entertaining the Citizen: When Politics and Popular Culture Converge* (Rowman and Littlefield, 2005).
40. Michael Berry, *A History of Pain: Trauma in Modern Chinese Literature and Film* (Columbia University Press, 2008).
41. Alex S. Edelstein, *Total Propaganda: From Mass Culture to Popular Culture* (Routledge, 1997); Anne-Marie Brady, *Marketing Dictatorship: Propaganda and Thought Work in Contemporary China* (Rowman and Littlefield, 2008); and Sheng Zou, "Restyling Propaganda: Popularized Party Press and the Making of Soft Propaganda in China," *Information Communication and Society* 26, no. 1 (2023): 201–17.
42. Thomas Chen, "The Workshop of the World: Censorship and the Internet Novel 'Such Is This World,'" in *China's Contested Internet*, ed. Guobin Yang (NIAS, 2015).
43. Michel Hockx, *Internet Literature in China* (Columbia University Press, 2015), 1–2.
44. Aldous Huxley, *Brave New World* (Harper and Row, 1946).
45. Neil Postman, *Amusing Ourselves to Death: Public Discourse in the Age of Show Business* (Penguin, 2005), xix–xx.
46. Shouzhi Xia, "Amusing Ourselves to Loyalty? Entertainment, Propaganda, and Regime Resilience in China," *Political Research Quarterly* 75, no. 4 (2022): 1096–112.
47. David Welch, *The Third Reich: Politics and Propaganda* (Routledge, 2008), 29.
48. Yanjun Shao, *Wangluo Shidai de Wenxue Yindu* [Literature Guide in the Digital Age] (Guangxi Normal University Press, 2015); and Yuan, *Web of Meaning*.
49. Adam Przeworski, "Formal Models of Authoritarian Regimes: A Critique," *Perspectives on Politics* 21, no. 3 (2022): 979–88.
50. Lears, "Concept of Cultural Hegemony," 569.
51. Lears, "Concept of Cultural Hegemony," 568.
52. Leo Ou-Fan Lee, "Dissent Literature from the Cultural Revolution," *Chinese Literature: Essays, Articles, Reviews* 1 (1979): 59–79; and Vivienne Shue, *The Reach of the State: Sketches of the Chinese Body Politic* (Stanford University Press, 1988).
53. Louis Althusser, "Ideology and Ideological State Apparatus (Notes Towards an Investigation)," in *Lenin and Philosophy and Other Essays* (Monthly Review, 2001).
54. Guo, *Evolution of the Chinese Internet*, 61. See also Jing Wang, *High Culture Fever: Politics, Aesthetics, and Ideology in Deng's China* (University of California Press, 1996).
55. Xiao Xu, "A Comprehensive Review of the River Elegy Debate," *Chinese Sociology and Anthropology* 25, no. 1 (1992): 6–27; and Fong-Ching Chen and Guantao Jin,

From Youthful Manuscripts to River Elegy: The Chinese Popular Cultural Movement and Political Transformation, 1979–1989 (Chinese University Press, 1997).
56. Markus K. Brunnermeier et al., "China's Gradualistic Economic Approach and Financial Markets," *American Economic Review* 107, no. 5 (2017): 608–13.
57. Guo, *Evolution of the Chinese Internet*; and Veg, *Minjian*.
58. Pingyuan Chen, "Jin Bainian Zhongguo Jingying Wenhua de Shiluo" [The Loss of China's Elite Culture in the Past Century], *Twenty-First Century*, no. 17 (1993): 12.
59. Ashley Esarey and Rongbin Han, eds., *The Xi Jinping Effect* (University of Washington Press, 2024).
60. Economist, "Xi Jinping and the Chinese Dream," *The Economist*, no. 8834 (2013): 13.
61. King et al., "How the Chinese Government Fabricates Social Media Posts."
62. Gramsci, *Selections from the Prison Notebooks of Antonio Gramsci*.
63. I am grateful to Alexsia Chan for the inspiration.
64. That said, the internet is not a winner-take-all space, and less successful products often have their chance of survival, too. See Chris Anderson, *The Long Tail: Why the Future of Business Is Selling Less of More* (Hyperion, 2006).
65. Han, *Contesting Cyberspace in China*; and Yang, *Power of the Internet in China*.

1. INTERNET LITERATURE IN CHINA

1. On a digital contention perspective, see Guobin Yang, *The Power of the Internet in China: Citizen Activism Online* (Columbia University Press, 2009); Johan Lagerkvist, *The Internet in China: Unlocking and Containing the Public Sphere* (Lund University, 2007); and Philip N. Howard and Muzammil M. Hussain, *Democracy's Fourth Wave? Digital Media and the Arab Spring* (Oxford University Press, 2013). On controlling and manipulating information, see Gary King et al., "How Censorship in China Allows Government Criticism but Silences Collective Expression," *American Political Science Review* 107, no. 2 (2013): 326–43; Margaret E. Roberts, *Censored: Distraction and Diversion Inside China's Great Firewall* (Princeton University Press, 2018); Peter Lorentzen, "China's Strategic Censorship," *American Journal of Political Science* 58, no. 2 (2014): 402–14; Seva Gunitsky, "Corrupting the Cyber-Commons: Social Media as a Tool of Autocratic Stability," *Perspectives on Politics* 13, no. 1 (2015): 42–54; and Ronald Deibert, "Cyberspace Under Siege," *Journal of Democracy* 26, no. 3 (2015): 64–78.
2. Bingchun Meng, *The Politics of Chinese Media: Consensus and Contestation* (Palgrave Macmillan, 2018); Paola Voci, *China on Video: Smaller-Screen Realities* (Routledge, 2010); David Kurt Herold and Peter Marolt, eds., *Online Society in China: Creating, Celebrating, and Instrumentalising the Online Carnival* (Routledge, 2011); Shaohua Guo, *The Evolution of the Chinese Internet: Creative Visibility in the Digital Public* (Stanford University Press, 2020); Lin Zhang, *The Labor of Reinvention: Entrepreneurship in the New Chinese Digital Economy* (Columbia University Press, 2023).
3. On multi-interactionism, see Yang, *Power of the Internet in China*. On the conception of "field," see Pierre Bourdieu, *The Field of Cultural Production: Essays on Art and Literature* (Columbia University Press, 1993).
4. Michel Hockx, *Internet Literature in China* (Columbia University Press, 2015), 4.
5. Guobin Yang, "Chinese Internet Literature and the Changing Field of Print Culture," in *From Woodblocks to the Internet: Chinese Publishing and Print Culture in*

Transition, circa 1800 to 2008, ed. Cynthia Brokaw and Christopher A. Reed (Brill, 2010), 333.

6. On electronic literature in the West, see N. Katherine Hayles, *Electronic Literature: New Horizons for the Literary* (University of Notre Dame Press, 2008); and Scott Rettberg, *Electronic Literature* (Polity, 2019). I by no means suggest that internet literature lacks creativity in writing styles or techniques. On internet literature in China, see Youquan Ouyang, ed., *Wangluo Wenxue Wunian Pucha (2009–2013)* [*Five Year Census of Internet Literature (2009–2013)*] (Central Compilation and Translation, 2014).
7. China Internet Network Information Center, *Di 52 Ci Zhogguo Hulian Wangluo Fazhan Zhuangkuang Tongji Baogao* [*The 52nd China Statistical Report on Internet Development*], CNNIC, August 28, 2023, https://www.cnnic.cn/n4/2023/0828/c88-10829.html.
8. China Internet Network Information Center, *Di 44 Ci Zhogguo Hulian Wangluo Fazhan Zhuangkuang Tongji Baogao* [*The 44th China Statistical Report on Internet Development*], CNNIC, August 30, 2019, https://www.cnnic.cn/n4/2022/0401/c88-1116.html.
9. Originally, both *China News Digest* and *New Threads* were available only through email subscription. Web access was developed later. Youquan Ouyang and Xingjie Yuan, eds., *Zhongguo Wangluo Wenxue Biannian Shi* (*A Chronical History of Chinese Internet literature*) (China Federation of Literary and Art Circles, 2015).
10. The club also used the platform to facilitate the organization of literature competitions among college students and many of those who participated were literature enthusiasts on campus BBS forums.
11. See Sina, http://news.sina.com.cn/richtalk/news/cbt/index.html.
12. Zhixiong Zhou, "Wangluo Wenxue Dasai yu Wangluo Wenxue de Fazhan" [Internet Literature Contests and the Development of Internet Literature], China Writer Net, January 22, 2010, http://www.chinawriter.com.cn/2010/2010-01-22/81753.html.
13. Shaohua Guo argues that the novel "marked the beginning of the Internet literature era." See Guo, *Evolution of the Chinese Internet*, 70.
14. Murong Xuechun, "Chengdu, Jinye qing Jiang Wo Yiwang" [Chengdu, Remember Me Not Tonight], Tianya.cn, April 5, 2002, http://bbs.tianya.cn/post-culture-48701-1.shtml.
15. Its description on the Amazon product page shows that the novel has accumulated more than one billion clicks on Tianya alone and sold almost one million copies. See Amazon, https://www.amazon.cn/dp/B07PHJS3CK.
16. Yang, "Chinese Internet Literature," 333.
17. Fanghang Han, "'Rongshuxia' Ruhe Kaiqi yige Wangwen Shidai, you Ruhe Zouxiang Moluo" [How "Under the Banyan Tree" Started the Internet Literature Era and How It Goes Downhill], *QDaily*, August 27, 2917, https://www.qdaily.com/articles/44533.html.
18. Han, "'Rongshuxia' Ruhe Kaiqi."
19. Xiaoming Wang, "A Realm Divided in Six: Chinese Literature Today," in *On China's Cultural Transformation*, ed. Keping Yu (Brill, 2015), 184.
20. Luoyefeitian, "Lun Zhongguo Wangluo Wenxue de Fazhan yu Xianzhuang" [On the Development and State of Chinese Online Literature], Jiangshan Literature Net, October 13, 2008, http://www.vsread.com/index.php/article/showread?id=3617&pn2=1&pn=1.

21. Han, "'Rongshuxia' Ruhe Kaiqi."
22. According to William Zhu, UBT attempted to sell e-books by its writers at the very affordable price of 1 to 2 RMB (roughly 15 to 25 cents in US dollars). See Han, "'Rongshuxia' Ruhe Kaiqi"; Wei Ji, "Hulianwang Shidai de Qiji: Zhongguo Wangluo Wenxue" [Miracle of the Internet Age: Chinese Online Literature], *BBC Chinese*, March 5, 2010, https://www.bbc.com/zhongwen/simp/indepth/2010/03/100302_internetliterature1.
23. Michael S. C. Tse and Maleen Z. Gong, "Online Communities and Commercialization of Chinese Internet Literature," *Journal of Internet Commerce* 11, no. 2 (2012): 100–116.
24. Pusu, "Wangluo Wenxue de Ming yu An: Yi Tianya Shequ Weili" [The Light and Dark Aspects of Online Literature: Tianya Community as an Example], Tianya.cn, November 15, 2017, http://bbs.tianya.cn/post-1178-5201-1.shtml.
25. Qidian was not the first platform to try the pay-to-read model. Its success might be because (1) the model was rolled out when a reliable online payment system was ready, and (2) it allowed readers to test-read before paying. For more on the model, see Hockx, *Internet Literature in China*, 110–12.
26. Many platforms still rely on ad revenue, including forums as well as sites that attract readers by providing free access to pirated novels.
27. Writers' income depends on their platform contracts. Following are three typical options: (1) revenue-sharing (i.e., writers and platforms share all revenue from the work); (2) buy-out, under which the platform pays the writer royalties at a negotiated rate and enjoys exclusive rights to the work; and (3) base-pay, under which the platform pays writers royalties at a lower rate than the buy-out rate; writers can share the revenue should their works generate more pay-to-read revenue than the royalties, and can also benefit from intellectual property (IP) transactions. According to the 2019 Chinese Internet Literature Development Report, writers' monthly average income was RMB 5,133 yuan; among them, about 69 percent had a monthly income below 5,000 yuan, 11 percent earned more than 10,000 yuan, and 4.1 percent earned more than 20,000 yuan. See Jingyuan Wang, "Yue Shouru Pingjun 5133 Yuan?" [Average Monthly Income being 5,133 Yuan?], *CCTV News*, September 11, 2020, https://news.cctv.com/2020/09/11/ARTIMTA6NxjvmxjHLaWV8dFX200911.shtml.
28. Sina Tech, "Shengda Chengli Wenxue Gongsi, Xinlang Hou Xiaoqiang Jiameng" [Shanda Sets Up Literature Company and Joined by Sina's Hou Xiaoqiang], *Sina Tech*, July 4, 2008, http://tech.sina.com.cn/i/2008-07-04/12302304830.shtml.
29. Liming Zhang, "Wangluo Xieshou, Bushi Shui Dou Neng Xiecheng 'Baiwan Fuweng'" [Online Writers, Not Everyone Can Become a "Millionaire"], *Beijing Morning News*, August 2, 2010.
30. Shijia Ouyang, "IP Drives Pan-entertainment Sector Change," *China Daily*, November 28, 2018, https://www.chinadaily.com.cn/a/201811/28/WS5bfded43a310eff30328b718.html.
31. Baidu Literature was sold back to Perfect World in 2016. See Xuemei Yang, "Zhuanfang Zongheng CEO: Baidu Wenxue Bianshen hou Guzhi 45 Yi, Huo Beiwentou Touzhi"[Exclusive Interview With Zongheng CEO: Baidu Literature Now Valued at 4.5 billion After Transformation With Investment from Beijing Cultural Investment Group], *Sina Tech*, October 9, 2018, https://tech.sina.com.cn/i/2018-10-09/doc-ihkvrhpt2529421.shtml.

32. Jinglin Li, "Wangluo Wenxue Wu Zhanshi" [All Quiet in Internet Literature Realm], *Deep Echo*, January 10, 2022, https://m.jiemian.com/article/6997420.html.
33. Linhu Mo, *Dazhong Wenhua Xinlun* [*New Discussion on Mass Culture*] (Tsinghua University Press, 2016); Zhuoxiao Xie et al., "Materializing Storyworld, Battles of Transmedia Storytelling: Trans-Fandom Cultures of The King's Avatar on Chinese Social Media Platform," *International Journal of Cultural Studies* 28, no. 2 (2024): 497–519; Heather Inwood, "What's in a Game? Transmedia Storytelling and the Web-Game Genre of Online Chinese Popular Fiction," *Asia Pacific Perspectives*, Spring/Summer 2014, 6–29.
34. "2019–2020 Niandu Wangluo Wenxue IP Yingshiju Gaibian Qianli Pinggu Baogao" [2019–2020 Internet Literature IP Film and Television Adaptation Potential Evaluation Report], People.com.cn, January 29, 2021, http://unn.people.com.cn/n1/2021/0129/c420625-32016929.html.
35. Amy Qin, "Making Online Literature Pay Big in China," *New York Times*, November 1, 2016, https://www.nytimes.com/2016/11/01/world/asia/china-online-literature-zhang-wei.html.
36. Jianwei Zheng, "Zhongguo Wangluo Wenxue de Haiwai Jieshou yu Wangluo Fanyi Moshi" [A Study on the Overseas Reception and Internet Translation Mode of Chinese Internet Literature], *Modern Chinese Literature and Culture*, no. 5 (2018): 119–25.
37. Yang, *Power of the Internet in China*, 7.
38. Loic J. D. Wacquant, "Towards a Reflexive Sociology: A Workshop with Pierre Bourdieu," *Sociological Theory* 7, no. 1 (1989): 39.
39. Bourdieu, *Field of Cultural Production*.
40. John Levi Martin, "What Is Field Theory?," *American Journal of Sociology* 109, no. 1 (2015): 1–49.
41. Wacquant, "Towards a Reflexive Sociology," 40.
42. The commodified political field is embedded in cyberspace. Therefore, there is also a technological aspect as the given background, although it is not visualized in figure 1.2.
43. Shaohua Guo, "Ruled by Attention: A Case Study of Professional Digital Attention Agents at Sina.Com and the Chinese Blogosphere," *International Journal of Cultural Studies* 19, no. 4 (2016): 407–23; Thomas H. Davenport and John C. Beck, *Attention Economy: Understanding the New Currency of Business* (Harvard Business School Press, 2001); and Michael H. Goldhaber, "The Attention Economy and the Net," *First Monday* 2, no. 4 (1997), https://doi.org/10.5210/fm.v2i4.519.
44. This does not mean that there is no room for other literary forms. For instance, online poetry is quite popular. See Heather Inwood, *Verse Going Viral: China's New Media Scenes* (University of Washington Press, 2014).
45. Although literature portals adopt similar categories, the categorization is not devised for analytical purposes. In particular, historical fiction in this case is different from alt-history fiction, although they overlap significantly.
46. Jin Feng, *Romancing the Internet: Producing and Consuming Chinese Web Romance* (Brill, 2013).
47. iResearch, "Wangwen Jianghu Qunying Pu: Zhongguo Wangluo Wenxue Zuozhe Dongcha Baogao" [Heroes in the Internet Literature Rivers and Lakes: Insight Report on Chinese Online Writers], *iResearch*, December 27, 2016, https://report.iresearch.cn/report/201612/2696.shtml.

48. iResearch, "Wangwen Jianghu Qunying Pu."
49. Yue Wang, "China's Tencent Has Quietly Built an Entertainment Empire That Western Tech Giants Can Only Envy," *Forbes*, December 19, 2017, https://www.forbes.com/sites/ywang/2017/12/19/chinas-tencent-has-quietly-built-an-entertainment-empire-that-western-tech-giants-can-only-envy.
50. Lili Du, "Wangwen Zuozhe Lianhe Qilai, Yuewen Kandao le Fangjian li de Daxiang" [Online Writers Are United and Yuewen Sees the Elephant in the Room], *PingWest*, May 8, 2020, https://www.pingwest.com/a/209911.
51. This was the old practice before Qidian popularized the pay-to-read model. Although it was not successful then, it reportedly has become more sustainable in recent years. Compared with fee-free literature portals and apps, pirate platforms do not share the revenue with writers and typically do not enable writer-reader interactions. Piracy may help writers attract attention to their works, and perhaps serve as a temporary haven for them in cases of censorship because literature portals are more likely to comply with state control.
52. Ling Li, "Yuewen Jietuan Huiying Zuozhe Heyue Zhengyi" [Yuewen Group Responds to Writer Contract Controversy], *Southern Metropolis Daily*, May 3, 2020, https://www.sohu.com/a/392790893_161795.
53. Platforms also often provide extra incentives for writers to produce, such as offering them a monthly "full-attendance bonus" if they manage to publish a certain amount every day. This functions like a guaranteed minimal income for writers who are not yet popular.
54. Yushu Song, "Wangluo Wenxue: Shangye Xiezuo zhong de Ziyou Zheyi" [Internet Literature: The Broken Wings of Freedom in Commercialized Writing], *Wenyi Zhengming*, no. 11 (2012): 110–13; and Yanyan Zhao, "Qianxi Wangluo Wenxue de Kuaican Shuxing" A Brief Analysis of the Fast-Food Attributes of Online Literature], *Peony*, no. 18 (2015): 102–3.
55. Michel Hockx, "Virtual Chinese Literature: A Comparative Case Study of Online Poetry Communities," *China Quarterly*, no. 183 (2005): 670–91; and Tse and Gong, "Online Communities and Commercialization of Chinese Internet Literature."
56. Tensions sometimes arise between writers and readers. One source of such tensions is the pressure to update. Writers failing to meet the expectation would typically explain, citing reasons such as health situations, family emergencies, or having other priorities—many only write in their spare time. While most readers would understand, not all of them play nice. Also, as will be discussed in chapter 5, readers may confront writers in their comments for nationalist and ideological reasons.
57. On interactive, adaptive, and improvisational writing and reading, see Alexander Lugg, "Chinese Online Fiction: Taste Publics, Entertainment, and Candle in the Tomb," *Chinese Journal of Communication* 4, no. 2 (2011): 121–36; and Hockx, *Internet Literature in China*. On "value-enhancing labor," see Mark Andrejevic, "Watching Television Without Pity: The Productivity of Online Fans," *Television and New Media* 9, no. 1 (2008): 24–46.
58. Lin Zhang and Elaine J. Yuan, "Entrepreneurs in China's 'Silicon Valley': State-Led Financialization and Mass Entrepreneurship/Innovation," *Information, Communication and Society* 26, no. 2 (2022): 286–303; and Zhang, *Labor of Reinvention*.
59. On the number of writers, see Jinglin Li, "Wangluo Wenxue Wu Zhanshi." On realizing their literary dreams, see Xinkai Huang, "To Become Immortal: Chinese Fantasy Literature Online," *Intercultural Communication Studies* 20, no. 2 (2011): 119–30.

60. John Christopher Hamm, *Paper Swordsmen: Jin Yong and the Modern Chinese Martial Arts Novel* (University of Hawaiʻi Press, 2006); and Ann Huss and Jianmei Liu, eds., *The Jin Yong Phenomenon: Chinese Martial Arts Fiction and Modern Chinese Literary History* (Cambria, 2007).
61. Hockx, *Internet Literature in China*; and Michel Hockx, "Truth, Goodness, and Beauty: Literary Policy in Xi Jinping's China," *Law and Literature* 35, no. 3 (2023): 515–31.
62. According to Bourdieu, "apparatus" implies a functionalist perspective, suggesting that "it is an infernal machine, programmed to accomplish certain purposes." See Wacquant, "Towards a Reflexive Sociology," 40. Therefore, "field" may be less controversial here; however, Althusser sees the ideological state apparatuses not just "the *stake*, but also the *site* of class struggle." See Louis Althusser, "Ideology and Ideological State Apparatus (Notes Towards an Investigation)," in *Lenin and Philosophy and Other Essays* (Monthly Review, 2001), 99.
63. Guo, *Evolution of the Chinese Internet*, 104; Henry Jenkins, *Convergence Culture: Where Old and New Media Collide* (New York University Press, 2006), 97–98; and Inwood, "What's in a Game?"
64. Sebastian Veg, *Minjian: The Rise of China's Grassroots Intellectuals* (Columbia University Press, 2019), 13.
65. Antonio Gramsci, *Selections from the Prison Notebooks of Antonio Gramsci*, ed. Quintin Hoare and Geoffrey Nowell Smith (International Publishers, 1971).

2. DANCING WITH SHACKLES ON

1. Mao Zedong, *Selected Works of Mao Tse-Tung*, vol. 3 (Foreign Languages Press, 1965), 69–98.
2. Xi Jinping, "Xi Jinping zai Wenyi Zuotanhui shang de Jianghua" [Xi Jinping's Speech at the Forum on Literature and Art], *CPC News*, October 15, 2014, http://cpc.people.com.cn/n/2015/1015/c64094-27699249.html. For an introduction to the talk in English, see "Xi Jinping's Talks at the Beijing Forum on Literature and Art," October 16, 2014, https://chinacopyrightandmedia.wordpress.com/2014/10/16/xi-jinpings-talks-at-the-beijing-forum-on-literature-and-art.
3. Timothy Cheek, "Xi Jinping's Counter-Reformation: The Reassertion of Ideological Governance in Historical Perspective," *Journal of Contemporary China* 30, no. 132 (2021): 875–87.
4. See David Holm, "The Strange Case of Liu Zhidan," *Australian Journal of Chinese Affairs* 27 (1992): 77–96.
5. Mao Zedong, *Selected Works of Mao Tse-Tung*, vol. 8 (Foreign Languages Press, 2020), 443.
6. Mao, *Selected Works of Mao Tse-Tung*, 8:443.
7. Joseph Torigian, "A Squabble About History Almost Killed Xi Jinping's Father," *Foreign Policy*, November 25, 2021, https://foreignpolicy.com/2021/11/25/xi-father-history-ccp.
8. Michel Hockx, *Internet Literature in China* (Columbia University Press, 2015), 108.
9. Rongbin Han, *Contesting Cyberspace in China: Online Expression and Authoritarian Resilience* (Columbia University Press, 2018).
10. For instance, see Rebecca MacKinnon, "China's Censorship 2.0: How Companies Censor Bloggers," *First Monday* 14, no. 2 (2009), https://firstmonday.org/article/view

/2378/2089; and Lotus Ruan et al., "The Intermingling of State and Private Companies: Analysing Censorship of the 19th National Communist Party Congress on WeChat," *China Quarterly*, no. 246 (2021): 497–526.

11. Yonggang Li, *Women de Fanghuoqiang: Wangluo Shidai de Biaoda Yu Jianguan* [*Our Great Firewall: Expression and Governance in the Era of the Internet*] (Guangxi Normal University Press, 2009); Margaret E. Roberts, *Censored: Distraction and Diversion Inside China's Great Firewall* (Princeton University Press, 2018); Yun Tai and King-wa Fu, "Specificity, Conflict, and Focal Point: A Systematic Investigation into Social Media Censorship in China," *Journal of Communication* 70, no. 6 (2020): 842–867; and Jason Gainous et al., *Directed Digital Dissidence in Autocracies: How China Wins Online* (Oxford University Press, 2023).
12. Rongbin Han, "Manufacturing Consent in Cyberspace: China's 'Fifty-Cent Army,'" *Journal of Current Chinese Affairs* 44, no. 2 (2015): 105–34; Gary King et al., "How the Chinese Government Fabricates Social Media Posts for Strategic Distraction, Not Engaged Argument," *American Political Science Review* 111, no. 3 (2017): 484–501; Johan Lagerkvist, "Internet Ideotainment in the PRC: National Responses to Cultural Globalization," *Journal of Contemporary China* 17, no. 54 (2008): 121–40; Sheng Zou, "Restyling Propaganda: Popularized Party Press and the Making of Soft Propaganda in China," *Information Communication and Society* 26, no. 1 (2023): 201–17; and Daniel C. Mattingly and Elaine Yao, "How Soft Propaganda Persuades," *Comparative Political Studies* 55, no. 9 (2022): 1569–94.
13. Maximilian Mayer and Frederik Schmitz, eds., *The Digitalisation of Memory Practices in China: Contesting the Curating State* (Bristol University Press, 2025); and Florian Schneider, *China's Digital Nationalism* (Oxford University Press, 2018).
14. Ashley Esarey, "Winning Hearts and Minds? Cadres as Microbloggers in China," *Journal of Current Chinese Affairs* 44, no. 2 (2015): 69–103; Genia Kostka, "China's Social Credit Systems and Public Opinion: Explaining High Levels of Approval," *New Media and Society* 21, no. 7 (2019): 1565–93; Nele Noesselt, "Microblogs and the Adaptation of the Chinese Party-State's Governance Strategy," *Governance* 27, no. 3 (2014): 449–68; Jesper Schlæger and Min Jiang, "Official Microblogging and Social Management by Local Governments in China," *China Information* 28, no. 2 (2014): 189–213.
15. Kai Deng et al., "Xi Jinping's Surveillance State: Merging Digital Technology and Grassroots Organizations," in *The Xi Jinping Effect*, ed. Ashley Esarey and Rongbin Han (University of Washington Press, 2024); and Qiang Xiao, "The Road to Digital Unfreedom: President Xi's Surveillance State," *Journal of Democracy* 30, no. 1 (2019): 53–67.
16. Michel Hockx, "Truth, Goodness, and Beauty: Literary Policy in Xi Jinping's China," *Law and Literature* 35, no. 3 (2023): 515–31.
17. Rachel E. Stern and Jonathan Hassid, "Amplifying Silence: Uncertainty and Control Parables in Contemporary China," *Comparative Political Studies* 45, no. 10 (2012): 1230–54.
18. Many banned books fall into this category. For instance, *Tomb Stone* (墓碑) by Yang Jisheng is about the Great Famine.
19. For example, see National Eliminate Pornography and Illegal Publications Work Team Office, "Guanyu Yanli Chachu Wangluo Yinhui Seqing Xiaoshuo de Jinji Tongzhi" [Urgent Notice on Strictly Investigating and Punishing Online Pornographic Fiction], GAPP Web, August 1, 2007, http://www.gapp.gov.cn/news/1663/102998.shtml.

This was not the first or last time that the state attempted to "clean the Web." As early as 2004, there was such a campaign that lasted for three months and resulted in 428 arrests. See Ying Zhang, "Bushi Diyici, Ye Bushi Zuihou Yici, Wangluo Wenxue 'Saohuang Dafei' Shinian Ji" [Not the First Time, Nor the Last, Ten-Year 'Anti-Pornography and Anti-Illegal' Record of Internet Literature], *Southern Weekend*, May 29, 2014, http://www.infzm.com/content/101018.

20. BBC Beijing Bureau, "China's Fledgling Hip-Hop Culture Faces Official Crackdown," *BBC News*, January 24, 2018, http://www.bbc.com/news/blogs-china-blog-42800032.
21. Jun Mai, "China Deletes 2 Million Online Posts for 'Historical Nihilism' as Communist Party Centenary Nears," *South China Morning Post*, May 11, 2021, https://www.scmp.com/news/china/politics/article/3132957/china-deletes-2-million-online-posts-historical-nihilism; and Qiang Zhang and Robert Weatherley, "The Rise of 'Republican Fever' in the PRC and the Implications for CCP Legitimacy," *China Information* 27, no. 3 (2013): 277–300.
22. This constraint makes some stories simply illogical. For example, *The Rise of a Great Writer in Republic Era* (*Minguo zhi Wenhao Jueqi* 民国之文豪崛起) is about a young man traveling back to 1926 who intervenes in numerous social, political, economic, and cultural events. Yet all the changes fail to effect the pace of the anti-Japanese War, the Second United Front between CCP and KMT, and, presumably, CCP seizing power in 1949.
23. Jinpingmei, "Zhexie Nian, Guangdian Zongju Caole Naxie Xin" [What Has the State Administration of Radio, Film and Television Been Worrying about Over the Years?], Sina.com.cn, December 3, 2014, http://news.sina.com.cn/c/zg/jpm/2014-12-03/1825441.html.
24. Zhihu, "Ruhe Pingjia Wangluo Xiaoshuo Chise Liming?" [How to Evaluate the Online Novel *Red Dawn*?], *Zhihu*, July 7, 2014, https://www.zhihu.com/question/24406194; and Zhihu, "Chise Liming Zheben Xuanchuan Makesi Zhuyi de Xiaoshuo Zenme Yang?" [What Is Your Take of the Novel *Red Dawn* That Promotes Marxism?], *Zhihu*, October 12, 2015, https://www.zhihu.com/question/36411398.
25. Starting from 2018, college-based Marxist associations across the nation, including those of Peking University, Nanjing University, and Remin University, were restructured or ceased operations, with some of their members taken into custody. See Jenny Chan, "A Precarious Worker-Student Alliance in Xi's China," *China Review* 20, no. 1 (2020): 165–90; and Jérôme Doyon and Konstantinos Tsimonis, "Apathy Is Not Enough: Changing Modes of Student Management in Post-Mao China," *Europe—Asia Studies* 74, no. 7 (2022): 1123–46.
26. Source not provided to protect the writer.
27. Source not provided to protect the writer.
28. Gary King et al., "How Censorship in China Allows Government Criticism but Silences Collective Expression," *American Political Science Review* 107, no. 2 (2013): 326–43; Peter Lorentzen, "China's Strategic Censorship," *American Journal of Political Science* 58, no. 2 (2014): 402–14.
29. Many anti-Manchu titles are Han-chauvinistic. The state seems concerned less with than with Islam and Xinjiang, or Tibet.
30. Han, *Contesting Cyberspace in China*, chap. 3; MacKinnon, "China's Censorship 2.0: How Companies Censor Bloggers"; and Ruan et al., "The Intermingling of State and Private Companies."

31. Source not provided to protect the writer.
32. MacKinnon, "China's Censorship 2.0."
33. See Rongbin Han and Li Shao, "Scaling Authoritarian Information Control: How China Adjusts the Level of Online Censorship," *Political Research Quarterly* 75, no. 4 (2022): 1345–59.
34. Ying Zhang, "'Jing Wang' Er Yue Jian" [Two Months of 'Cleaning the Web'], *Xinmin Weekly*, June 12, 2014, http://www.xinminweekly.com.cn/wenhua/2014/06/12/3950.html. This case is not anonymized because the source is a state media outlet.
35. Buerzi Lin, "Xiaohou Yinfa Gongming, IP Zhuixu Ruhe zai Dazhong Shichang Nixi" [Resonance After Laughter, How the "Zhui Xu' IP Achieved Mainstream Success"], Sohu.com, February 17, 2021, https://www.sohu.com/a/451127706_116132.
36. Source not provided to protect the writer.
37. Bruce J. Dickson, "Cooptation and Corporatism in China: The Logic of Party Adaptation," *Political Science Quarterly* 115, no. 4 (2000): 517–40; Jennifer Gandhi, *Political Institutions Under Dictatorship* (Cambridge University Press, 2010); Beatriz Magaloni, "Credible Power-Sharing and the Longevity of Authoritarian Rule," *Comparative Political Studies* 41, no. 4–5 (2008): 715–41; and Edmund Malesky and Paul Schuler, "Nodding or Needling: Analyzing Delegate Responsiveness in an Authoritarian Parliament," *American Political Science Review* 104, no. 3 (2010): 482–502.
38. On the way co-optation targets groups, see Yuen Yuen Ang, "Co-Optation and Clientelism: Nested Distributive Politics in China's Single-Party Dictatorship," *Studies in Comparative International Development* 51, no. 3 (2016): 235–56. On long-term credible commitments, see Magaloni, "Credible Power-Sharing and the Longevity of Authoritarian Rule."
39. Han, *Contesting Cyberspace in China*, 63.
40. State Administration of Press, Publication, Radio, Film and Television, "Guanyu Yinfa Guanyu Tuidong Wangluo Wenxue Jiankang Fazhan de Zhidao Yijian de Tongzhi" [Notice on the Issuance of Guiding Opinions Concerning Promoting the Healthy Development of Online Literature], Cyber Administration of China Web, January 6, 2015, http://www.cac.gov.cn/2015-01/06/c_1113893482.htm.
41. State Administration of Press, Publication, Radio, Film and Television, "Guanyu Yinfa Wangluo Wenxue Chuban Fuwu Danwei Shehui Xiaoyi Pinggu Shixing Banfa de Tongzhi" [Notice on Issuance of Provisional Methods for Evaluating Social Benefits of Online Literature Publication Service Platforms], National Press and Publication Administration, June 27, 2017, https://www.nppa.gov.cn/xxfb/tzgs/201706/t20170627_666172.html.
42. This specific scheme reflects the general trend of "quantification of governance" in China, which uses metrics to compare and rank targeted entities. For more, see Yingdan Lu and Jennifer Pan, "Capturing Clicks: How the Chinese Government Uses Clickbait to Compete for Visibility," *Political Communication* 38, no. 1–2 (2020): 23–54; and Angèle Christin, "Counting Clicks: Quantification and Variation in Web Journalism in the United States and France," *American Journal of Sociology* 123, no. 5 (2018): 1382–415.
43. Zhiyan Wang, "Xinwen Chuban Guangdian Zongju Fabu 'Wangluo Wenxue Chuban Fuwu Danwei Shehui Xiaoyi Pinggu Shixing Banfa'" [SAPPRFT Issues Provisional Methods for Evaluating Social Benefits of Online Literature Publication Service], Xinhua Net, June 26, 2017, http://www.xinhuanet.com/politics/2017-06/26/c_129640672.htm.

44. State Administration of Press, Publication, Radio, Film and Television, "Guanyu Yinfa Wangluo Wenxue Chuban."
45. Dazhi Lu, "Zhongguo Zuoxie Chengli Wangluo Wenxue Weiyuanhui" [China Writers Association establishes Internet Literature Committee], *China Reading Weekly*, December 30, 2015.
46. Ning Hui and David Wertime, "Is This the New Face of China's Silent Majority?," *Foreign Policy*, October 22, 2014, http://foreignpolicy.com/2014/10/22/is-this-the-new-face-of-chinas-silent-majority.
47. Zheng Zhang, "Shenmi Xinxing Qunti Wangluo Zuojia Jueqi" [A Mysterious Emerging Group of Online Writers Rises], *China Youth Daily*, March 19, 2018.
48. Huairang Yue, "Zhongyang Tongzhanbu Juban Di Er Qi Wangluo Renshi Lilun Yantaoban" [CCCPC United Front Work Department Held the Second Theoretical Symposium for Internet Personalities], *The Paper*, March 24, 2018, http://m.thepaper.cn/newsDetail_forward_2041005.
49. Yue, "Zhongyang Tongzhanbu Juban."
50. Tongzhanxinyu, "Zhihu CEO Zhou Yuan, Mi Meng Deng 52 Ming Wangluo Renshi Chuxi Tongzhanbu Lilun Yantaoban" [Zhihu CEO Zhou Yuan, Mi Meng and Other 52 Internet Personalities Attended the United Front Work Department Theoretical Symposium], *The Paper*, March 26, 2018, http://m.thepaper.cn/newsDetail_forward_2043049.
51. These tactics can be a means to co-opt writers and platforms. By promotion, however, I intend to highlight how some writers and works are selected and highlighted by the state to signal its approval and attract more attention from the audience.
52. Kun Yin, "Rang Tuijie Huodong Fahui 'Zhishi Deng' Xiaoying" [Let the Promotion Function as "Signal Light"], China Writer Net, March 28, 2016, http://www.chinawriter.com.cn/news/2016/2016-03-28/268511.html.
53. NPPA continues to promote Internet literature works it deems recommendable after 2019, just under a different banner. See Li Gao, "Youxiu Xianshi Ticai he Lishi Ticai Wangluo Wenxue Chuban Gongcheng Qidong" [Excellent Realistic and Historical Themed Online Literature Publishing Project Launched], Xinhua Net, June 12, 2020, http://m.xinhuanet.com/ent/2020-06/12/c_1126104828.htm.
54. Shuangqi Fu, "2016 Nian Beijing Shi Youxiu Wangluo Wenxue Yuanchuang Zuopin Fabu" [List of 2016 Beijing Municipality Excellent Online Literary Original Works Publicized], *Guangmin Daily*, October 26, 2016.
55. Lagerkvist, "Internet Ideotainment in the PRC"; Mattingly and Yao, "How Soft Propaganda Persuades"; and Zou, "Restyling Propaganda."
56. Linan Yao, "Popular Propaganda in Pop Culture: How China Sells Its Ideology" (PhD diss., Columbia University, 2023); and Weijun Ma, "Chinese Main Melody TV Drama: Hollywoodization and Ideological Persuasion," *Television and New Media* 15, no. 6 (2013): 523–37.
57. "2019–2020 Niandu Wangluo Wenxue IP Yingshiju Gaibian Qianli Pinggu Baogao" [2019–2020 Internet Literature IP Film and Television Adaptation Potential Evaluation Report], People.com.cn, January 29, 2021, http://unn.people.com.cn/n1/2021/0129/c420625-32016929.html.
58. Zhiyan Wang et al., "25 Bu Wangwen Jiazuo Huo Guojia Xinwen Chubanshu he Zhongguo Zuoxie Lianhe Tuijie" [25 Online Fiction Received Joint Recommendation by NPPA and the China Writers Association], Xinhua Net, October 11, 2019, http://www.xinhuanet.com/politics/2019-10/11/c_1210308698.htm.

59. Li Li, "Wangluo Wenxue Zuopin 'Daguo Zhonggong' Huo Zhongguo Chuban Zhengfu Jiang" [Online Literature Work "Great Power Heavy Industry" Won China's Government Publishing Award], *Beijing Daily*, July 29, 2021.
60. Xiaojing Liu and Min Zhou, "Wangluo Wenxue Yongbao 'Xianshi' 24 Bu Wangwen Lizuo zai Jiangsu Huojiang" [Online Literature Embraces "Reality," 24 Masterpieces Won Awards in Jiangsu], China Writer Net, November 4, 2019, https://www.chinawriter.com.cn/n1/2019/1104/c404023-31436018.html.
61. Zhang, "Bushi Diyici."
62. See chapter 1044 of the fiction. Source not provided to protect the writer.
63. Edward Wong, "Pushing China's Limits on Web, if Not on Paper." *New York Times*, November 7, 2011.
64. Thomas Chen, "The Workshop of the World: Censorship and the Internet Novel 'Such Is This World,'" in *China's Contested Internet*, ed. Guobin Yang (NIAS, 2015), 19–43.
65. Zhang, "'Jing Wang' Er Yue Jian."
66. Ashley Esarey and Qiang Xiao, "Political Expression in the Chinese Blogosphere: Below the Radar," *Asian Survey* 48, no. 5 (2008): 752–72; Han, *Contesting Cyberspace in China*; and Guobin Yang, *The Power of the Internet in China: Citizen Activism Online* (Columbia University Press, 2009).
67. Source not provided to protect the writer.
68. Hockx, "Truth, Goodness, and Beauty," 516.
69. Jeffrey L. Brudney and Robert E. England, "Toward a Definition of the Coproduction Concept," *Public Administration Review* 43, no. 1 (1983): 59–65; and Elinor Ostrom, "Crossing the Great Divide: Coproduction, Synergy, and Development," *World Development* 24, no. 6 (1996): 1073–87.
70. I acknowledge that the term *coproduction* contains an implicit value judgment, which is not my intent.
71. Liang Chen, "IP Shengtai Wenyu Fenghui: Kuangshi Yanhuo Zuozhe Chen Liang de 'Xianli' Zhuti Yanjiang" [IP Ecological Entertainment Summit: Keynote Speech by Chen Liang, Author of Unparalleled Fireworks], *Netease*, August 23, 2019, https://www.163.com/dy/article/ENA0CQ6705387W7O.html.
72. Chen, "IP Shengtai Wenyu Fenghui."
73. Wei Du, "Yibu Daju Neng Yingxiang Yijia Shangshi Gongsi Yeji!" [A Big Drama Can Affect the Performance of a Listed Company!], *National Business Daily*, March 24, 2019, http://www.nbd.com.cn/articles/2019-03-24/1313505.html.
74. See chapter 520 of the fiction.
75. Source not provided to protect the users.
76. Jingnan Shi, "2020 Nian 'Youxiu Xianshi Ticai he Lishi Ticai Wangluo Wenxue Chuban Gongcheng' Ruxuan Zuopin Jiexiao" [2020 Selected Works of "Excellent Realistic and Historical Themed Online Literature Publishing Project" Announced], Sohu.com, August 23, 2021, https://www.sohu.com/a/485186786_267106.
77. Lisa Wedeen, *Authoritarian Apprehensions: Ideology, Judgment, and Mourning in Syria* (University of Chicago Press, 2019).

3. MAKE CHINA GREAT AGAIN

1. On romance, see Jin Feng, *Romancing the Internet: Producing and Consuming Chinese Web Romance* (Brill, 2013); and Shaohua Guo, "Startling by Each Click:

'Word-of-Mouse' Publicity and Critically Manufacturing Time-Travel Romance Online," *Chinese Literature Today* 5, no. 1 (2015): 74–83. On poetry, see Heather Inwood, *Verse Going Viral: China's New Media Scenes* (University of Washington Press, 2014). On game-based fiction, see Heather Inwood, "What's in a Game? Transmedia Storytelling and the Web-Game Genre of Online Chinese Popular Fiction," *Asia Pacific Perspectives*, no. Spring/Summer (2014): 6–29. On fantasy literature, see Xinkai Huang, "To Become Immortal: Chinese Fantasy Literature Online," *Intercultural Communication Studies* 20, no. 2 (2011): 119–30.

2. Most alt-history titles do not engage in the philosophical or scientific discussion of the implications of changing history.
3. See iResearch, "2018 Nian Zhongguo Wangluo Wenxue Zuozhe Baogao" [2018 Report on Chinese Internet Literature Writers], *iResearch*, May 9, 2018, 7, http://www.iresearch.com.cn/Detail/report?id=3208&isfree=0.
4. Chia-Fu Sung, "The Official Historiographical Operation of the Song Dynasty," *Journal of Song-Yuan Studies* 45 (2015): 175–206; and Denis Twitchett, *The Writing of Official History under the T'ang* (Cambridge University Press, 2002).
5. On the shaping of history, see Benedict Anderson, *Imagined Communities: Reflections on the Origin and Spread of Nationalism* (Verso, 1991); Ernest Gellner, *Nations and Nationalism* (Cornell University Press, 2008); Anthony D. Smith, *The Ethnic Origins of Nations* (Blackwell, 1986); and Anthony D. Smith, *National Identity* (Penguin, 1991). On routine symbols and habits, see Michael Billig, *Banal Nationalism* (SAGE, 1995).
6. On the impact of history on national identity, see Haifeng Huang and Xinsheng Liu, "Historical Knowledge and National Identity: Evidence from China," *Research and Politics* 5, no. 3 (2018): 1–8. On sufferings in modern times, see Yinan He, "History, Chinese Nationalism and the Emerging Sino-Japanese Conflict," *Journal of Contemporary China* 16, no. 50 (2007): 1–24; Florian Schneider, *China's Digital Nationalism* (Oxford University Press, 2018); and Yi Wang and Matthew M. Chew, "State, Market, and the Manufacturing of War Memory: China's Television Dramas on the War of Resistance Against Japan," *Memory Studies* 14, no. 4 (2021): 877–91.
7. I exclude titles that focus on other countries (e.g., Soviet Union, Germany, or the United States), pursuit of personal desires (wealth, fame, and romantic relations), or royal court struggle (concubines competing for the emperor's favor), because they are less political than MCGA titles. This by no means suggests that they play no function in ideological governance.
8. There is a literature on nostalgia, which often glorifies the past as a critique of the present. See Guobin Yang, "China's Zhiqing Generation: Nostalgia, Identity, and Cultural Resistance in the 1990s," *Modern China* 29, no. 3 (2003): 267–96; and Maria Todorova and Zsuzsa Gille, eds., *Post-Communist Nostalgia* (Berghahn, 2010).
9. This term was originally coined by President Xi Jinping and has been widely referred to in China and beyond. For instance, see Rush Doshi, *The Long Game: China's Grand Strategy to Displace American Order* (Oxford University Press, 2021).
10. Xiaomei Chen, *Staging Chinese Revolution: Theater, Film, and the Afterlives of Propaganda* (Columbia University Press, 2016); Alison Landsberg, *Engaging the Past: Mass Culture and the Production of Historical Knowledge* (Columbia University Press, 2015); and Rudolf G. Wagner, *The Contemporary Chinese Historical Drama: Four Studies* (University of California Press, 1990).

11. Tom Fisher, "'The Play's the Thing': Wu Han and Hai Rui Revisited," *Australian Journal of Chinese Affairs*, no. 7 (1982): 1–35; and Jiaqi Yan and Gao Gao, *Turbulent Decade*, ed. Daniel W. Y. Kwok (University of Hawai'i Press, 1996).
12. Yan and Gao, *Turbulent Decade*, chap. 1.
13. Ian Johnson, *Sparks: China's Underground Historians and Their Battle for the Future* (Oxford University Press, 2023).
14. Mobo C. F. Gao, *The Battle for China's Past: Mao and the Cultural Revolution* (Pluto, 2008); and Jun Liu, "Who Speaks for the Past? Social Media, Social Memory, and the Production of Historical Knowledge in Contemporary China," *International Journal of Communication* 12 (2018): 1675–95.
15. Howard Choy, *Remapping the Past: Fictions of History in Deng's China, 1979–1997* (Brill, 2008).
16. Geremie R. Barmé and Jeremy Goldkorn, eds., "Party Policies from One to Ten," in *China Story Yearbook 2013: Civilising China* (Australian National University, 2013), 116.
17. Chen, *Staging Chinese Revolution.*
18. Jian Xu, Qian Gong, and Wen Yin, "Maintaining Ideological Security and Legitimacy in Digital China: Governance of Cyber Historical Nihilism," *Media International Australia* 185, no. 1 (2022): 26–40.
19. Thomas J. Christensen, "Chinese Realpolitik," *Foreign Affairs* 75, no. 5 (1996): 37–52.
20. Anderson, *Imagined Communities*; Smith, *The Ethnic Origins of Nations*; and Smith, *National Identity*; Gellner, *Nations and Nationalism.*
21. Montserrat Guibernau, "Anthony D. Smith on Nations and National Identity: A Critical Assessment," *Nations and Nationalism* 10, no. 1–2 (2004): 137.
22. Schneider, *China's Digital Nationalism*, 45.
23. George Orwell, *1984* (Houghton Mifflin Harcourt, 2017).
24. Peter Hays Gries, "Chinese Nationalism: Challenging the State?," *Current History* 104, no. 683 (2005): 251–56; and Florian Schneider, *China's Digital Nationalism*; Zheng Wang, *Never Forget National Humiliation: Historical Memory in Chinese Politics and Foreign Relations* (Columbia University Press, 2014).
25. Clark Hulse, *The Rule of Art: Literature and Painting in the Renaissance* (University of Chicago Press, 1990).
26. Thomas M. Kavanagh, *Esthetics of the Moment: Literature and Art in the French Enlightenment* (University of Pennsylvania Press, 1996).
27. Mingwei Song, "Preface to 'Chinese Science Fiction: Late Qing and the Contemporary,'" *Renditions*, no. 77/78 (2012): 7; and Mingwei Song, "Variations on Utopia in Contemporary Chinese Science Fiction," *Science-Fiction Studies* 40, no. 1 (2013): 86.
28. Nathaniel Isaacson, *Celestial Empire: The Emergence of Chinese Science Fiction* (Wesleyan University Press, 2017).
29. Kenneth Liberthal, *Governing China: From Revolution Through Reform* (W. W. Norton, 2004); and Tony Saich, *Governance and Politics of China* (Palgrave Macmillan, 2015).
30. Wenfang Tang, *Populist Authoritarianism: Chinese Political Culture and Regime Sustainability* (Oxford University Press, 2016).
31. Mao Zedong, *Selected Works of Mao Tse-Tung, vol. 5* (Foreign Languages Press, 1977), 22.
32. On modernity, see David Der-Wei Wang, *Fin-de-Siècle Splendor: Repressed Modernities of Late Qing Fiction, 1849–1911* (Stanford University Press, 1997); and Nathaniel

Isaacson, *Celestial Empire*; Mingwei Song, *Young China: National Rejuvenation and the Bildungsroman, 1900–1959* (Harvard University Asia Center, 2015). An example of contemporary national revival sci-fi title is *Mars over America* (火星照耀美国), published in 2012 by Han Song, which depicts a world in which China has replaced the United States as the only superpower.

33. See Jianmei Liu, *Revolution Plus Love: Literary History, Women's Bodies, and Thematic Repetition in Twentieth-Century Chinese Fiction* (University of Hawai'i Press, 2003); and Weijun Ma, "Chinese Main Melody TV Drama: Hollywoodization and Ideological Persuasion," *Television and New Media* 15, no. 6 (2013): 523–37.
34. Cora Kaplan, *Victoriana: Histories, Fictions, Criticism* (Columbia University Press, 2007).
35. Again, alt-history titles are more male-oriented. Female-oriented works that involve time traveling often care little about changing history and instead typically fit the romance fiction genre. See Feng, *Romancing the Internet*.
36. See the concluding chapter of *Tang Cavaliers*, Qidian, https://www.qidian.com/chapter/1496095/77418401.
37. See *Tang Cavaliers*, Qidian, March 15, 2022, https://book.qidian.com/info/1496095.
38. See *Ruling Under Heaven*, Zongheng, http://book.zongheng.com/book/69507.html.
39. See *Pointing South*, 17K, March 15, 2022, https://www.17k.com/chapter/4988/422724.html.
40. For a discussion of the event, see ifeng, "Yan Chongnian Daodi Gaibugai Da?" (Does Yan Chongnian Deserve the Slap?), *Ifeng News*, October 10, 2008, https://news.ifeng.com/history/special/yanchongnian/.
41. See Wen Zhao, " 'Gongye Dang' Ruhe zai Gaizao 'Gudai' Shijie de Tongshi Gaizao Ziji: Lingao Qiming de Qimeng Xushi Shiyan" [How the "Industrial Party" Transforms Itself Through Reforming the "Ancient World": The Illuminating Narrative Experiment by Lingao Qiming], *Dongfang Journal*, no. 4 (2019): 130–41.
42. See *F—k Qing*, Qidian, https://book.qidian.com/info/2050926.
43. See the introduction to *F—k Qing*, Qidian, https://book.qidian.com/info/2050926. Also see the writer's afterword to *F—k Qing*, Qidian, https://read.qidian.com/chapter/KqXWQzrWQDw1/8kGSYxMq5MgexoRJOkJclQ2.
44. See the introduction to *F—k Qing*, Qidian, https://book.qidian.com/info/2050926.
45. See *Red Dawn*, Yousuu, April 2, 2019, https://web.archive.org/web/20190402090849/https://www.yousuu.com/book/4166.
46. The ranking score is calculated through multiplying the average rating by the number of raters. This means the book might rank higher should it not be censored.
47. See the concluding chapter of *The Industrial Tycoon*, Qidian, https://www.qidian.com/chapter/2104576/42993513.
48. William Zheng, "China's Officials Play Up 'Rise of the East, Decline of the West,' " *South China Morning Post*, March 9, 2021, https://www.scmp.com/news/china/diplomacy/article/3124752/chinas-officials-play-rise-east-decline-west.
49. Sarah Zhang, "Xi Jinping Takes Leading Role in Hit Propaganda Film Extolling 'Amazing' China," *South China Morning Post*, March 14, 2018, https://www.scmp.com/news/china/society/article/2137168/xi-jinping-takes-leading-role-hit-propaganda-film-extolling.
50. Susan L. Shirk, *Overreach: How China Derailed Its Peaceful Rise* (Oxford University Press, 2022).

51. For state curation of history and memory, see Maximilian Mayer and Karolina Pawlik, "Politics of Memory, Heritage, and Diversity in Modern China," *Journal of Current Chinese Affairs* 52, no. 2 (2023): 139–62.
52. Suisheng Zhao, "A State-Led Nationalism: The Patriotic Education Campaign in Post-Tiananmen China," *Communist and Post-Communist Studies* 31, no. 3 (1998): 287–302.
53. "Taizu Shi Chuanyue Huilai de" [Taizu Is a Time Traveler], Cchere.com, October 24, 2009, https://cchere.com/article/2501713.
54. "2019–2020 Niandu Wangluo Wenxue IP Yingshiju Gaibian Qianli Pinggu Baogao" [2019–2020 Internet Literature IP Film and Television Adaptation Potential Evaluation Report], People.com.cn, January 29, 2021, http://unn.people.com.cn/n1/2021/0129/c420625-32016929.html.
55. Chris Buckley, "In China, an Action Hero Beats Box Office Records (and Arrogant Westerners)," *New York Times*, August 16, 2017, https://www.nytimes.com/2017/08/16/world/asia/china-wolf-warrior-2-film.html.
56. Tuvia Gering, "A Xinderella Story: Turning the Chinese Dream into China's Master Narrative," *China Report* 59, no. 3 (2023): 243–58; and Wei Shi and Shih Diing Liu, "Pride as Structure of Feeling: Wolf Warrior II and the National Subject of the Chinese Dream," *Chinese Journal of Communication* 13, no. 3 (2020): 329–43.
57. This explains why Mike Pompeo's strategy to distinguish between Chinese people and the government was not effective.
58. Wing Shan Ho, *Screening Post-1989 China: Critical Analysis of Chinese Film and Television* (Palgrave Macmillan, 2015); Zala Volcic and Mark Andrejevic, eds., *Commercial Nationalism: Selling the Nation and Nationalizing the Sell* (Palgrave Macmillan, 2016); and Mei Ling Yang, "Selling Patriotism," *American Journalism* 12, no. 3 (2013): 304–20.

4. THE VARIETY OF CHINESE DREAMS

1. Yipeng Shen, *Public Discourses of Contemporary China: The Narration of the Nation in Popular Literatures, Film, and Television* (Palgrave Macmillan, 2015), 176.
2. Antonio Gramsci, *Selections from the Prison Notebooks of Antonio Gramsci*, ed. Quintin Hoare and Geoffrey Nowell Smith (International Publishers, 1971), 323, 327.
3. T. J. Jackson Lears, "The Concept of Cultural Hegemony: Problems and Possibilities," *American Historical Review* 90, no. 3 (1985): 568–69, 571.
4. Louis Althusser, "Ideology and Ideological State Apparatus (Notes Towards an Investigation)," in *Lenin and Philosophy and Other Essays* (Monthly Review, 2001), 85–126.
5. Karl Marx, *A Contribution to the Critique of Political Economy* (Progress, 1977).
6. Teresa Wright, *Accepting Authoritarianism: State-Society Relations in China's Reform Era* (Stanford University Press, 2010).
7. On a state-initiated ideological evolution, see Alan R. Kluver, *Legitimating the Chinese Economic Reforms: A Rhetoric of Myth and Orthodoxy* (State University of New York Press, 1996). On media commercialization and weakening of state control over ideological state apparatus, see Daniela Stockmann, *Media Commercialization and Authoritarian Rule in China* (Cambridge University Press, 2013). On alternate

ideations and spiritual pollution, see Thomas B. Gold, "'Just in Time!': China Battles Spiritual Pollution on the Eve of 1984," *Asian Survey* 24, no. 9 (1984): 947–74.

8. On "money worship," see Huaihong He, *Social Ethics in a Changing China: Moral Decay or Ethical Awakening?* (Brookings Institution, 2015). On "bourgeois liberalization," see Richard Baum, "Deng Liqun and the Struggle Against 'Bourgeois Liberalization,' 1979–1993," *China Information* 9, no. 4 (1995): 1–35. On "high culture fever," see Jing Wang, *High Culture Fever: Politics, Aesthetics, and Ideology in Deng's China* (University of California Press, 1996).
9. Chen Feng, "Order and Stability in Social Transition: Neoconservative Political Thought in Post-China," *China Quarterly* 151 (1997): 593–613.
10. Lears, "Concept of Cultural Hegemony," 568.
11. For an introduction, see Wei Shan et al., "Layering Ideologies from Deng Xiaoping to Xi Jinping: Tracing Ideological Changes of the Communist Party of China Using Text Analysis," *China: An International Journal* 21, no. 2 (2023): 26–50.
12. See Guobin Yang, *The Power of the Internet in China: Citizen Activism Online* (Columbia University Press, 2009); Jesper Schlæger, *E-Government in China: Technology, Power and Local Government Reform* (Routledge, 2013); Jun Liu, *Shifting Dynamics of Contention in the Digital Age: Mobile Communication and Politics in China* (Oxford University Press, 2020).
13. The state was not absent at this stage, but its intervention was rather crude. See Rongbin Han, *Contesting Cyberspace in China: Online Expression and Authoritarian Resilience* (Columbia University Press, 2018).
14. Yanjun Shao and Yingxuan Xiao, eds., *Chuangshizhe Shuo: Wangluo Wenxue Wangzhan Chuangshiren Fangtanlu* [*The Founders Say: Interviews with Internet Literature Website Founders*] (Peking University Press, 2020).
15. See Johan Lagerkvist, *After the Internet, Before Democracy: Competing Norms in Chinese Media and Society* (Peter Lang, 2010); Shaohua Guo, *The Evolution of the Chinese Internet: Creative Visibility in the Digital Public* (Stanford University Press, 2020); and Sebastian Veg, *Minjian: The Rise of China's Grassroots Intellectuals* (Columbia University Press, 2019).
16. The internet is not the only reason driving the trend since the fade of "high cultural fever" and the rise of grassroots *minjian* intellectuals both started in the 1990s, before use of the internet became widely accessible in China.
17. Yousuu adopts a simple ranking metric: Each user can assign a star rating of one to five, and each star equals two points. The total scores it receives decides the title's ranking. Again, not all novels that involve time travel are MCGA. Among the 2,100 works, 175 involve time travel or rebirth but are not coded as MCGA. Most of these titles focus on personal adventures.
18. Michael Szonyi, "Ming Fever: The Past in the Present in the People's Republic of China at Sixty," in *The People's Republic of China at 60: An International Assessment*, ed. William C. Kirby (Harvard University Asia Center, 2011).
19. James Leibold, "More Than a Category: Han Supremacism on the Chinese Internet," *China Quarterly* 203 (2010): 539–59.
20. Xiaoling Zhang et al., "No CCP, No New China: Pastoral Power in Official Narratives in China," *China Quarterly* 235 (2018): 784–803.
21. Heike Holbig, "China After Reform: The Ideological, Constitutional, and Organisational Makings of a New Era," *Journal of Current Chinese Affairs* 47, no. 3 (2018): 187–207.

22. See volume 6 of *Pointing South*, section 10, chap. 3, https://www.17k.com/book/4988.html.
23. See volume 6 of *Pointing South*, section 1, chap. 2.
24. See finishing remarks of *Qin Revolution*, https://www.qidian.com/chapter/1024655112/697810522.
25. William J. Hurst, "The Power of the Past: Nostalgia and Popular Discontent in Contemporary China," in *Laid-Off Workers in a Workers' State: Unemployment with Chinese Characteristics*, ed. Thomas B. Gold et al. (Palgrave Macmillan, 2009), 115–32.
26. Yiting Chu, "Constructing Minzu: The Representation of Minzu and Zhonghua Minzu in Chinese Elementary Textbooks," *Discourse: Studies in the Cultural Politics of Education* 39, no. 6 (2017): 941–53.
27. Zhao Xiaochun, "In Pursuit of a Community of Shared Future: China's Global Activism in Perspective," *China Quarterly of International Strategic Studies* 4, no. 1 (2018): 23–37.
28. See volume 6 of *Pointing South*, section 11, chap. 3.
29. See volume 6 of *Pointing South*, section 9, chap. 4.
30. This may remain a major factor. A 2016 survey suggests that around 50.9 percent of online novelists began writing because they had dreamed of being an author since they were young. See iResearch, "Wangwen Jianghu Qunying Pu: Zhongguo Wangluo Wenxue Zuozhe Dongcha Baogao" [Heroes in the Internet Literature Rivers and Lakes: Insight Report on Chinese Online Writers], *iResearch*, December 27, 2016, https://report.iresearch.cn/report/201612/2696.shtml.
31. Heather Inwood, "The Happiness of Unrealizable Dreams: On the Pursuit of Pleasure in Contemporary Chinese Popular Fiction," in *Chinese Discourses on Happiness*, ed. Gerda Wielander and Derek Hird (Hong Kong University Press, 2018).
32. Xi Jinping, "Xi Jinping Zhe Shiduan Hua Dingyi Zhongguomeng Neihan" [These Ten Quotes from Xi Jinping Defines the Connotations of Chinese Dream], Xinhua Net, November 29, 2017, http://www.xinhuanet.com//politics/2017-11/29/c_1122031311.htm; and Xi Jinping, "Achieving Rejuvenation Is the Dream of the Chinese People," National People's Congress, November 29, 2012, http://www.npc.gov.cn/englishnpc/c23934/202006/32191c5bbdb04cbab6df01e5077d1c60.shtml.
33. Kirk Denton, "China Dreams and the 'Road to Revival,'" *Origins: Current Events in Historical Perspective* 8, no. 3 (November 2014), https://origins.osu.edu/article/china-dreams-and-road-revival?.
34. Timothy Cheek, "Xi Jinping's Counter-Reformation: The Reassertion of Ideological Governance in Historical Perspective," *Journal of Contemporary China* 30, no. 132 (2021): 875–87.
35. See volume 6 of *Pointing South*, section 2, chap. 2.
36. Ashley Esarey and Qiang Xiao, "Political Expression in the Chinese Blogosphere: Below the Radar," *Asian Survey* 48, no. 5 (2008): 752–72.
37. Kevin J. O'Brien and Lianjiang Li, *Rightful Resistance in Rural China* (Cambridge University Press, 2006).
38. Willy Lam, "Xi Jinping's Ideology and Statecraft," *Chinese Law and Government* 48, no. 6 (2016): 409–17.
39. Suisheng Zhao, *A Nation-State by Construction: Dynamics of Modern Chinese Nationalism* (Stanford University Press, 2004); Peter Hays Gries, *China's New Nationalism: Pride, Politics, and Diplomacy* (University of California Press, 2004); Hongxing Yang and Dingxin Zhao, "Performance Legitimacy, State Autonomy and

China's Economic Miracle," *Journal of Contemporary China* 24, no. 91 (2015): 64–82; and Heike Holbig and Bruce Gilley, "Reclaiming Legitimacy in China," *Politics and Policy* 38, no. 3 (2010): 395–422.

40. Yuezhi Zhao, "The Struggle for Socialism in China," *Monthly Review: An Independent Socialist Magazine* 64, no. 5 (2012): 1–17; and Jude Blanchette, *China's New Red Guards: The Return of Radicalism and the Rebirth of Mao Zedong* (Oxford University Press, 2019).
41. Rongbin Han, "Passing on the Red Genes: Communism Nostalgia in Online Fictions and Ideological Governance in China," *Regulation and Governance* (2024). https://doi.org/10.1111/rego.12622.
42. Maria Repnikova, *Media Politics in China: Improvising Power Under Authoritarianism* (Cambridge University Press, 2017).
43. Shouzhi Xia, "Amusing Ourselves to Loyalty? Entertainment, Propaganda, and Regime Resilience in China," *Political Research Quarterly* 75, no. 4 (2022): 1096–112; Neil Postman, *Amusing Ourselves to Death: Public Discourse in the Age of Show Business* (Penguin, 2005).
44. See Yanqi Tong and Shaohua Lei, "War of Position and Microblogging in China," *Journal of Contemporary China* 22, no. 80 (2013): 292–311.
45. Ian Johnson, *Sparks: China's Underground Historians and Their Battle for the Future* (Oxford University Press, 2023).
46. Ziyue Zhao, "'Lishi Xiezuo yu Chuanbo de Duoyangxing—Xugou yu Feixugou de Xiezuo' Luntan Jiyao" ["Diversity of Historical Writing and Communication—Fictional and Non-Fictional Writing" Forum Minutes], *The Paper*, November 7, 2023, https://m.thepaper.cn/newsDetail_forward_25196253.
47. Johan Lagerkvist, "Internet Ideotainment in the PRC: National Responses to Cultural Globalization," *Journal of Contemporary China* 17, no. 54 (2008): 121–40.
48. On the realist reasoning of Chinese foreign policy, see Daniel Lynch, "Chinese Thinking on the Future of International Relations: Realism as the Ti, Rationalism as the Yong?," *China Quarterly*, no. 197 (2009): 87–107. On official slogans, see Yi Wang, "'The Backward Will Be Beaten': Historical Lesson, Security, and Nationalism in China," *Journal of Contemporary China* 29, no. 126 (2020): 887–900.
49. Jeffrey Javed, *Righteous Revolutionaries: Morality, Mobilization, and Violence in the Making of the Chinese State* (University of Michigan Press, 2022).
50. O'Brien and Li, *Rightful Resistance in Rural China*; and Lily L. Tsai, "Constructive Noncompliance," *Comparative Politics* 47, no. 3 (2015): 253–79.
51. Rongbin Han, "Withering Gongzhi: Cyber Criticism of Chinese Public Intellectuals," *International Journal of Communication* 12 (2018): 1966–87; and Rongbin Han and Linan Jia, "Rescuing Authoritarian Rule: The Anti-Gongzhi Discourse in Chinese Cyberspace," in *The Routledge Handbook of Chinese Discourse Analysis*, ed. Chris Shei (Routledge, 2019), 415–27.
52. Michel Hockx, "Truth, Goodness, and Beauty: Literary Policy in Xi Jinping's China," *Law and Literature* 35, no. 3 (2023): 515–31; and Amy Hawkins and Jeffrey Wasserstrom, "Why *1984* and *Animal Farm* Aren't Banned in China," *The Atlantic*, January 13, 2019, https://www.theatlantic.com/ideas/archive/2019/01/why-1984-and-animal-farm-arent-banned-china/580156. This is not to deny that there can be an influential foreign audience, even if China is less worried about international pressure or sanctions than most other states.

53. Han, "Withering Gongzhi"; and Margaret E. Roberts, *Censored: Distraction and Diversion Inside China's Great Firewall* (Princeton University Press, 2018).
54. Shao and Xiao, *Chuangshizhe Shuo*, 28.
55. Yanjun Shao, *Wangluo Shidai de Wenxue Yindu* [*Literature Guide in the Digital Age*] (Guangxi Normal University Press, 2015).
56. Han and Jia, "Rescuing Authoritarian Rule."
57. Aldous Huxley, *Brave New World* (Harper and Row, 1946).
58. Alex Chan, "From Propaganda to Hegemony: Jiaodian Fangtan and China's Media Policy," *Journal of Contemporary China* 11, no. 30 (2002): 35–51; Peter Lorentzen, "Designing Contentious Politics in Post-1989 China," *Modern China* 43, no. 5 (2017): 459–93; and Rongbin Han et al., "Opportunistic Bargaining: Negotiating Distribution in China," *China Quarterly* 253 (2023): 141–57.

5. MORE THAN AUDIENCE

1. Sebastian Veg, *Minjian: The Rise of China's Grassroots Intellectuals* (Columbia University Press, 2019).
2. Alvin Toffler, *The Third Wave* (Bantam, 1980).
3. For an excellent review, see George Ritzer et al., "The Coming of Age of the Prosumer," *American Behavioral Scientist* 56, no. 4 (2012): 379–80.
4. Ritzer et al., "Coming of Age of the Prosumer," 383. See also Aaron Shaw and Yochai Benkler, "A Tale of Two Blogospheres: Discursive Practices on the Left and Right," *American Behavioral Scientist* 56, no. 4 (2012): 459–87; P. J. Rey, "Alienation, Exploitation, and Social Media," *American Behavioral Scientist* 56, no. 4 (2012): 399–420; and Christian Fuchs, "Class, Knowledge and New Media," *Media, Culture and Society* 32, no. 1 (2010): 141–50.
5. iResearch, "Wangwen Jianghu Qunying Pu: Zhongguo Wangluo Wenxue Zuozhe Dongcha Baogao" [Heroes in the Internet Literature Rivers and Lakes: Insight Report on Chinese Online Writers], *iResearch*, December 27, 2016, https://report.iresearch.cn/report/201612/2696.shtml.
6. Michael S. C. Tse and Maleen Z. Gong, "Online Communities and Commercialization of Chinese Internet Literature," *Journal of Internet Commerce* 11, no. 2 (2012): 100–116.
7. Kailiang Sun and Qiang Li, "Jiti Ruhe Zhihui: 'Lingao Qiming' de Luntan Wenhua yu 'Tongren Zhuanzheng' Jizhi" [How the Collective Becomes Intelligent: Forum Culture and the 'Fan Production' Mechanism of 'Lingao Qiming'], *Zhongguo Wenxue Piping* (*Chinese Journal of Literary Criticism*), no. 1 (2018): 124–25; and Qiang Li, "'Jiti Zhihui' de Duochongbianzhou: You 'Lingao Qiming' Kan Wangwen Shengchan Jizhi yu Yishixingtai zhi Guanxi" [Multiple Variations of 'Collective Wisdom:' Examining the Relationship between Internet Literature Production Mechanism and Ideology from 'Lingao Qiming'], *Wenyi Lilun yu Piping* [*Theory and Criticism of Literature and Art*], no. 2 (2018): 130–137.
8. Thomas H. Davenport and John C. Beck, *The Attention Economy: Understanding the New Currency of Business* (Harvard Business School Press, 2001).
9. Alexander Lugg, "Chinese Online Fiction: Taste Publics, Entertainment, and Candle in the Tomb," *Chinese Journal of Communication* 4, no. 2 (2011): 121–36.

10. Yilu Liang and Wanqi Shen, "Fan Economy in the Chinese Media and Entertainment Industry: How Feedback from Super Fans Can Propel Creative Industries' Revenue," *Global Media and China* 1, no. 4 (2016): 331–49.
11. Yiwen Wang, "Chinese Internet Fictions in the Transmedia World," in *A World History of Chinese Literature*, ed. Yingjin Zhang (Routledge, 2023), 377–87; and Heather Inwood, "What's in a Game? Transmedia Storytelling and the Web-Game Genre of Online Chinese Popular Fiction," *Asia Pacific Perspectives*, Spring/Summer 2014, 6–29.
12. For details, see "Bangzhu yu Kefu" [Help and Customer Service], Qidian, https://www.qidian.com/help.
13. See *My Heroic Husband*, Qidian, https://www.qidian.com/book/1979049.
14. Also, because tipping may affect the ranking, writers may game the system by manufacturing tipping.
15. Many writers drop a project unfinished when it fails to attract enough readers, as this not only renders it financially unsustainable but also makes writing an incredibly lonely and unfulfilling endeavor.
16. See "Wo de Shijie Shu (27 Sui Suibi, Baoqian Meineng Gengxin)" [My World Tree (Essay on Turning 27 and Sorry for No Updates)], Qidian, https://www.qidian.com/chapter/1979049/38699083/.
17. See Anthony Gierzynski and Kathryn Eddy, *Harry Potter and the Millennials: Research Methods and the Politics of the Muggle Generation* (Johns Hopkins University Press, 2013).
18. See chapter 4 for the introduction to the title. See also Xiaofang Yang, "Chuanyue Xiaoshuo 'Qie Ming' Dianfu Lishi Yin Zhengyi" [Time Travel Fiction "Usurping Ming" Subverts History and Sparks Controversy], *China Press Publication Radio Film and Television Journal*, June 23, 2008.
19. Otherwise, I would have had to go to different platforms for different works and circumvent their antipiracy mechanisms that would have made data collection very challenging.
20. Some comments are missing in the non-MCGA comments dataset because the website blocked access to them. Because the missing data rate was less than 0.5 percent, it should not have affected the findings.
21. Norman Fairclough, *Analysing Discourse: Textual Analysis for Social Research* (Psychology Press, 2003).
22. David M. Blei et al., "Latent Dirichlet Allocation," *Journal of Machine Learning Research* 3 (2003): 993–1022.
23. Heather Inwood, "Internet Literature: From YY to MOOC," in *The Columbia Companion to Modern Chinese Literature*, ed. Kirk Denton (Columbia University Press, 2016).
24. I requested R to report the top three hundred words (packages used included chinese.misc and JiebaR). A few more terms were reported in both cases because of tied results. Both frequent word lists excluded stop words and terms like 作者 (author) and 主角 (main character) that were omnipresent, thus of little analytical value.
25. Tai-Yee Wu, Anne Oeldorf-Hirsch, and David Atkin, "A Click Is Worth a Thousand Words: Probing the Predictors of Using Click Speech for Online Opinion Expression," *International Journal of Communication* 14 (2020): 2687–706; and Florian Schneider, *China's Digital Nationalism* (Oxford University Press, 2018).

26. User comment number 801.
27. Mimi Lau, "Why Does China React So Strongly over the South Korea-Based Anti-Missile System?" *South China Morning Post*, February 11, 2016, https://www.scmp.com/news/china/diplomacy-defence/article/1911857/why-does-china-react-so-strongly-over-south-korea-based.
28. Dier, "Miaoni Wei Zhichi Jin Taiyan Daoqian: Yanlun Guoji, Fandui Sade" [Maoni Apologizes for Supporting Kim Taeyeon: Opinion Overly Extreme and Against Deployment of THAAD], Sina.cn, March 13, 2017, https://ent.sina.cn/star/tv/2017-03-13/detail-ifychhus1080467.d.html.
29. User comment number 114.
30. User comment number 4735.
31. Functioning like "cheat codes" in gaming, "golden finger," although often criticized, enables a greater degree of personal gratification for readers who often identify with the protagonists.
32. Not all readers have such expectations. The stories to save and glorify China and the rise of protagonists, reasonable or not, are simply gratifying for many. In fact, many read online fictions precisely to escape reality and pursue pleasure.
33. These terms appear in the frequently used word lists of both MCGA and non-MCGA comments. See appendix tables A.2 and A.3. Though it is beyond the scope of discussion, it is worth noting that some genres catering to female readers tend to sexualize men.
34. User comment number 1.
35. Jiang Chang and Hao Tian, "Girl Power in Boy Love: Yaoi, Online Female Counterculture, and Digital Feminism in China," *Feminist Media Studies* 21, no. 4 (2021): 604–20; Jia Tan, "Digital Masquerading: Feminist Media Activism in China," *Crime, Media, Culture* 13, no. 2 (2017): 171–86.
36. On commenting as social practice, see Fairclough, *Analysing Discourse*. Readers may engage the platforms by commenting. For instance, many readers criticized Qidian (the capital) when the platform proposed a free-reading business model that could be detrimental to writers' income. Because this typically is not a key theme, I do not discuss it in detail.
37. I do not intend to suggest that this is the only market preference.
38. User comment number 1121.
39. User comment number 1122.
40. Yi Wang and Matthew M. Chew, "State, Market, and the Manufacturing of War Memory: China's Television Dramas on the War of Resistance against Japan," *Memory Studies* 14, no. 4 (2021): 877–91.
41. User comment number 3321.
42. User comment number 4001.
43. User comment number 2923.
44. Rongbin Han, "Cyber Nationalism and Regime Support under Xi Jinping: The Effects of the 2018 Constitutional Revision," *Journal of Contemporary China* 30, no. 131 (2021): 717–33; and Suisheng Zhao, *A Nation-State by Construction: Dynamics of Modern Chinese Nationalism* (Stanford University Press, 2004).
45. User comment number 2669.
46. Rongbin Han, "Passing on the Red Genes: Communism Nostalgia in Online Fictions and Ideological Governance in China," *Regulation and Governance* (2024). https://doi.org/10.1111/rego.12622.

47. User comment number 763.
48. User comment number 773.
49. Willy Lam, "Xi Jinping's Ideology and Statecraft," *Chinese Law and Government* 48, no. 6 (2016): 409–17.
50. Han, "Cyber Nationalism and Regime Support." See also chapter 4.
51. User comment number 573.
52. See Gary King et al., "How the Chinese Government Fabricates Social Media Posts for Strategic Distraction, Not Engaged Argument," *American Political Science Review* 111, no. 3 (2017): 484–501; Rongbin Han, "Manufacturing Consent in Cyberspace: China's 'Fifty-Cent Army,'" *Journal of Current Chinese Affairs* 44, no. 2 (2015): 105–34; and Rongbin Han and Linan Jia, "Governing by the Internet: Local Governance in the Digital Age," *Journal of Chinese Governance* 3, no. 1 (2018): 67–85.
53. See Han, "Manufacturing Consent in Cyberspace."
54. On young Marxists, see Jenny Chan, "A Precarious Worker-Student Alliance in Xi's China," *China Review* 20, no. 1 (2020): 165–90. On "red genes," see Han, "Passing on the Red Genes." On the "make China Marxist again" strategy, see Timothy Cheek and David Ownby, "Make China Marxist Again," *Dissent* 65, no. 4 (2018): 71–77; and Yuezhi Zhao, "The Struggle for Socialism in China," *Monthly Review: An Independent Socialist Magazine* 64, no. 5 (2012): 1–17.
55. On "the mandate to supervise and guide citizens," see Michel Hockx, *Internet Literature in China* (Columbia University Press, 2015), 3; and Mei Zhang, *Pornography, Ideology, and the Internet: A Japanese Adult Video Actress in Mainland China* (Lexington, 2019). On "cultural governance and source of legitimacy," see Bin Xu, "Moral Performance and Cultural Governance in China: The Compassionate Politics of Disasters," *China Quarterly* 226 (2016): 407–30; and Aleksandra Kubat, "Morality as Legitimacy Under Xi Jinping: The Political Functionality of Traditional Culture for the Chinese Communist Party," *Journal of Current Chinese Affairs* 47, no. 3 (2018): 47–86.
56. Neil Postman, *Amusing Ourselves to Death: Public Discourse in the Age of Show Business* (Penguin, 2005); and Shouzhi Xia, "Amusing Ourselves to Loyalty? Entertainment, Propaganda, and Regime Resilience in China," *Political Research Quarterly* 75, no. 4 (2022): 1096–112.

CONCLUSION

1. Eva Dou, "New Phone Sparks Worry China Has Found a Way Around U.S. Tech Limits," *Washington Post*, September 2, 2023, https://www.washingtonpost.com/technology/2023/09/02/huawei-raimondo-phone-chip-sanctions.
2. "Huawei Mate 60 Pro Triggers Buying Spree Among Chinese Consumers," *Global Times*, September 7, 2023, https://www.globaltimes.cn/page/202309/1297757.shtml.
3. Voice of America, "China's Propaganda Victory Over US Sanctions: Huawei's Mate 60 Pro," VOA, September 12, 2023, https://www.voanews.com/a/fact-check-china-launches-propaganda-campaign-portraying-mate-60-pro-as-huawei-s-victory-over-us-sanctions/7265226.html.
4. Richard Baum and Alexei Shevchenko, "The 'State of the State,'" in *The Paradox of China's Post-Mao Reforms*, ed. Merle Goldman and Roderick MacFarquhar (Harvard University Press, 1999), 354.

5. Recent studies have started exploring mundane political-socialization and its implications, especially for political trust or regime support. See Haifeng Huang et al., "In Government We Trust: Implicit Political Trust and Regime Support in China," *Perspectives on Politics* 21, no. 4 (2022): 1357–75; and Rongbin Han, "Debating China Beyond the Great Firewall: Digital Disenchantment and Authoritarian Resilience," *Journal of Chinese Political Science* 28, no. 1 (2023): 85–103.
6. For instance, Gary King et al., "How Censorship in China Allows Government Criticism but Silences Collective Expression," *American Political Science Review* 107, no. 2 (2013): 326–43; and Peter Lorentzen, "China's Strategic Censorship," *American Journal of Political Science* 58, no. 2 (2014): 402–14.
7. Bruce Gilley, "Paradigms of Chinese Politics: Kicking Society Back Out," *Journal of Contemporary China* 20, no. 70 (2011): 517–33.
8. On cultural hegemony, see Antonio Gramsci, *Selections from the Prison Notebooks of Antonio Gramsci*, ed. Quintin Hoare and Geoffrey Nowell Smith (International Publishers, 1971). On ideological interpellation, see Louis Althusser, "Ideology and Ideological State Apparatus (Notes Towards an Investigation)," in *Lenin and Philosophy and Other Essays* (Monthly Review, 2001), 85–126.
9. Ying Miao, "Romanticising the Past: Core Socialist Values and the China Dream as Legitimisation Strategy," *Journal of Current Chinese Affairs* 49, no. 2 (2021): 162–84; and Michael Gow, "The Core Socialist Values of the Chinese Dream: Towards a Chinese Integral State," *Critical Asian Studies* 49, no. 1 (2017): 92–116.
10. Johan Lagerkvist, *After the Internet, Before Democracy: Competing Norms in Chinese Media and Society* (Peter Lang, 2010).
11. Guobin Yang, *The Wuhan Lockdown* (Columbia University Press, 2022); Dali L. Yang, *Wuhan: How the COVID-19 Outbreak in China Spiraled Out of Control* (Oxford University Press, 2023); and Cary Wu et al., "Chinese Citizen Satisfaction with Government Performance During COVID-19," *Journal of Contemporary China* 30, no. 132 (2021): 930–44.
12. On co-opting social participation, see Bruce J. Dickson, *Red Capitalists in China: The Party, Private Entrepreneurs, and Prospects for Political Change* (Cambridge University Press, 2003); and Dimitar Gueorguiev, *Retrofitting Leninism: Participation Without Democracy in China* (Oxford University Press, 2021). On disliking regime critics, see Rongbin Han, *Contesting Cyberspace in China: Online Expression and Authoritarian Resilience* (Columbia University Press, 2018).
13. On the burgeoning scholarly enterprise on cultural politics, see Paola Voci, *China on Video: Smaller-Screen Realities* (Routledge, 2010); David Kurt Herold and Peter Marolt, eds., *Online Society in China: Creating, Celebrating, and Instrumentalising the Online Carnival* (Routledge, 2011); Luzhou Li, *Zoning China: Online Video, Popular Culture, and the State* (MIT Press, 2019); Dan Chen, "Seeing Politics Through Popular Culture," *Journal of Chinese Political Science* 29, no. 1 (2024): 185–205; Karl Gerth, *Unending Capitalism: How Consumerism Negated China's Communist Revolution* (Cambridge University Press, 2020); Christy Wampole, *Degenerative Realism: Novel and Nation in Twenty-First-Century France* (Columbia University Press, 2020); and Caren Irr, *Toward the Geopolitical Novel: U.S. Fiction in the Twenty-First Century* (Columbia University Press, 2013). On the politics of history and memory, see Thomas Chen, *Made in Censorship: The Tiananmen Movement in Chinese Literature and Film* (Columbia University Press, 2022); Ian Johnson, *Sparks: China's*

Underground Historians and Their Battle for the Future (Oxford University Press, 2023); Ban Wang, *Illuminations from the Past: Trauma, Memory, and History in Modern China* (Stanford University Press, 2004); Jeffrey C. Kinkley, *Visions of Dystopia in China's New Historical Novels* (Columbia University Press, 2014); and Bin Xu, *Chairman Mao's Children: Generation and the Politics of Memory in China* (Cambridge University Press, 2021).

14. On proregime patriotic arts and literature, see Xiaomei Chen, *Staging Chinese Revolution: Theater, Film, and the Afterlives of Propaganda* (Columbia University Press, 2016); and Jianmei Liu, *Revolution Plus Love: Literary History, Women's Bodies, and Thematic Repetition in Twentieth-Century Chinese Fiction* (University of Hawai'i Press, 2003). On traditional types of intellectuals, see Johnson, *Sparks*; and Perry Link and Dazhi Wu, *I Have No Enemies: The Life and Legacy of Liu Xiaobo* (Columbia University Press, 2023).
15. On the challenging authoritarian rule, see Clay Shirky, "The Political Power of Social Media," *Foreign Affairs* 90, no. 1 (2011): 28–41; Philip N. Howard and Muzammil M. Hussain, *Democracy's Fourth Wave? Digital Media and the Arab Spring* (Oxford University Press, 2013); and Philip N. Howard, *The Digital Origins of Dictatorship and Democracy: Information Technology and Political Islam* (Oxford University Press, 2010). On the rise of digital authoritarianism, see Marc Owen Jones, *Digital Authoritarianism in the Middle East: Deception, Disinformation and Social Media* (Oxford University Press, 2022); Steven Feldstein, *The Rise of Digital Repression: How Technology Is Reshaping Power, Politics, and Resistance* (Oxford University Press, 2021); Ronald Deibert, "Cyberspace Under Siege," *Journal of Democracy* 26, no. 3 (2015): 64–78; and Seva Gunitsky, "Corrupting the Cyber-Commons: Social Media as a Tool of Autocratic Stability," *Perspectives on Politics* 13, no. 1 (2015): 42–54.
16. Aim Sinpeng, *Opposing Democracy in the Digital Age: The Yellow Shirts in Thailand* (University of Michigan Press, 2021); Shoshana Zuboff, *The Age of Surveillance Capitalism: The Fight for a Human Future at the New Frontier of Power* (Public Affairs, 2019); Nathaniel Persily and Joshua A. Tucker, eds., *Social Media and Democracy: The State of the Field, Prospects for Reform* (Cambridge University Press, 2020); and Yochai Benkler et al., *Network Propaganda: Manipulation, Disinformation, and Radicalization in American Politics* (Oxford University Press, 2018).
17. William A. Callahan, "Dreaming as a Critical Discourse of National Belonging: China Dream, American Dream and World Dream," *Nations and Nationalism* 23, no. 2 (2017): 248–70.
18. Michael Lucken, *The Japanese and the War: Expectation, Perception, and the Shaping of Memory*, trans. Karen Grimwade (Columbia University Press, 2017), xvii.
19. Jonathan Unger, ed., *Using the Past to Serve the Present: Historiography and Politics in Contemporary China* (M. E. Sharpe, 1993).
20. BBC Beijing Bureau, "Wolf Warrior 2: The Nationalist Action Film Storming China." *BBC News*, August 4, 2017, https://www.bbc.com/news/blogs-china-blog-40811952.
21. Finishing remarks of the fiction *Catching Gu* (捉蛊记), Hetushu, https://www.hetushu.com/book/2395/1652203.html.
22. See *Crazy Stories from Hmong Frontiers*, sequel 2, Laikan, https://www.laikan.com/book/68382.
23. Benedict Anderson, *Imagined Communities: Reflections on the Origin and Spread of Nationalism* (Verso, 1991).

24. Anne-Marie Brady, "'We Are All Part of the Same Family': China's Ethnic Propaganda," *Journal of Current Chinese Affairs* 41, no. 4 (2012): 159–81.
25. Samuel P. Huntington, *The Clash of Civilizations and the Remaking of World Order* (Simon & Schuster, 1996).
26. It is the last of a trilogy that started in 2019. The two prequels are *My People, My Country* (2019) and *My People, My Homeland* (2020).
27. The lyrics are available at Faye Wang, "Ruyuan" [As You Wish], Spotify, https://open.spotify.com/track/4x9retPoJqKa35zZZhNhNS.
28. Elizabeth Economy, *The Third Revolution: Xi Jinping and the New Chinese State* (Oxford University Press, 2018); and Susan L. Shirk, *Overreach: How China Derailed Its Peaceful Rise* (Oxford University Press, 2022).
29. Jude Blanchette, *China's New Red Guards: The Return of Radicalism and the Rebirth of Mao Zedong* (Oxford University Press, 2019); Yuezhi Zhao, "The Struggle for Socialism in China," *Monthly Review: An Independent Socialist Magazine* 64, no. 5 (2012): 1–17; and Bingchun Meng, "Political Scandal at the End of Ideology? The Mediatized Politics of the Bo Xilai Case," *Media, Culture, and Society* 38, no. 6 (2016): 811–26.
30. According to Daniel Bell, China features a system of political meritocracy. See Daniel A. Bell, *The China Model: Political Meritocracy and the Limits of Democracy* (Princeton University Press, 2015).
31. Sebastian L Mazzuca, "Access to Power Versus Exercise of Power: Reconceptualizing Democratization in Latin America," *Studies in Comparative International Development* 45, no. 3 (2010): 334–57; and Kevin J. O'Brien and Rongbin Han, "Path to Democracy? Assessing Village Elections in China," *Journal of Contemporary China* 18, no. 60 (2009): 359–78.
32. Yu-long Ling, "Dr. Sun Yat-Sen's Doctrine and Impact on the Modern World," *American Journal of Chinese Studies* 19, no. 1 (2012): 1–11.
33. Gengsong Gao, "Post-Tiananmen Chinese Liberal Intellectuals' Political Uses of Confucian Tradition and Chinese History," *Journal of Contemporary China* 31, no. 137 (2022): 709.
34. Lagerkvist, *After the Internet*; and Qiang Xiao, "The Battle for the Chinese Internet," *Journal of Democracy* 22, no. 2 (2011): 47–61.
35. Michael Mann, "The Autonomous Power of the State: Its Origins, Mechanisms and Results," *European Journal of Sociology* 25, no. 02 (1984): 190; and James Ron, *Frontiers and Ghettos: State Violence in Serbia and Israel* (University of California Press, 2003), 18–20.
36. Dingxin Zhao, "'Zhonghua Diguo de Xingshuai' zhi Bing" [The Ills of 'The Rise and Fall of Imperial China'], *Dushu*, no. 7(2023): 3–11.
37. Suzanne E. Scoggins, *Policing China: Street-Level Cops in the Shadow of Protest* (Cornell University Press, 2021).
38. Jianfeng Zheng, "Jiepo Lishi Xuwuzhuyi de 'Taolu'" [Exposing the Traps of Historical Nihilism], *Guangming Daily Online*, April 2, 2020, https://theory.gmw.cn/2020-04/02/content_33708033.htm.
39. Alt-history titles are significantly affected by the state's effort to crack down historical nihilism. In response, platforms and writers, although worried about crossing the "red line," were unwilling to give up the genre. For instance, see Yang Chen, "Shenme shi Cuangai Lishi? Zenme Xie Hui Weijin? Liangda Yuanze Jiaoni Panduan" [What

Is Tampering with History? How Does Writing Become Prohibited? Two Principles to Help You Judge], *Zhihu*, June 19, 2017, https://zhuanlan.zhihu.com/p/27472255.

40. Minxin Pei, "China: Totalitarianism's Long Shadow," *Journal of Democracy* 32, no. 2 (2021): 5–21.
41. Elaine J. Yuan, *The Web of Meaning: The Internet in a Changing Chinese Society* (University of Toronto Press, 2021), 4.
42. Sebastian Veg, *Minjian: The Rise of China's Grassroots Intellectuals* (Columbia University Press, 2019); Johnson, *Sparks*; and Jonathan Hassid, *China's Unruly Journalists: How Committed Professionals Are Changing the People's Republic* (Routledge, 2015).
43. Matt Taibbi, "Donald Trump Claims Authorship of Legendary Reagan Slogan; Has Never Heard of Google," *Rolling Stone*, March 25, 2015, https://www.rollingstone.com/politics/politics-news/donald-trump-claims-authorship-of-legendary-reagan-slogan-has-never-heard-of-google-193834; and Emma Margolin, "'Make America Great Again'—Who Said It First?," *NBC News*, September 9, 2016, https://www.nbcnews.com/politics/2016-election/make-america-great-again-who-said-it-first-n645716.
44. Cas Mudde, "The Populist Zeitgeist," *Government and Opposition* 39, no. 4 (2004): 541–63; and Ghita Ionescu and Ernest Gellner, eds., *Populism: Its Meaning and National Characteristics* (Macmillan, 1969).
45. Ruth Wodak et al., *Right-Wing Populism in Europe: Politics and Discourse* (Bloomsbury, 2013); Victoria McCollum, ed., *Make America Hate Again: Trump-Era Horror and the Politics of Fear* (Routledge, 2019); and Richard C. Fording and Sanford F. Schram, *Hard White: The Mainstreaming of Racism in American Politics* (Oxford University Press, 2020).
46. Steven Erlanger and Christina Anderson, "How the Far Right Bagged Election Success in Sweden," *New York Times*, September 19, 2022.
47. Davide Vampa, *Brothers of Italy: A New Populist Wave in an Unstable Party System* (Palgrave Macmillan, 2023).
48. Cas Mudde, *Populist Radical Right Parties in Europe* (Cambridge University Press, 2007); Cas Mudde and Cristobal Rovira Kaltwasser, *Populism: A Very Short Introduction* (Oxford University Press, 2017); and Abdul Noury and Gerard Roland, "Identity Politics and Populism in Europe," *Annual Review of Political Science* 23 (2020): 421–39.
49. See Rongbin Han, "Passing on the Red Genes: Communism Nostalgia in Online Fictions and Ideological Governance in China," *Regulation and Governance* (2024). https://doi.org/10.1111/rego.12622.
50. On populist authoritarianism, see Wenfang Tang, *Populist Authoritarianism: Chinese Political Culture and Regime Sustainability* (Oxford University Press, 2016). On Xi as a populist president, see Salvatore Babones, "Xi Jinping: Communist China's First Populist President," *Forbes*, October 20, 2017, https://www.forbes.com/sites/salvatore babones/2017/10/20/populism-chinese-style-xi-jinping-cements-his-status-as-chinas-first-populist-president.
51. James Leibold, "Blogging Alone: China, the Internet, and the Democratic Illusion?," *Journal of Asian Studies* 70, no. 4 (2011): 1023–41.
52. The *International Journal of Communication* published a special issue in 2023 on digital memory and populism in different contexts and countries. See Manuel Menke and Berber Hagedoorn, "Digital Memory and Populism—Introduction," *International Journal of Communication* 17 (2023): 2101.

53. I use “West” and “Western” in a general sense, although I acknowledge that both are contested concepts and there are huge variations within the West.
54. Helen V. Milner, “Voting for Populism in Europe: Globalization, Technological Change, and the Extreme Right,” *Comparative Political Studies* 54, no. 13 (2021): 2267–441.
55. I do not intend to engage in the debate on whether such perceptions are factually correct.
56. Brian L. Ott and Greg Dickinson, *The Twitter Presidency: Donald J. Trump and the Politics of White Rage* (Routledge, 2019).
57. On empathy, see Arlie Russell Hochschild, *Strangers in Their Own Land: Anger and Mourning on the American Right* (New Press, 2018). On the “clash of civilizations,” Huntington, *Clash of Civilizations*.
58. James Leibold, “More Than a Category: Han Supremacism on the Chinese Internet,” *China Quarterly* 203 (2010): 542.
59. Ryan Powers and Austin Strange, “Can Rising Powers Reassure? Shifting Power, Foreign Economic Policy, and Perceptions of Revisionist Intent,” *Journal of Peace Research* (2025), https://doi.org/10.1177/00223433241303414.
60. State Council Information Office of the People's Republic of China, “China and the World in the New Era,” Xinhua Net, September 27, 2019, http://www.xinhuanet.com/english/2019-09/27/c_138427541.htm; and Ministry of Foreign Affairs of PRC, “President Xi Jinping Meets with U.S. President Joe Biden in Bali,” FMPRC, November 14, 2022, https://www.fmprc.gov.cn/mfa_eng/zxxx_662805/202211/t20221114_10974686.html. Arguably China under President Xi deviates from its previous low-profile strategy and pursues a more active global role. See Hal Brands and Jake Sullivan, “China Has Two Paths to Global Domination,” *Foreign Policy*, no. 237 (2020): 46–51; Kerry Brown, *The World According to Xi: Everything You Need to Know About the New China* (Bloomsbury Academic, 2018); Xuetong Yan, “From Keeping a Low Profile to Striving for Achievement,” *Chinese Journal of International Politics* 7, no. 2 (2014): 153–84; and Elizabeth Economy, *The World According to China* (Polity, 2022).
61. For an interesting discussion, see Yuan Kong, “‘Ruguan’ yu ‘Fazhou’: Guanyu Zhongguo Jueqi de Liangzhong Zhishilun Tujing” [“Ruguan” and “Crusade Against King Zhou”: Two Epistemological Approaches of China Rise], *Dongfang Journal*, no. 9 (2020): 25–31.
62. This is not to argue that Chinese foreign policy is not subject to popular influences. See Jessica Chen Weiss, *Powerful Patriots: Nationalist Protest in China's Foreign Relations* (Oxford University Press, 2014); and James Reilly, *Strong Society, Smart State: The Rise of Public Opinion in China's Japan Policy* (Columbia University Press, 2013).
63. Maria Repnikova, “Rethinking China's Soft Power: ‘Pragmatic Enticement’ of Confucius Institutes in Ethiopia,” *China Quarterly* 250 (2022): 440–63; Ching Kwan Lee, *The Specter of Global China: Politics, Labor, and Foreign Investment in Africa* (University of Chicago Press, 2017); David Shambaugh, *China Goes Global: The Partial Power* (Oxford University Press, 2013); and Wen Hsuan Tsai, “Enabling China's Voice to Be Heard by the World: Ideas and Operations of the Chinese Communist Party's External Propaganda,” *Problems of Post-Communism* 64, no. 3–4 (2017): 203–13.
64. Maria Repnikova, *Chinese Soft Power* (Cambridge University Press, 2022); and Hongying Wang and James N. Rosenau, “China and Global Governance,” *Asian Perspective* 33, no. 3 (2009): 5–39.

65. Sheena Chestnut Greitens, "Dealing with Demand for China's Global Surveillance Exports," Brookings Institution Global China Report, April 2020, https://www.brookings.edu/articles/dealing-with-demand-for-chinas-global-surveillance-exports.
66. Min Jiang and Luca Belli, eds., *Digital Sovereignty in the BRICS Countries: How the Global South and Emerging Power Alliances Are Reshaping Digital Governance* (Cambridge University Press, 2024).
67. Julia Pohle and Thorsten Thiel, "Digital Sovereignty," *Internet Policy Review* 9, no. 4 (2020): 1–19.
68. Zuboff, *Age of Surveillance Capitalism*.
69. See Friedrich Hayek, *The Road to Serfdom: Text and Documents* (University of Chicago Press, 2007).

BIBLIOGRAPHY

Almond, Gabriel A., and Sidney Verba. *The Civic Culture: Political Attitudes and Democracy in Five Nations*. Princeton University Press, 1963.

Althusser, Louis. "Ideology and Ideological State Apparatus (Notes Towards an Investigation)." In *Lenin and Philosophy and Other Essays*. Monthly Review, 2001.

Anderson, Benedict. *Imagined Communities: Reflections on the Origin and Spread of Nationalism*. Verso, 1991.

Anderson, Chris. *The Long Tail: Why the Future of Business Is Selling Less of More*. Hyperion, 2006.

Andrejevic, Mark. "Watching Television Without Pity: The Productivity of Online Fans." *Television and New Media* 9, no. 1 (2008): 24–46.

Ang, Yuen Yuen. "Co-Optation and Clientelism: Nested Distributive Politics in China's Single-Party Dictatorship." *Studies in Comparative International Development* 51, no. 3 (2016): 235–56.

Babones, Salvatore. "Xi Jinping: Communist China's First Populist President." *Forbes*, October 20, 2017. https://www.forbes.com/sites/salvatorebabones/2017/10/20/populism-chinese-style-xi-jinping-cements-his-status-as-chinas-first-populist-president.

Barmé, Geremie R., and Jeremy Goldkorn, eds. "Party Policies from One to Ten." In *China Story Yearbook 2013: Civilising China*. Australian National University, 2013.

Baum, Richard. "Deng Liqun and the Struggle Against 'Bourgeois Liberalization,' 1979–1993." *China Information* 9, no. 4 (1995): 1–35.

Baum, Richard, and Alexei Shevchenko. "The 'State of the State.'" In *The Paradox of China's Post-Mao Reforms*, ed. Merle Goldman and Roderick MacFarquhar. Harvard University Press, 1999.

BBC Beijing Bureau. "China's Fledgling Hip-Hop Culture Faces Official Crackdown." *BBC News*, January 24, 2018. http://www.bbc.com/news/blogs-china-blog-42800032.

BBC Beijing Bureau. "Wolf Warrior 2: The Nationalist Action Film Storming China." *BBC News*, August 4, 2017. https://www.bbc.com/news/blogs-china-blog-40811952.

Bell, Daniel A. *The China Model: Political Meritocracy and the Limits of Democracy*. Princeton University Press, 2015.

Benkler, Yochai, Robert Faris, and Hal Roberts. *Network Propaganda: Manipulation, Disinformation, and Radicalization in American Politics*. Oxford University Press, 2018.

Berry, Michael. *A History of Pain: Trauma in Modern Chinese Literature and Film*. Columbia University Press, 2008.

Billig, Michael. *Banal Nationalism*. SAGE, 1995.

Blanchette, Jude. *China's New Red Guards: The Return of Radicalism and the Rebirth of Mao Zedong*. Oxford University Press, 2019.

Blei, David M., Andrew Ng, and Michael Jordan. "Latent Dirichlet Allocation." *Journal of Machine Learning Research* 3 (2003): 993–1022.

Bourdieu, Pierre. *The Field of Cultural Production: Essays on Art and Literature*. Columbia University Press, 1993.

Brady, Anne-Marie. *Marketing Dictatorship: Propaganda and Thought Work in Contemporary China*. Rowman and Littlefield, 2008.

Brady, Anne-Marie. "'We Are All Part of the Same Family': China's Ethnic Propaganda." *Journal of Current Chinese Affairs* 41, no. 4 (2012): 159–81.

Brands, Hal, and Jake Sullivan. "China Has Two Paths to Global Domination." *Foreign Policy*, no. 237 (2020): 46–51.

Brown, Kerry. *The World According to Xi: Everything You Need to Know About the New China*. Bloomsbury Academic, 2018.

Brudney, Jeffrey L., and Robert E. England. "Toward a Definition of the Coproduction Concept." *Public Administration Review* 43, no. 1 (1983): 59–65.

Brunnermeier, Markus K., Michael Sockin, and Wei Xiong. "China's Gradualistic Economic Approach and Financial Markets." *American Economic Review* 107, no. 5 (2017): 608–13.

Buckley, Chris. "In China, an Action Hero Beats Box Office Records (and Arrogant Westerners)." *New York Times*, August 16, 2017.

Callahan, William A. "Dreaming as a Critical Discourse of National Belonging: China Dream, American Dream and World Dream." *Nations and Nationalism* 23, no. 2 (2017): 248–70.

Certeau, Michel de, and Steven Rendall. *The Practice of Everyday Life*. University of California Press, 1984.

Chan, Alex. "From Propaganda to Hegemony: Jiaodian Fangtan and China's Media Policy." *Journal of Contemporary China* 11, no. 30 (2002): 35–51.

Chan, Jenny. "A Precarious Worker-Student Alliance in Xi's China." *China Review* 20, no. 1 (2020): 165–90.

Chang, Jiang, and Hao Tian. "Girl Power in Boy Love: Yaoi, Online Female Counterculture, and Digital Feminism in China." *Feminist Media Studies* 21, no. 4 (2021): 604–20.

Cheek, Timothy. "Xi Jinping's Counter-Reformation: The Reassertion of Ideological Governance in Historical Perspective." *Journal of Contemporary China* 30, no. 132 (2021): 875–87.

Cheek, Timothy, and David Ownby. "Make China Marxist Again." *Dissent* 65, no. 4 (2018): 71–77.

Chen, Dan. "Seeing Politics Through Popular Culture." *Journal of Chinese Political Science* 29, no. 1 (2024): 185–205.

Chen, Feng. "Order and Stability in Social Transition: Neoconservative Political Thought in Post-China." *China Quarterly* 151 (1997): 593–613.

Chen, Fong-Ching, and Guantao Jin. *From Youthful Manuscripts to River Elegy: The Chinese Popular Cultural Movement and Political Transformation, 1979–1989*. Chinese University Press, 1997.

Chen, Liang. "IP Shengtai Wenyu Fenghui: Kuangshi Yanhuo Zuozhe Chen Liang de 'Xianli' Zhuti Yanjiang" [IP Ecological Entertainment Summit: Keynote Speech by Chen Liang, Author of Unparalleled Fireworks]. *Netease*, August 23, 2019. https://www.163.com/dy/article/ENA0CQ6705387W7O.html.

Chen, Pingyuan. "Jin Bainian Zhongguo Jingying Wenhua de Shiluo" [The Loss of China's Elite Culture in the Past Century]. *Twenty-First Century*, no. 17 (1993): 11–22.

Chen, Thomas. *Made in Censorship: The Tiananmen Movement in Chinese Literature and Film*. Columbia University Press, 2022.

Chen, Thomas. "The Workshop of the World: Censorship and the Internet Novel 'Such Is This World.'" In *China's Contested Internet*, ed. Guobin Yang. NIAS, 2015.

Chen, Xiaomei. *Staging Chinese Revolution: Theater, Film, and the Afterlives of Propaganda*. Columbia University Press, 2016.

Chen, Yang. "Shenme shi Cuangai Lishi? Zenme Xie Hui Weijin? Liangda Yuanze Jiaoni Panduan" [What Is Tampering with History? How Does Writing Become Prohibited? Two Principles to Help You Judge]. *Zhihu*, June 19, 2017. https://zhuanlan.zhihu.com/p/27472255.

China Internet Network Information Center. *Di 44 Ci Zhogguo Hulian Wangluo Fazhan Zhuangkuang Tongji Baogao* [*The 44th China Statistical Report on Internet Development*]. CNNIC, August 30, 2019. https://www.cnnic.cn/n4/2022/0401/c88-1116.html.

China Internet Network Information Center. *Di 52 Ci Zhogguo Hulian Wangluo Fazhan Zhuangkuang Tongji Baogao* [*The 52nd China Statistical Report on Internet Development*]. CNNIC, August 28, 2023. https://www.cnnic.cn/n4/2023/0828/c88-10829.html.

Choy, Howard. *Remapping the Past: Fictions of History in Deng's China, 1979–1997*. Brill, 2008.

Christensen, Thomas J. "Chinese Realpolitik." *Foreign Affairs* 75, no. 5 (1996): 37–52.

Christin, Angèle. "Counting Clicks: Quantification and Variation in Web Journalism in the United States and France." *American Journal of Sociology* 123, no. 5 (2018): 1382–415.

Chu, Yiting. "Constructing Minzu: The Representation of Minzu and Zhonghua Minzu in Chinese Elementary Textbooks." *Discourse: Studies in the Cultural Politics of Education* 39, no. 6 (2017): 941–53.

Ci, Jiwei. *Democracy in China: The Coming Crisis*. Harvard University Press, 2019.

Dahlgren, Peter. "The Internet, Public Spheres, and Political Communication: Dispersion and Deliberation." *Political Communication* 22, no. 2 (2005): 147–62.

Damm, Jens. "The Internet and the Fragmentation of Chinese Society." *Critical Asian Studies* 39, no. 2 (2007): 273–94.

Davenport, Thomas H., and John C. Beck. *The Attention Economy: Understanding the New Currency of Business*. Harvard Business School Press, 2001.

Dean, Jonathan. "Left Politics and Popular Culture in Britain: From Left-Wing Populism to 'Popular Leftism.'" *Politics* 43, no. 1 (2023): 3–17.

Deibert, Ronald. "Cyberspace Under Siege." *Journal of Democracy* 26, no. 3 (2015): 64–78.

Deibert, Ronald, John Palfrey, Rafal Rohozinski, and Jonathan Zittrain, eds. *Access Contested: Security, Identity, and Resistance in Asian Cyberspace*. MIT Press, 2011.

Deibert, Ronald, John Palfrey, Rafal Rohozinski, and Jonathan Zittrain, eds. *Access Controlled: The Shaping of Power, Rights, and Rule in Cyberspace*. MIT Press, 2010.

Deibert, Ronald, John Palfrey, Rafal Rohozinski, and Jonathan Zittrain, eds. *Access Denied: The Practice and Policy of Global Internet Filtering*. MIT Press, 2008.

Deng, Kai, David Demes, and Chih-Jou Jay Chen. "Xi Jinping's Surveillance State: Merging Digital Technology and Grassroots Organizations." In *The Xi Jinping Effect*, ed. Ashley Esarey and Rongbin Han. University of Washington Press, 2024.

Denton, Kirk. "China Dreams and the 'Road to Revival.'" *Origins: Current Events in Historical Perspective* 8, no. 3 (November 2014). https://origins.osu.edu/article/china-dreams-and-road-revival?.

Dickson, Bruce J. "Cooptation and Corporatism in China: The Logic of Party Adaptation." *Political Science Quarterly* 115, no. 4 (2000): 517–40.

Dickson, Bruce J. *Red Capitalists in China: The Party, Private Entrepreneurs, and Prospects for Political Change*. Cambridge University Press, 2003.

Dier. "Miaoni Wei Zhichi Jin Taiyan Daoqian: Yanlun Guoji, Fandui Sade" [Maoni Apologizes for Supporting Kim Taeyeon: Opinion Overly Extreme and Against Deployment of THAAD]. *Sina.cn*, March 13, 2017. https://ent.sina.cn/star/tv/2017-03-13/detail-ifychhus1080467.d.html.

Ding, Iza Yue. *The Performative State: Public Scrutiny and Environmental Governance in China*. Cornell University Press, 2022.

Doshi, Rush. *The Long Game: China's Grand Strategy to Displace American Order*. Oxford University Press, 2021.

Dou, Eva. "New Phone Sparks Worry China Has Found a Way around U.S. Tech Limits." *Washington Post*, September 2, 2023. https://www.washingtonpost.com/technology/2023/09/02/huawei-raimondo-phone-chip-sanctions.

Doyon, Jérôme, and Konstantinos Tsimonis. "Apathy Is Not Enough: Changing Modes of Student Management in Post-Mao China." *Europe—Asia Studies* 74, no. 7 (2022): 1123–46.

Du, Lili. "Wangwen Zuozhe Lianhe Qilai, Yuewen Kandao le Fangjian li de Daxiang" ("Online Writers Are United and Yuewen Sees the Elephant in the Room"). *PingWest*, May 8, 2020. https://www.pingwest.com/a/209911.

Du, Wei. "Yibu Daju Neng Yingxiang Yijia Shangshi Gongsi Yeji!" [A Big Drama Can Affect the Performance of a Listed Company!]. *National Business Daily*, March 24, 2019. http://www.nbd.com.cn/articles/2019-03-24/1313505.html.

Economy, Elizabeth. *The Third Revolution: Xi Jinping and the New Chinese State*. Oxford University Press, 2018.

Economy, Elizabeth. *The World According to China*. Polity, 2022.

Edelstein, Alex S. *Total Propaganda: From Mass Culture to Popular Culture*. Routledge, 1997.

Enstad, Nan. *Ladies of Labor, Girls of Adventure: Working Women, Popular Culture, and Labor Politics at the Turn of the Twentieth Century*. Columbia University Press, 1999.

Erlanger, Steven, and Christina Anderson. "How the Far Right Bagged Election Success in Sweden." *New York Times*, September 19, 2022.

Esarey, Ashley. "Winning Hearts and Minds? Cadres as Microbloggers in China." *Journal of Current Chinese Affairs* 44, no. 2 (2015): 69–103.

Esarey, Ashley, and Rongbin Han, eds. *The Xi Jinping Effect*. University of Washington Press, 2024.

Esarey, Ashley, and Qiang Xiao. "Political Expression in the Chinese Blogosphere: Below the Radar." *Asian Survey* 48, no. 5 (2008): 752–72.

Fairclough, Norman. *Analysing Discourse: Textual Analysis for Social Research*. Psychology Press, 2003.

Fang, Kecheng, and Maria Repnikova. "Demystifying 'Little Pink': The Creation and Evolution of a Gendered Label for Nationalistic Activists in China." *New Media and Society* 20, no. 6 (2017): 2162–85.

Feldstein, Steven. *The Rise of Digital Repression: How Technology Is Reshaping Power, Politics, and Resistance*. Oxford University Press, 2021.

Feng, Jin. *Romancing the Internet: Producing and Consuming Chinese Web Romance*. Brill, 2013.

Fisher, Aleksandr. "Demonizing the Enemy: The Influence of Russian State-Sponsored Media on American Audiences." *Post-Soviet Affairs* 36, no. 4 (2020): 281–96.

Fisher, Tom. " 'The Play's the Thing': Wu Han and Hai Rui Revisited." *Australian Journal of Chinese Affairs*, no. 7 (1982): 1–35.

Fording, Richard C., and Sanford F. Schram. *Hard White: The Mainstreaming of Racism in American Politics*. Oxford University Press, 2020.

Freelon, Deen, Michael Bossetta, Chris Wells, Josephine Lukito, Yiping Xia, and Kirsten Adams. "Black Trolls Matter: Racial and Ideological Asymmetries in Social Media Disinformation." *Social Science Computer Review* 40, no. 3 (2022): 560–78.

Fu, Shuangqi. "2016 Nian Beijing Shi Youxiu Wangluo Wenxue Yuanchuang Zuopin Fabu" [List of 2016 Beijing Municipality Excellent Online Literary Original Works Publicized]. *Guangmin Daily*, October 26, 2016.

Fuchs, Christian. "Class, Knowledge and New Media." *Media, Culture, and Society* 32, no. 1 (2010): 141–50.

Gainous, Jason, Rongbin Han, Andrew W. MacDonald, and Kevin M. Wagner. *Directed Digital Dissidence in Autocracies: How China Wins Online*. Oxford University Press, 2023.

Gallagher, Mary, and Blake Miller. "Who Not What: The Logic of China's Information Control Strategy." *China Quarterly* 248, no. 1 (2021): 1011–36.

Gandhi, Jennifer. *Political Institutions under Dictatorship*. Cambridge University Press, 2010.

Gao, Gengsong. "Post-Tiananmen Chinese Liberal Intellectuals' Political Uses of Confucian Tradition and Chinese History." *Journal of Contemporary China* 31, no. 137 (2022): 709–25.

Gao, Li. "Youxiu Xianshi Ticai he Lishi Ticai Wangluo Wenxue Chuban Gongcheng Qidong" [Excellent Realistic and Historical Themed Online Literature Publishing Project Launched]. Xinhua Net, June 12, 2020. http://m.xinhuanet.com/ent/2020-06/12/c_1126104828.htm.

Gao, Mobo C. F. *The Battle for China's Past: Mao and the Cultural Revolution*. Pluto, 2008.

Gellner, Ernest. *Nations and Nationalism*. Ithaca: Cornell University Press, 2008.

Gering, Tuvia. "A Xinderella Story: Turning the Chinese Dream Into China's Master Narrative." *China Report* 59, no. 3 (2023): 243–58.

Gerth, Karl. *Unending Capitalism: How Consumerism Negated China's Communist Revolution*. Cambridge University Press, 2020.

Gierzynski, Anthony, and Kathryn Eddy. *Harry Potter and the Millennials: Research Methods and the Politics of the Muggle Generation*. Johns Hopkins University Press, 2013.

Gilley, Bruce. "Paradigms of Chinese Politics: Kicking Society Back Out." *Journal of Contemporary China* 20, no. 70 (2011): 517–33.

Gitlin, Todd. *How the Torrent of Images and Sounds Overwhelms Our Lives*. Macmillan, 2007.

Gold, Thomas B. "'Just in Time!': China Battles Spiritual Pollution on the Eve of 1984." *Asian Survey* 24, no. 9 (1984): 947–74.

Goldhaber, Michael H. "The Attention Economy and the Net." *First Monday* 2, no. 4 (1997). https://doi.org/10.5210/fm.v2i4.519.

Gow, Michael. "The Core Socialist Values of the Chinese Dream: Towards a Chinese Integral State." *Critical Asian Studies* 49, no. 1 (2017): 92–116.

Gramsci, Antonio. *Selections from the Prison Notebooks of Antonio Gramsci*, ed. Quintin Hoare and Geoffrey Nowell Smith. International Publishers, 1971.

Greitens, Sheena Chestnut. "Dealing with Demand for China's Global Surveillance Exports." Brookings Institution Global China Report (2020). https://www.brookings.edu/articles/dealing-with-demand-for-chinas-global-surveillance-exports.

Gries, Peter Hays. *China's New Nationalism: Pride, Politics, and Diplomacy*. University of California Press, 2004.

Gries, Peter Hays. "Chinese Nationalism: Challenging the State?" *Current History* 104, no. 683 (2005): 251–56.

Gueorguiev, Dimitar. *Retrofitting Leninism: Participation Without Democracy in China*. Oxford University Press, 2021.

Guibernau, Montserrat. "Anthony D. Smith on Nations and National Identity: A Critical Assessment." *Nations and Nationalism* 10, no. 1–2 (2004): 125–41.

Gunitsky, Seva. "Corrupting the Cyber-Commons: Social Media as a Tool of Autocratic Stability." *Perspectives on Politics* 13, no. 1 (2015): 42–54.

Guo, Shaohua. "Ruled by Attention: A Case Study of Professional Digital Attention Agents at Sina.Com and the Chinese Blogosphere." *International Journal of Cultural Studies* 19, no. 4 (2016): 407–23.

Guo, Shaohua. "Startling by Each Click: 'Word-of-Mouse' Publicity and Critically Manufacturing Time-Travel Romance Online." *Chinese Literature Today* 5, no. 1 (2015): 74–83.

Guo, Shaohua. *The Evolution of the Chinese Internet: Creative Visibility in the Digital Public*. Stanford University Press, 2020.

Hall, Stuart. "Popular Culture, Politics and History." *Cultural Studies* 32, no. 6 (2018): 929–52.

Hamm, John Christopher. *Paper Swordsmen: Jin Yong and the Modern Chinese Martial Arts Novel*. University of Hawai'i Press, 2006.

Han, Fanghang. "'Rongshuxia' Ruhe Kaiqi yige Wangwen Shidai, you Ruhe Zouxiang Moluo" [How *Under the Banyan Tree* Started the Internet Literature Era and How It Goes Downhill]. *QDaily*, August 27, 2017. https://www.qdaily.com/articles/44533.html.

Han, Rongbin. *Contesting Cyberspace in China: Online Expression and Authoritarian Resilience*. Columbia University Press, 2018.

Han, Rongbin. "Cyber Nationalism and Regime Support Under Xi Jinping: The Effects of the 2018 Constitutional Revision." *Journal of Contemporary China* 30, no. 131 (2021): 717–33.

Han, Rongbin. "Debating China Beyond the Great Firewall: Digital Disenchantment and Authoritarian Resilience." *Journal of Chinese Political Science* 28, no. 1 (2023): 85–103.

Han, Rongbin. "Manufacturing Consent in Cyberspace: China's 'Fifty-Cent Army.'" *Journal of Current Chinese Affairs* 44, no. 2 (2015): 105–34.

Han, Rongbin. "Passing on the Red Genes: Communism Nostalgia in Online Fictions and Ideological Governance in China." *Regulation and Governance* (2024). https://doi.org/10.1111/rego.12622.

Han, Rongbin. "Withering Gongzhi: Cyber Criticism of Chinese Public Intellectuals." *International Journal of Communication* 12 (2018): 1966–87.

Han, Rongbin, Juan Du, and Li Shao. "Opportunistic Bargaining: Negotiating Distribution in China." *China Quarterly* 253 (2023): 141–57.

Han, Rongbin, and Linan Jia. "Governing by the Internet: Local Governance in the Digital Age." *Journal of Chinese Governance* 3, no. 1 (2018): 67–85.

Han, Rongbin, and Linan Jia. "Rescuing Authoritarian Rule: The Anti-Gongzhi Discourse in Chinese Cyberspace." In *The Routledge Handbook of Chinese Discourse Analysis*, ed. Chris Shei. Routledge, 2019.

Han, Rongbin, and Li Shao. "Scaling Authoritarian Information Control: How China Adjusts the Level of Online Censorship." *Political Research Quarterly* 75, no. 4 (2022): 1345–59.

Hassid, Jonathan. *China's Unruly Journalists: How Committed Professionals Are Changing the People's Republic*. Routledge, 2015.

Hawkins, Amy, and Jeffrey Wasserstrom. "Why *1984* and *Animal Farm* Aren't Banned in China." *The Atlantic*, January 13, 2019. https://www.theatlantic.com/ideas/archive/2019/01/why-1984-and-animal-farm-arent-banned-china/580156.

Hayek, Friedrich. *The Road to Serfdom: Text and Documents*. University of Chicago Press, 2007.

Hayles, N. Katherine. *Electronic Literature: New Horizons for the Literary*. University of Notre Dame Press, 2008.

He, Huaihong. *Social Ethics in a Changing China: Moral Decay or Ethical Awakening?* Brookings Institution, 2015.

He, Yinan. "History, Chinese Nationalism and the Emerging Sino-Japanese Conflict." *Journal of Contemporary China* 16, no. 50 (2007): 1–24.

Heberer, Thomas, and Gunter Schubert, eds. *Regime Legitimacy in Contemporary China: Institutional Change and Stability*. Routledge, 2008.

Herold, David Kurt, and Peter Marolt, eds. *Online Society in China: Creating, Celebrating, and Instrumentalising the Online Carnival*. Routledge, 2011.

Herpen, Marcel H. Van. *Putin's Propaganda Machine: Soft Power and Russian Foreign Policy*. Rowman and Littlefield, 2016.

Ho, Wing Shan. *Screening Post-1989 China: Critical Analysis of Chinese Film and Television*. Palgrave Macmillan, 2015.

Hochschild, Arlie Russell. *Strangers in Their Own Land: Anger and Mourning on the American Right*. New Press, 2018.

Hockx, Michel. *Internet Literature in China*. Columbia University Press, 2015.

Hockx, Michel. "Truth, Goodness, and Beauty: Literary Policy in Xi Jinping's China." *Law and Literature* 35, no. 3 (2023): 515–31.
Holbig, Heike. "China After Reform: The Ideological, Constitutional, and Organisational Makings of a New Era." *Journal of Current Chinese Affairs* 47, no. 3 (2018): 187–207.
Holbig, Heike, and Bruce Gilley. "Reclaiming Legitimacy in China." *Politics and Policy* 38, no. 3 (2010): 395–422.
Holm, David. "The Strange Case of Liu Zhidan." *Australian Journal of Chinese Affairs* 27 (1992): 77–96.
Howard, Philip N. *The Digital Origins of Dictatorship and Democracy: Information Technology and Political Islam.* Oxford University Press, 2010.
Howard, Philip N., and Muzammil M. Hussain. *Democracy's Fourth Wave? Digital Media and the Arab Spring.* Oxford University Press, 2013.
Huang, Haifeng, Chanita Intawan, and Stephen P. Nicholson. "In Government We Trust: Implicit Political Trust and Regime Support in China." *Perspectives on Politics* 21, no. 4 (2022): 1357–75.
Huang, Haifeng, and Xinsheng Liu. "Historical Knowledge and National Identity: Evidence from China." *Research and Politics* 5, no. 3 (2018): 1–8.
Huang, Xinkai. "To Become Immortal: Chinese Fantasy Literature Online." *Intercultural Communication Studies* 20, no. 2 (2011): 119–30.
"Huawei Mate 60 Pro Triggers Buying Spree Among Chinese Consumers." *Global Times*, September 7, 2023. https://www.globaltimes.cn/page/202309/1297757.shtml.
Hui, Ning, and David Wertime. "Is This the New Face of China's Silent Majority?" *Foreign Policy*, October 22, 2014. http://foreignpolicy.com/2014/10/22/is-this-the-new-face-of-chinas-silent-majority.
Hulse, Clark. *The Rule of Art: Literature and Painting in the Renaissance.* University of Chicago Press, 1990.
Huntington, Samuel P. *The Clash of Civilizations and the Remaking of World Order.* Simon and Schuster, 1996.
Hurst, William J. "The Power of the Past: Nostalgia and Popular Discontent in Contemporary China." In *Laid-Off Workers in a Workers' State: Unemployment with Chinese Characteristics*, ed. Thomas B. Gold, William J. Hurst, Jaeyoun Won, and Li Qiang. Palgrave Macmillan, 2009.
Huss, Ann, and Jianmei Liu, eds. *The Jin Yong Phenomenon: Chinese Martial Arts Fiction and Modern Chinese Literary History.* Cambria, 2007.
Huxley, Aldous. *Brave New World.* Harper and Row, 1946.
Inglehart, Ronald. "The Renaissance of Political Culture." *American Political Science Review* 82, no. 4 (1988): 1203–30.
Inwood, Heather. "Internet Literature: From YY to MOOC." In *The Columbia Companion to Modern Chinese Literature*, ed. Kirk Denton. Columbia University Press, 2016.
Inwood, Heather. "The Happiness of Unrealizable Dreams: On the Pursuit of Pleasure in Contemporary Chinese Popular Fiction." In *Chinese Discourses on Happiness*, ed. Gerda Wielander and Derek Hird. Hong Kong University Press, 2018.
Inwood, Heather. *Verse Going Viral: China's New Media Scenes.* University of Washington Press, 2014.
Inwood, Heather. "What's in a Game? Transmedia Storytelling and the Web-Game Genre of Online Chinese Popular Fiction." *Asia Pacific Perspectives* (Spring/Summer 2014): 6–29.

Ionescu, Ghita, and Ernest Gellner, eds. *Populism: Its Meaning and National Characteristics*. Macmillan, 1969.

iResearch. "Wangwen Jianghu Qunying Pu: Zhongguo Wangluo Wenxue Zuozhe Dongcha Baogao" [Heroes in the Internet Literature Rivers and Lakes: Insight Report on Chinese Online Writers]. *iResearch*, December 27, 2016. https://report.iresearch.cn/report/201612/2696.shtml.

iResearch. "2018 Nian Zhongguo Wangluo Wenxue Zuozhe Baogao" [2018 Report on Chinese Internet Literature Writers]. iResearch, May 9, 2018. http://www.iresearch.com.cn/Detail/report?id=3208&isfree=0.

Irr, Caren. *Toward the Geopolitical Novel: U.S. Fiction in the Twenty-First Century*. Columbia University Press, 2013.

Isaacson, Nathaniel. *Celestial Empire: The Emergence of Chinese Science Fiction*. Wesleyan University Press, 2017.

Javed, Jeffrey. *Righteous Revolutionaries: Morality, Mobilization, and Violence in the Making of the Chinese State*. University of Michigan Press, 2022.

Jenkins, Henry. *Convergence Culture: Where Old and New Media Collide*. New York University Press, 2006.

Jiang, Min, and Luca Belli, eds. *Digital Sovereignty in the BRICS Countries: How the Global South and Emerging Power Alliances Are Reshaping Digital Governance*. Cambridge University Press, 2024.

Jiang, Ying. *Cyber-Nationalism in China: Challenging Western Media Portrayals of Internet Censorship in China*. University of Adelaide Press, 2012.

Ji, Wei. "Hulianwang Shidai de Qiji: Zhongguo Wangluo Wenxue" [Miracle of the Internet Age: Chinese Online Literature]. BBC Chinese, March 5, 2010. https://www.bbc.com/zhongwen/simp/indepth/2010/03/100302_internetliterature1.

Jinpingmei. "Zhexie Nian, Guangdian Zongju Caole Naxie Xin" [What Has the State Administration of Radio, Film and Television Been Worrying About Over the Years?]. Sina.com.cn, December 3, 2014. http://news.sina.com.cn/c/zg/jpm/2014-12-03/1825441.html.

Johnson, Ian. *Sparks: China's Underground Historians and Their Battle for the Future*. Oxford University Press, 2023.

Jones, Marc Owen. *Digital Authoritarianism in the Middle East: Deception, Disinformation and Social Media*. Oxford University Press, 2022.

Kaplan, Cora. *Victoriana: Histories, Fictions, Criticism*. Columbia University Press, 2007.

Kavanagh, Thomas M. *Esthetics of the Moment: Literature and Art in the French Enlightenment*. University of Pennsylvania Press, 1996.

King, Gary, Jennifer Pan, and Margaret E. Roberts. "How Censorship in China Allows Government Criticism but Silences Collective Expression." *American Political Science Review* 107, no. 2 (2013): 326–43.

King, Gary, Jennifer Pan, and Margaret E. Roberts. "How the Chinese Government Fabricates Social Media Posts for Strategic Distraction, Not Engaged Argument." *American Political Science Review* 111, no. 3 (2017): 484–501.

Kinkley, Jeffrey C. *Visions of Dystopia in China's New Historical Novels*. Columbia University Press, 2014.

Kluver, Alan R. *Legitimating the Chinese Economic Reforms: A Rhetoric of Myth and Orthodoxy*. State University of New York Press, 1996.

Kong, Yuan. "'Ruguan' yu 'Fazhou': Guanyu Zhongguo Jueqi de Liangzhong Zhishilun Tujing" ["Ruguan" and "Crusade Against King Zhou": Two Epistemological Approaches of China Rise]. *Dongfang Journal*, no. 9 (2020): 25–31.

Kostka, Genia. "China's Social Credit Systems and Public Opinion: Explaining High Levels of Approval." *New Media and Society* 21, no. 7 (2019): 1565–1593.

Kubat, Aleksandra. "Morality as Legitimacy Under Xi Jinping: The Political Functionality of Traditional Culture for the Chinese Communist Party." *Journal of Current Chinese Affairs* 47, no. 3 (2018): 47–86.

Lagerkvist, Johan. *After the Internet, Before Democracy: Competing Norms in Chinese Media and Society*. Peter Lang, 2010.

Lagerkvist, Johan. "Internet Ideotainment in the PRC: National Responses to Cultural Globalization." *Journal of Contemporary China* 17, no. 54 (2008): 121–40.

Lagerkvist, Johan. *The Internet in China: Unlocking and Containing the Public Sphere*. Lund: Lund University, 2007.

Lam, Willy. "Xi Jinping's Ideology and Statecraft." *Chinese Law and Government* 48, no. 6 (2016): 409–17.

Landsberg, Alison. *Engaging the Past : Mass Culture and the Production of Historical Knowledge*. Columbia University Press, 2015.

Lau, Mimi. "Why Does China React so Strongly over the South Korea-Based Anti-Missile System?" *South China Morning Post*, February 11, 2016. https://www.scmp.com/news/china/diplomacy-defence/article/1911857/why-does-china-react-so-strongly-over-south-korea-based.

Lears, T. J. Jackson. "The Concept of Cultural Hegemony: Problems and Possibilities." *American Historical Review* 90, no. 3 (1985): 567–93.

Lee, Ching Kwan. *The Specter of Global China: Politics, Labor, and Foreign Investment in Africa*. University of Chicago Press, 2017.

Lee, Leo Ou-Fan. "Dissent Literature from the Cultural Revolution." *Chinese Literature: Essays, Articles, Reviews* 1 (1979): 59–79.

Leibold, James. "Blogging Alone: China, the Internet, and the Democratic Illusion?" *Journal of Asian Studies* 70, no. 4 (2011): 1023–41.

Leibold, James. "More Than a Category: Han Supremacism on the Chinese Internet." *China Quarterly* 203 (2010): 539–59.

Li, Jinglin. "Wangluo Wenxue Wu Zhanshi: Shui Zai Kan? Shui Zai Xie? Shui Zai Zuan?" [All Quiet in Internet Literature Realm: Who Writes, Who Reads, and Who Makes the Profit?]. *Deep Echo*, January 10, 2022. https://m.jiemian.com/article/6997420.html.

Li, Li. "Wangluo Wenxue Zuopin 'Daguo Zhonggong' Huo Zhongguo Chuban Zhengfu Jiang" [Online Literature Work "Great Power Heavy Industry" Won China's Government Publishing Award]. *Beijing Daily*, July 29, 2021.

Li, Ling. "Yuewen Jietuan Huiying Zuozhe Heyue Zhengyi: Fouren Quanbu Mianfei Yuedu, Bu Heli Tiaokuan Jiang Xiugai" [Yuewen Group Responds to Writer Contract Controversy: Denies All-for-Free Read and Unreasonable Stipulations Will Be Revised]. *Southern Metropolis Daily*, May 3, 2020. https://www.sohu.com/a/392790893_161795.

Li, Luzhou. *Zoning China: Online Video, Popular Culture, and the State*. MIT Press, 2019.

Li, Qiang. "'Jiti Zhihui' de Duochongbianzhou: You 'Lingao Qiming' Kan Wangwen Shengchan Jizhi yu Yishixingtai zhi Guanxi" [Multiple Variations of "Collective

Wisdom": Examining the Relationship Between Internet Literature Production Mechanism and Ideology from "Lingao Qiming"]. *Wenyi Lilun yu Piping* [*Theory and Criticism of Literature and Art*], no. 2 (2018): 130–37.

Li, Yonggang. *Women de Fanghuoqiang: Wangluo Shidai de Biaoda Yu Jianguan* [*Our Great Firewall: Expression and Governance in the Era of the Internet*]. Guangxi Normal University Press, 2009.

Liang, Yilu, and Wanqi Shen. "Fan Economy in the Chinese Media and Entertainment Industry: How Feedback from Super Fans Can Propel Creative Industries' Revenue." *Global Media and China* 1, no. 4 (2016): 331–49.

Liberthal, Kenneth. *Governing China: From Revolution Through Reform*. W. W. Norton, 2004.

Lin, Buerzi. "Xiaohou Yinfa Gongming, IP Zhuixu Ruhe zai Dazhong Shichang Nixi" [Resonance After Laughter, How the "Zhui Xu" IP Achieved Mainstream Success]. Sohu.com, February 17, 2021. https://www.sohu.com/a/451127706_116132.

Ling, Yu-long. "Dr. Sun Yat-Sen's Doctrine and Impact on the Modern World." *American Journal of Chinese Studies* 19, no. 1 (2012): 1–11.

Link, Perry, and Dazhi Wu. *I Have No Enemies: The Life and Legacy of Liu Xiaobo*. Columbia University Press, 2023.

Liu, Hailong, ed. *From Cyber-Nationalism to Fandom Nationalism: The Case of Diba Expedition In China*. Routledge, 2019.

Liu, Jianmei. *Revolution Plus Love: Literary History, Women's Bodies, and Thematic Repetition in Twentieth-Century Chinese Fiction*. University of Hawai'i Press, 2003.

Liu, Jun. *Shifting Dynamics of Contention in the Digital Age: Mobile Communication and Politics in China*. Oxford University Press, 2020.

Liu, Jun. "Who Speaks for the Past? Social Media, Social Memory, and the Production of Historical Knowledge in Contemporary China." *International Journal of Communication* 12 (2018): 1675–95.

Liu, Lizhi. *From Click to Boom: The Political Economy of E-Commerce in China*. Princeton University Press, 2024.

Liu, Xiaojing, and Min Zhou. "Wangluo Wenxue Yongbao 'Xianshi' 24 Bu Wangwen Lizuo zai Jiangsu Huojiang" [Online Literature Embraces "Reality," 24 Masterpieces Won Awards in Jiangsu], China Writer Net, November 4, 2019. https://www.chinawriter.com.cn/n1/2019/1104/c404023-31436018.html.

Lorentzen, Peter. "China's Strategic Censorship." *American Journal of Political Science* 58, no. 2 (2014): 402–14.

Lorentzen, Peter. "Designing Contentious Politics in Post-1989 China." *Modern China* 43, no. 5 (2017): 459–93.

Lu, Dazhi. "Zhongguo Zuoxie Chengli Wangluo Wenxue Weiyuanhui" [China Writers Association Establishes Internet Literature Committee]. *China Reading Weekly*, December 30, 2015.

Lu, Nanfeng, and Jing Wu. "Lishi Zhuanzhe zhong de Hongda Xushi: Gongyedang Wangluo Sichao de Zhengzhi Fenxi" [Grand Narrative at History's Turning Point: Political Analysis of the Internet Ideology of China's Industrial Party]. *Dongfang Journal* no. 1 (2018): 49–60, 118–19.

Lu, Yingdan, and Jennifer Pan. "Capturing Clicks: How the Chinese Government Uses Clickbait to Compete for Visibility." *Political Communication* 38, no. 1–2 (2020): 23–54.

Lucken, Michael. *The Japanese and the War: Expectation, Perception, and the Shaping of Memory*, trans. Karen Grimwade. Columbia University Press, 2017.

Lugg, Alexander. "Chinese Online Fiction: Taste Publics, Entertainment, and Candle in the Tomb." *Chinese Journal of Communication* 4, no. 2 (2011): 121–36.

Luoyefeitian. "Lun Zhongguo Wangluo Wenxue de Fazhan yu Xianzhuang" [On the Development and State of Chinese Online Literature]. Jiangshan Literature Net, October 13, 2008. http://www.vsread.com/index.php/article/showread?id=3617&pn2=1&pn=1.

Lynch, Daniel. "Chinese Thinking on the Future of International Relations: Realism as the Ti, Rationalism as the Yong?" *China Quarterly*, no. 197 (2009): 87–107.

Ma, Weijun. "Chinese Main Melody TV Drama: Hollywoodization and Ideological Persuasion." *Television and New Media* 15, no. 6 (2013): 523–37.

Ma, Yifan. "'Ruguanxue' de Huayu Shengcheng Jiegou jiqi Chulu" [The Discourse-Generating Structure of "Ruguanism" and Its Way Out]. *Dongfang Journal*, no. 9 (2020): 53–63.

MacKinnon, Rebecca. "China's Censorship 2.0: How Companies Censor Bloggers." *First Monday* 14, no. 2 (2009). https://firstmonday.org/article/view/2378/2089.

Magaloni, Beatriz. "Credible Power-Sharing and the Longevity of Authoritarian Rule." *Comparative Political Studies* 41, no. 4–5 (2008): 715–41.

Mai, Jun. "China Deletes 2 Million Online Posts for 'Historical Nihilism' as Communist Party Centenary Nears." *South China Morning Post*, May 11, 2021. https://www.scmp.com/news/china/politics/article/3132957/china-deletes-2-million-online-posts-historical-nihilism.

Malesky, Edmund, and Paul Schuler. "Nodding or Needling: Analyzing Delegate Responsiveness in an Authoritarian Parliament." *American Political Science Review* 104, no. 3 (2010): 482–502.

Mann, Michael. "The Autonomous Power of the State: Its Origins, Mechanisms and Results." *European Journal of Sociology* 25, no. 02 (1984): 185–213.

Mao, Zedong. *Selected Works of Mao Tse-Tung*. Vol. 3. Foreign Languages Press, 1965.

Mao, Zedong. *Selected Works of Mao Tse-Tung*. Vol. 5. Foreign Languages Press, 1977.

Mao, Zedong. *Selected Works of Mao Tse-Tung*. Vol. 8. Foreign Languages Press, 2020.

Margolin, Emma. "'Make America Great Again'—Who Said It First?" *NBC News*, September 9, 2016. https://www.nbcnews.com/politics/2016-election/make-america-great-again-who-said-it-first-n645716.

Martin, John Levi. "What Is Field Theory?" *American Journal of Sociology* 109, no. 1 (2015): 1–49.

Marx, Karl. *A Contribution to the Critique of Political Economy*. Progress, 1977.

Mattingly, Daniel C., and Elaine Yao. "How Soft Propaganda Persuades." *Comparative Political Studies* 55, no. 9 (2022): 1569–94.

Mayer, Maximilian, and Karolina Pawlik. "Politics of Memory, Heritage, and Diversity in Modern China." *Journal of Current Chinese Affairs* 52, no. 2 (2023): 139–62.

Mayer, Maximilian, and Frederik Schmitz, eds. *The Digitalisation of Memory Practices in China: Contesting the Curating State*. Bristol University Press, 2025.

Mazzuca, Sebastian L. "Access to Power Versus Exercise of Power: Reconceptualizing Democratization in Latin America." *Studies in Comparative International Development* 45, no. 3 (2010): 334–57.

McCollum, Victoria, ed. *Make America Hate Again: Trump-Era Horror and the Politics of Fear*. Routledge, 2019.

Meng, Bingchun. "Political Scandal at the End of Ideology? The Mediatized Politics of the Bo Xilai Case." *Media, Culture, and Society* 38, no. 6 (2016): 811–26.

Meng, Bingchun. *The Politics of Chinese Media: Consensus and Contestation*. Palgrave Macmillan, 2018.

Menke, Manuel, and Berber Hagedoorn. "Digital Memory and Populism—Introduction." *International Journal of Communication* 17 (2023): 2101–12.

Miao, Ying. "Romanticising the Past: Core Socialist Values and the China Dream as Legitimisation Strategy." *Journal of Current Chinese Affairs* 49, no. 2 (2021): 162–84.

Michel Hockx. "Virtual Chinese Literature: A Comparative Case Study of Online Poetry Communities." *China Quarterly*, no. 183 (2005): 670–91.

Milner, Helen V. "Voting for Populism in Europe: Globalization, Technological Change, and the Extreme Right." *Comparative Political Studies* 54, no. 13 (2021): 2267–441.

Ministry of Foreign Affairs of PRC. "President Xi Jinping Meets with U.S. President Joe Biden in Bali." November 14, 2022. https://www.fmprc.gov.cn/mfa_eng/zxxx_662805/202211/t20221114_10974686.html.

Mo, Linhu. *Dazhong Wenhua Xinlun* [*New Discussion on Mass Culture*]. Tsinghua University Press, 2016.

Mudde, Cas. *Populist Radical Right Parties in Europe*. Cambridge University Press, 2007.

Mudde, Cas. "The Populist Zeitgeist." *Government and Opposition* 39, no. 4 (2004): 541–63.

Mudde, Cas, and Cristobal Rovira Kaltwasser. *Populism: A Very Short Introduction*. Oxford University Press, 2017.

Murong, Xuechun. "Chengdu, Jinye qing Jiang Wo Yiwang" [Chengdu, Remember Me Not Tonight]. Tianya.cn, April 5, 2002. http://bbs.tianya.cn/post-culture-48701-1.shtml.

Nathan, Andrew J. "China's Changing of the Guard: Authoritarian Resilience." *Journal of Democracy* 14, no. 1 (2003): 6–17.

Nathan, Andrew J. "The Alternate History of China: Could Beijing Have Taken a Different Path?" *Foreign Affairs* 101, no. 5 (2022): 234–40.

National Eliminate Pornography and Illegal Publications Work Team Office. "Guanyu Yanli Chachu Wangluo Yinhui Seqing Xiaoshuo de Jinji Tongzhi" [Urgent Notice on Strictly Investigating and Punishing Online Pornographic Fictions]. GAPP Web, August 1, 2007. http://www.gapp.gov.cn/news/1663/102998.shtml.

Noesselt, Nele. "Microblogs and the Adaptation of the Chinese Party-State's Governance Strategy." *Governance* 27, no. 3 (2014): 449–68.

Noury, Abdul, and Gerard Roland. "Identity Politics and Populism in Europe." *Annual Review of Political Science* 23 (2020): 421–39.

O'Brien, Kevin J., and Rongbin Han. "Path to Democracy? Assessing Village Elections in China." *Journal of Contemporary China* 18, no. 60 (2009): 359–78.

O'Brien, Kevin J., and Lianjiang Li. *Rightful Resistance in Rural China*. Cambridge University Press, 2006.

Orwell, George. *1984*. Houghton Mifflin Harcourt, 2017.

Ostrom, Elinor. "Crossing the Great Divide: Coproduction, Synergy, and Development." *World Development* 24, no. 6 (1996): 1073–87.

Ott, Brian L., and Greg Dickinson. *The Twitter Presidency: Donald J. Trump and the Politics of White Rage*. Routledge, 2019.

Ouyang, Shijia. "IP Drives Pan-entertainment Sector Change." *China Daily*, November 28, 2018. https://www.chinadaily.com.cn/a/201811/28/WS5bfded43a310eff30328b718.html.

Ouyang, Youquan, ed. *Wangluo Wenxue Wunian Pucha (2009–2013)* [*Five Year Census of Internet Literature (2009–2013)*]. Central Compilation and Translation, 2014.

Ouyang, Youquan, and Xingjie Yuan, eds. *Zhongguo Wangluo Wenxue Biannian Shi* [*A Chronical History of Chinese Internet Literature*]. China Federation of Literary and Art Circles, 2015.

Pei, Minxin. "China: Totalitarianism's Long Shadow." *Journal of Democracy* 32, no. 2 (2021): 5–21.

Pei, Minxin. *China's Trapped Transition: The Limits of Developmental Autocracy*. Harvard University Press, 2009.

People.com.cn. "2019–2020 Niandu Wangluo Wenxue IP Yingshiju Gaibian Qianli Pinggu Baogao" [2019–2020 Internet Literature IP Film and Television Adaptation Potential Evaluation Report]. People.com.cn, January 29, 2021. http://unn.people.com.cn/n1/2021/0129/c420625-32016929.html.

Perry, Elizabeth J. "Cultural Governance in Contemporary China: 'Re-Orienting' Party Propaganda." In *To Govern China: Evolving Practices of Power*, ed. Vivienne Shue and Patricia M. Thornton. Cambridge University Press, 2017.

Persily, Nathaniel, and Joshua A. Tucker, eds. *Social Media and Democracy: The State of the Field, Prospects for Reform*. Cambridge University Press, 2020.

Pohle, Julia, and Thorsten Thiel. "Digital Sovereignty." *Internet Policy Review* 9, no. 4 (2020): 1–19.

Postman, Neil. *Amusing Ourselves to Death: Public Discourse in the Age of Show Business*. Penguin, 2005.

Powers, Ryan, and Austin Strange. "Can Rising Powers Reassure? Shifting Power, Foreign Economic Policy, and Perceptions of Revisionist Intent." *Journal of Peace Research* (2025). https://doi.org/10.1177/00223433241303414.

Przeworski, Adam. "Formal Models of Authoritarian Regimes: A Critique." *Perspectives on Politics* 21, no. 3 (2022): 979–88.

Pusu. "Wangluo Wenxue de Ming yu An: Yi Tianya Shequ Weili" [The Light and Dark Aspects of Online Literature: Tianya Community as an Example]. Tianya.cn, November 15, 2017. http://bbs.tianya.cn/post-1178-5201-1.shtml.

Qin, Amy. "Making Online Literature Pay Big in China." *New York Times*, November 1, 2016. https://www.nytimes.com/2016/11/01/world/asia/china-online-literature-zhang-wei.html.

Reilly, James. *Strong Society, Smart State: The Rise of Public Opinion in China's Japan Policy*. Columbia University Press, 2013.

Repnikova, Maria. *Chinese Soft Power*. Cambridge University Press, 2022.

Repnikova, Maria. *Media Politics in China: Improvising Power Under Authoritarianism*. Cambridge University Press, 2017.

Repnikova, Maria. "Rethinking China's Soft Power: 'Pragmatic Enticement' of Confucius Institutes in Ethiopia." *China Quarterly* 250 (2022): 440–63.

Rettberg, Scott. *Electronic Literature*. Polity, 2019.

Rey, P. J. "Alienation, Exploitation, and Social Media." *American Behavioral Scientist* 56, no. 4 (2012): 399–420.

Ritzer, George, Paul Dean, and Nathan Jurgenson. "The Coming of Age of the Prosumer." *American Behavioral Scientist* 56, no. 4 (2012): 379–98.

Roberts, Margaret E. *Censored: Distraction and Diversion Inside China's Great Firewall*. Princeton University Press, 2018.

Ron, James. *Frontiers and Ghettos: State Violence in Serbia and Israel*. University of California Press, 2003.

Rosenthal, Rob, and Richard Flacks. *Playing for Change: Music and Musicians in the Service of Social Movements*. Routledge, 2015.

Ruan, Lotus, Masashi Crete-Nishihata, Jeffrey Knockel, Ruohan Xiong, and Jakub Dalek. "The Intermingling of State and Private Companies: Analysing Censorship of the 19th National Communist Party Congress on WeChat." *China Quarterly*, no. 246 (2021): 497–526.

Saich, Tony. *Governance and Politics of China*. Palgrave Macmillan, 2015.

Sandby-Thomas, Peter. "How Do You Solve a Problem Like Legitimacy? Contributing to a New Research Agenda." *Journal of Contemporary China* 23, no. 88 (2014): 575–92.

Schlæger, Jesper. *E-Government in China: Technology, Power and Local Government Reform*. Routledge, 2013.

Schlæger, Jesper, and Min Jiang. "Official Microblogging and Social Management by Local Governments in China." *China Information* 28, no. 2 (2014): 189–213.

Schneider, Florian. *China's Digital Nationalism*. Oxford University Press, 2018.

Schubert, Gunter. "Political Legitimacy in Contemporary China Revisited: Theoretical Refinement and Empirical Operationalization." *Journal of Contemporary China* 23, no. 88 (2014): 593–611.

Scoggins, Suzanne E. *Policing China: Street-Level Cops in the Shadow of Protest*. Cornell University Press, 2021.

Shambaugh, David. *China Goes Global: The Partial Power*. Oxford University Press, 2013.

Shan, Wei, Yongxin Gu, and Juan Chen. "Layering Ideologies from Deng Xiaoping to Xi Jinping: Tracing Ideological Changes of the Communist Party of China Using Text Analysis." *China: An International Journal* 21, no. 2 (2023): 26–50.

Shao, Yanjun. *Wangluo Shidai de Wenxue Yindu [Literature Guide in the Digital Age]*. Guangxi Normal University Press, 2015.

Shao, Yanjun, and Yingxuan Xiao, eds. *Chuangshizhe Shuo: Wangluo Wenxue Wangzhan Chuangshiren Fangtanlu* [*The Founders Say: Interviews with Internet Literature Website Founders*]. Peking University Press, 2020.

Shaw, Aaron, and Yochai Benkler. "A Tale of Two Blogospheres: Discursive Practices on the Left and Right." *American Behavioral Scientist* 56, no. 4 (2012): 459–87.

Shen, Yipeng. *Public Discourses of Contemporary China: The Narration of the Nation in Popular Literatures, Film, and Television*. Palgrave Macmillan, 2015.

Shi, Jingnan. "2020 Nian 'Youxiu Xianshi Ticai he Lishi Ticai Wangluo Wenxue Chuban Gongcheng' Ruxuan Zuopin Jiexiao" [2020 Selected Works of "Excellent Realistic and Historical Themed Online Literature Publishing Project" Announced]. Sohu.com, August 23, 2021. https://www.sohu.com/a/485186786_267106.

Shi-Kupfer, Kristin, Mareike Ohlberg, Simon Lang, and Bertram Lang. "Ideas and Ideologies Competing for China's Political Future." *Merics Papers on China*, no. 5 (2017): 1–90.

Shi, Wei, and Shih Diing Liu. "Pride as Structure of Feeling: Wolf Warrior II and the National Subject of the Chinese Dream." *Chinese Journal of Communication* 13, no. 3 (2020): 329–43.

Shirk, Susan L. *Overreach: How China Derailed Its Peaceful Rise*. Oxford University Press, 2022.

Shirky, Clay. "The Political Power of Social Media." *Foreign Affairs* 90, no. 1 (2011): 28–41.

Shue, Vivienne. *The Reach of the State: Sketches of the Chinese Body Politic*. Stanford University Press, 1988.

Sina Tech. "Shengda Chengli Wenxue Gongsi, Xinlang Hou Xiaoqiang Jiameng" [Shanda Sets Up Literature Company and Joined by Sina's Hou Xiaoqiang]. *Sina Tech*, July 4, 2008. http://tech.sina.com.cn/i/2008-07-04/12302304830.shtml.

Sinpeng, Aim. *Opposing Democracy in the Digital Age: The Yellow Shirts in Thailand*. University of Michigan Press, 2021.

Smith, Anthony D. *National Identity*. Penguin, 1991.

Smith, Anthony D. *The Ethnic Origins of Nations*. Blackwell, 1986.

Soldatov, Andreĭ, and Irina Borogan. *The Red Web: The Struggle Between Russia's Digital Dictators and the New Online Revolutionaries*. PublicAffairs, 2015.

Song, Mingwei. "Preface to 'Chinese Science Fiction: Late Qing and the Contemporary.'" *Renditions*, no. 77/78 (2012): 7–14.

Song, Mingwei. "Variations on Utopia in Contemporary Chinese Science Fiction." *Science-Fiction Studies* 40, no. 1 (2013): 86–102.

Song, Mingwei. *Young China: National Rejuvenation and the Bildungsroman, 1900–1959*. Harvard University Asia Center, 2015.

Song, Yushu. "Wangluo Wenxue: Shangye Xiezuo zhong de Ziyou Zheyi" [Internet Literature: The Broken Wings of Freedom in Commercialized Writing]. *Wenyi Zhengming*, no. 11 (2012): 110–13.

Sorace, Christian P. "The Chinese Communist Party's Nervous System: Affective Governance from Mao to Xi." *China Quarterly* 248, no. 1 (2021): 29–51.

State Administration of Press, Publication, Radio, Film and Television. "Guanyu Yinfa Guanyu Tuidong Wangluo Wenxue Jiankang Fazhan de Zhidao Yijian de Tongzhi" [Notice on the Issuance of Guiding Opinions Concerning Promoting the Healthy Development of Online Literature]. Cyber Administration of China Web, January 6, 2015. http://www.cac.gov.cn/2015-01/06/c_1113893482.htm.

State Administration of Press, Publication, Radio, Film and Television. "Guanyu Yinfa Wangluo Wenxue Chuban Fuwu Danwei Shehui Xiaoyi Pinggu Shixing Banfa de Tongzhi" [Notice on Issuance of Provisional Methods for Evaluating Social Benefits of Online Literature Publication Service Platforms]. National Press and Publication Administration, June 27, 2017. https://www.nppa.gov.cn/xxfb/tzgs/201706/t20170627_666172.html.

State Council Information Office of the People's Republic of China. "China and the World in the New Era." Xinhua Net, September 27, 2019. http://www.xinhuanet.com/english/2019-09/27/c_138427541.htm.

Stern, Rachel E., and Jonathan Hassid. "Amplifying Silence: Uncertainty and Control Parables in Contemporary China." *Comparative Political Studies* 45, no. 10 (2012): 1230–54.

Stockmann, Daniela. *Media Commercialization and Authoritarian Rule in China*. Cambridge University Press, 2013.

Stockmann, Daniela, and Ting Luo. *Governing Digital China*. Cambridge University Press, 2025.

Sun, Kailiang, and Qiang Li. "Jiti Ruhe Zhihui: 'Lingao Qiming' de Luntan Wenhua yu 'Tongren Zhuanzheng' Jizhi" [How the Collective Becomes Intelligent: Forum Culture and the "Fan Production" Mechanism of "Lingao Qiming"]. *Zhongguo Wenxue Piping* [*Chinese Journal of Literary Criticism*], no. 1 (2018): 124–25.

Sung, Chia-Fu. "The Official Historiographical Operation of the Song Dynasty." *Journal of Song-Yuan Studies* 45 (2015): 175–206.

Szonyi, Michael. "Ming Fever: The Past in the Present in the People's Republic of China at Sixty." In *The People's Republic of China at 60: An International Assessment*, ed. William C. Kirby. Harvard University Asia Center, 2011.

Tai-Yee Wu, Anne Oeldorf-Hirsch, and David Atkin. "A Click Is Worth a Thousand Words: Probing the Predictors of Using Click Speech for Online Opinion Expression." *International Journal of Communication* 14 (2020): 2687–706.

Tai, Yun, and King-wa Fu. "Specificity, Conflict, and Focal Point: A Systematic Investigation into Social Media Censorship in China." *Journal of Communication* 70, no. 6 (2020): 842–67.

Taibbi, Matt. "Donald Trump Claims Authorship of Legendary Reagan Slogan; Has Never Heard of Google." *Rolling Stone*, March 25, 2015.

"Taizu Shi Chuanyue Huilai de" [Taizu Is a Time Traveler]. Cchere.com, October 24, 2009. https://cchere.com/article/2501713.

Tan, Jia. "Digital Masquerading: Feminist Media Activism in China." *Crime, Media, Culture* 13, no. 2 (2017): 171–86.

Tang, Wenfang. *Populist Authoritarianism: Chinese Political Culture and Regime Sustainability*. Oxford University Press, 2016.

Tarrow, Sidney. *Power in Movement: Social Movements and Contentious Politics*. Cambridge University Press, 1998.

Todorova, Maria, and Zsuzsa Gille, eds. *Post-Communist Nostalgia*. Berghahn, 2010.

Toffler, Alvin. *The Third Wave*. Bantam, 1980.

Tong, Yanqi, and Shaohua Lei. "War of Position and Microblogging in China." *Journal of Contemporary China* 22, no. 80 (2013): 292–311.

Tongzhanxinyu. "Zhihu CEO Zhou Yuan, Mi Meng Deng 52 Ming Wangluo Renshi Chuxi Tongzhanbu Lilun Yantaoban" [Zhihu CEO Zhou Yuan, Mi Meng and Other 52 Internet Personalities Attended the United Front Work Department Theoretical Symposium]. *The Paper*, March 26, 2018. http://m.thepaper.cn/newsDetail_forward_2043049.

Torigian, Joseph. "A Squabble About History Almost Killed Xi Jinping's Father." *Foreign Policy*, November 25, 2021. https://foreignpolicy.com/2021/11/25/xi-father-history-ccp.

Tsai, Lily L. "Constructive Noncompliance." *Comparative Politics* 47, no. 3 (2015): 253–79.

Tsai, Wen Hsuan. "Enabling China's Voice to Be Heard by the World: Ideas and Operations of the Chinese Communist Party's External Propaganda." *Problems of Post-Communism* 64, no. 3–4 (2017): 203–13.

Tse, Michael S. C., and Maleen Z. Gong. "Online Communities and Commercialization of Chinese Internet Literature." *Journal of Internet Commerce* 11, no. 2 (2012): 100–116.

Twitchett, Denis. *The Writing of Official History under the T'ang*. Cambridge University Press, 2002.

Unger, Jonathan, ed. *Using the Past to Serve the Present: Historiography and Politics in Contemporary China*. Armonk, M.E. Sharpe, 1993.

Vampa, Davide. *Brothers of Italy: A New Populist Wave in an Unstable Party System*. Palgrave Macmillan, 2023.

Veg, Sebastian. *Minjian: The Rise of China's Grassroots Intellectuals*. Columbia University Press, 2019.

Voci, Paola. *China on Video: Smaller-Screen Realities*. Routledge, 2010.

Voice of America. "China's Propaganda Victory Over US Sanctions: Huawei's Mate 60 Pro." VOA, September 12, 2023. https://www.voanews.com/a/fact-check-china-launches

-propaganda-campaign-portraying-mate-60-pro-as-huawei-s-victory-over-us-sanctions/7265226.html.

Volcic, Zala, and Mark Andrejevic, eds. *Commercial Nationalism: Selling the Nation and Nationalizing the Sell*. Palgrave Macmillan, 2016.

Wacquant, Loic J. D. "Towards a Reflexive Sociology: A Workshop with Pierre Bourdieu." *Sociological Theory* 7, no. 1 (1989): 26–63.

Wagner, Rudolf G. *The Contemporary Chinese Historical Drama: Four Studies*. University of California Press, 1990.

Wallis, Cara. "New Media Practices in China: Youth Patterns, Processes, and Politics." *International Journal of Communication* 5 (2011): 406–36.

Wampole, Christy. *Degenerative Realism: Novel and Nation in Twenty-First-Century France*. Columbia University Press, 2020.

Wang, Ban. *Illuminations from the Past: Trauma, Memory, and History in Modern China*. Stanford University Press, 2004.

Wang, David Der-Wei. *Fin-de-Siècle Splendor: Repressed Modernities of Late Qing Fiction, 1849–1911*. Stanford: Stanford University Press, 1997.

Wang, Hongying, and James N. Rosenau. "China and Global Governance." *Asian Perspective* 33, no. 3 (2009): 5–39.

Wang, Jing. *High Culture Fever: Politics, Aesthetics, and Ideology in Deng's China*. University of California Press, 1996.

Wang, Jingyuan. "Yue Shouru Pingjun 5133 Yuan? Wangwen Zuozhe: Zhikan Pingjunshu Meiyou Yiyi" [Average Monthly Income being 5,133 Yuan? Internet Writers: It Is Meaningless to Only Look at the Mean]. *CCTV News*, September 11, 2020. https://news.cctv.com/2020/09/11/ARTIMTA6NxjvmxjHLaWV8dFX200911.shtml.

Wang, Xiaoming. "A Realm Divided in Six: Chinese Literature Today." In *On China's Cultural Transformation*, ed. Keping Yu. Brill, 2015.

Wang, Yi. " 'The Backward Will Be Beaten': Historical Lesson, Security, and Nationalism in China." *Journal of Contemporary China* 29, no. 126 (2020): 887–900.

Wang, Yi, and Matthew M. Chew. "State, Market, and the Manufacturing of War Memory: China's Television Dramas on the War of Resistance Against Japan." *Memory Studies* 14, no. 4 (2021): 877–91.

Wang, Yiwen. "Chinese Internet Fictions in the Transmedia World." In *A World History of Chinese Literature*, ed. Yingjin Zhang. Routledge, 2023.

Wang, Yuan, and Rongbin Han. "Cosmetic Responsiveness: Why and How Local Authorities Respond to Mundane Online Complaints in China." *Journal of Chinese Political Science* 28, no. 2 (2023): 187–207.

Wang, Yue. "China's Tencent Has Quietly Built An Entertainment Empire That Western Tech Giants Can Only Envy." *Forbes*, December 19, 2017. https://www.forbes.com/sites/ywang/2017/12/19/chinas-tencent-has-quietly-built-an-entertainment-empire-that-western-tech-giants-can-only-envy.

Wang, Zheng. *Never Forget National Humiliation: Historical Memory in Chinese Politics and Foreign Relations*. Columbia University Press, 2014.

Wang, Zhiyan. "Xinwen Chuban Guangdian Zongju Fabu 'Wangluo Wenxue Chuban Fuwu Danwei Shehui Xiaoyi Pinggu Shixing Banfa' " [SAPPRFT Issues Provisional Methods for Evaluating Social Benefits of Online Literature Publication Service]. Xinhua Net, June 26, 2017. http://www.xinhuanet.com/politics/2017-06/26/c_129640672.htm.

Wang, Zhiyan, Ying Wang, and Yujiao Zhao. "25 Bu Wangwen Jiazuo Huo Guojia Xinwen Chubanshu he Zhongguo Zuoxie Lianhe Tuijie" [25 Online Fictions Received Joint Recommendation by NPPA and the China Writers Association]. Xinhua Net, October 11, 2019. http://www.xinhuanet.com/politics/2019-10/11/c_1210308698.htm.

Wasserstrom, Jeffrey N., and Elizabeth J. Perry, eds. *Popular Protest and Political Culture in Modern China*. Westview, 1994.

Wedeen, Lisa. *Authoritarian Apprehensions: Ideology, Judgment, and Mourning in Syria*. University of Chicago Press, 2019.

Weiss, Jessica Chen. *Powerful Patriots: Nationalist Protest in China's Foreign Relations*. Oxford University Press, 2014.

Welch, David. *The Third Reich: Politics and Propaganda*. Routledge, 2008.

Williams, Raymond. *Marxism and Literature*. Oxford University Press, 1977.

Wodak, Ruth, Majid KhosraviNik, and Brigitte Mral. *Right-Wing Populism in Europe: Politics and Discourse*. Bloomsbury, 2013.

Wolfsfeld, Gadi, Elad Segev, and Tamir Sheafer. "Social Media and the Arab Spring." *International Journal of Press/Politics* 18, no. 2 (2013): 115–37.

Wong, Edward. "Pushing China's Limits on Web, if Not on Paper." *New York Times*, November 7, 2011.

Wright, Teresa. *Accepting Authoritarianism: State-Society Relations in China's Reform Era*. Stanford University Press, 2010.

Wu, Cary, Zhilei Shi, Rima Wilkes, Jiaji Wu, Zhiwen Gong, Nengkun He, Zang Xiao, et al. "Chinese Citizen Satisfaction with Government Performance During COVID-19." *Journal of Contemporary China* 30, no. 132 (2021): 930–44.

Xi, Jinping. "Achieving Rejuvenation Is the Dream of the Chinese People." National People's Congress Website, November 29, 2012. http://www.npc.gov.cn/englishnpc/c23934/202006/32191c5bbdb04cbab6df01e5077d1c60.shtml.

Xi, Jinping. "Xi Jinping zai Wenyi Zuotanhui shang de Jianghua" [Xi Jinping's Speech at the Forum on Literature and Art]. *CPC News*, October 15, 2014. http://cpc.people.com.cn/n/2015/1015/c64094-27699249.html.

Xi, Jinping. "Xi Jinping Zhe Shiduan Hua Dingyi Zhongguomeng Neihan" [These Ten Quotes from Xi Jinping Defines the Connotations of Chinese Dream]. Xinhua Net, November 29, 2017. http://www.xinhuanet.com//politics/2017-11/29/c_1122031311.htm.

"Xi Jinping and the Chinese Dream." *The Economist*, no. 8834 (2013): 13.

Xia, Shouzhi. "Amusing Ourselves to Loyalty? Entertainment, Propaganda, and Regime Resilience in China." *Political Research Quarterly* 75, no. 4 (2022): 1096–112.

Xiao, Qiang. "The Battle for the Chinese Internet." *Journal of Democracy* 22, no. 2 (2011): 47–61.

Xiao, Qiang. "The Road to Digital Unfreedom: President Xi's Surveillance State." *Journal of Democracy* 30, no. 1 (2019): 53–67.

Xiaochun, Zhao. "In Pursuit of a Community of Shared Future: China's Global Activism in Perspective." *China Quarterly of International Strategic Studies* 4, no. 1 (2018): 23–37.

Xie, Zhuoxiao, Yiyi Yin, and Mengya Ni. "Materializing Storyworld, Battles of Transmedia Storytelling: Trans-Fandom Cultures of The King's Avatar on Chinese Social Media Platform." *International Journal of Cultural Studies* 28, no. 2 (2024): 497–519.

Xu, Bin. *Chairman Mao's Children: Generation and the Politics of Memory in China*. Cambridge University Press, 2021.

Xu, Bin. "Moral Performance and Cultural Governance in China: The Compassionate Politics of Disasters." *China Quarterly* 226 (2016): 407–30.

Xu, Jian, Qian Gong, and Wen Yin. "Maintaining Ideological Security and Legitimacy in Digital China: Governance of Cyber Historical Nihilism." *Media International Australia* 185, no. 1 (2022): 26–40.

Xu, Xiao. "A Comprehensive Review of the River Elegy Debate." *Chinese Sociology and Anthropology* 25, no. 1 (1992): 6–27.

Xu, Xu, Genia Kostka, and Xun Cao. "Information Control and Public Support for Social Credit Systems in China." *Journal of Politics* 84, no. 4 (2022): 2230–45.

Yan, Jiaqi, and Gao Gao. *Turbulent Decade*, ed. Daniel W. Y. Kwok. University of Hawaiʻi Press, 1996.

Yan, Peng. "'Gongyedang': Yige Wenhua Jingguan de Suxie" [The "Industrial Party": A Sketch of Cultural Landscape]. *Dongfang Journal* no. 4 (2019): 31–40.

Yang, Xiaofang. "Chuanyue Xiaoshuo 'Qie Ming' Dianfu Lishi Yin Zhengyi" [Time-Travel Fiction *Usurping Ming* Subverts History and Sparks Controversy]. *China Press Publication Radio Film and Television Journal*, June 23, 2008.

Yan, Xuetong. "From Keeping a Low Profile to Striving for Achievement." *Chinese Journal of International Politics* 7, no. 2 (2014): 153–84.

Yang, Dali L. *Wuhan: How the COVID-19 Outbreak in China Spiraled Out of Control.* Oxford University Press, 2023.

Yang, Guobin. "China's Zhiqing Generation: Nostalgia, Identity, and Cultural Resistance in the 1990s." *Modern China* 29, no. 3 (2003): 267–96.

Yang, Guobin. "Chinese Internet Literature and the Changing Field of Print Culture." In *From Woodblocks to the Internet: Chinese Publishing and Print Culture in Transition, circa 1800 to 2008*, ed. Cynthia Brokaw and Christopher A. Reed. Brill, 2010.

Yang, Guobin. "Technology and Its Contents: Issues in the Study of the Chinese Internet." *Journal of Asian Studies* 70, no. 4 (2011): 1043–50.

Yang, Guobin. *The Power of the Internet in China: Citizen Activism Online*. Columbia University Press, 2009.

Yang, Guobin. *The Wuhan Lockdown*. Columbia University Press, 2022.

Yang, Hongxing, and Dingxin Zhao. "Performance Legitimacy, State Autonomy and China's Economic Miracle." *Journal of Contemporary China* 24, no. 91 (2015): 64–82.

Yang, Mei-ling. "Selling Patriotism." *American Journalism* 12, no. 3 (2013): 304–20.

Yang, Xuemei. "Zhuanfang Zongheng CEO: Baidu Wenxue Bianshen hou Guzhi 45 Yi, Huo Beiwentou Touzhi"[Exclusive Interview With Zongheng CEO: Baidu Literature Now Valued at 4.5 billion After Transformation With Investment from Beijing Cultural Investment Group]. *Sina Tech*, October 9, 2018. https://tech.sina.com.cn/i/2018-10-09/doc-ihkvrhpt2529421.shtml

Yao, Linan. "Popular Propaganda in Pop Culture: How China Sells Its Ideology." PhD diss., Columbia University, 2023.

Yin, Kun. "Rang Tuijie Huodong Fahui 'Zhishi Deng' Xiaoying" [Let the Promotion Function as "Signal Light"]. Chinawriter.com.cn, March 28, 2016. http://www.chinawriter.com.cn/news/2016/2016-03-28/268511.html.

Yuan, Elaine J. *The Web of Meaning: The Internet in a Changing Chinese Society*. University of Toronto Press, 2021.

Yue, Huairang. "Zhongyang Tongzhanbu Juban Di Er Qi Wangluo Renshi Lilun Yantaoban" [CCCPC United Front Work Department Held the Second Theoretical

Symposium for Internet Personalities]. *The Paper*, March 24, 2018. http://m.thepaper.cn/newsDetail_forward_2041005.

Zhang, Liming. "Wangluo Xieshou, Bushi Shui Dou Neng Xiecheng 'Baiwan Fuweng'" [Online Writers, Not Everyone Can Become a Millionaire]. *Beijing Morning News*, August 2, 2010.

Zhang, Lin. *The Labor of Reinvention: Entrepreneurship in the New Chinese Digital Economy*. Columbia University Press, 2023.

Zhang, Lin, and Elaine J. Yuan. "Entrepreneurs in China's 'Silicon Valley': State-Led Financialization and Mass Entrepreneurship/Innovation." *Information, Communication, and Society* 26, no. 2 (2022): 286–303.

Zhang, Mei. *Pornography, Ideology, and the Internet: A Japanese Adult Video Actress in Mainland China*. Lexington, 2019.

Zhang, Qiang, and Robert Weatherley. "The Rise of 'Republican Fever' in the PRC and the Implications for CCP Legitimacy." *China Information* 27, no. 3 (2013): 277–300.

Zhang, Sarah. "Xi Jinping Takes Leading Role in Hit Propaganda Film Extolling 'Amazing' China." *South China Morning Post*, March 14, 2018. https://www.scmp.com/news/china/society/article/2137168/xi-jinping-takes-leading-role-hit-propaganda-film-extolling.

Zhang, Xiaoling, Melissa Shani Brown, and David O'Brien. "No CCP, No New China: Pastoral Power in Official Narratives in China." *China Quarterly* 235 (2018): 784–803.

Zhang, Ying. "Bushi Diyici, Ye Bushi Zuihou Yici, Wangluo Wenxue 'Saohuang Dafei' Shinian Ji" [Not the First Time, Nor the Last, Ten-Year "Anti-Pornography and Anti-Illegal" Record of Internet Literature]. *Southern Weekend*, May 29, 2014. http://www.infzm.com/content/101018.

Zhang, Ying. "'Jing Wang' Er Yue Jian" [Two Months of "Cleaning the Web"]. *Xinmin Weekly*, June 12, 2014. http://www.xinminweekly.com.cn/wenhua/2014/06/12/3950.html.

Zhang, Zheng. "Shenmi Xinxing Qunti Wangluo Zuojia Jueqi, Ruhe Zuoshang Shehui Zhuzhuo" [A Mysterious Emerging Group of Online Writers Rises, How They Get on the "Main Table" of the Society]. *China Youth Daily*, March 19, 2018.

Zhao, Dingxin. "'Zhonghua Diguo de Xingshuai' zhi Bing" [The Ills of "The Rise and Fall of Imperial China"]. *Dushu* no. 7 (2023): 3–11.

Zhao, Suisheng. *A Nation-State by Construction: Dynamics of Modern Chinese Nationalism*. Stanford University Press, 2004.

Zhao, Suisheng. "A State-Led Nationalism: The Patriotic Education Campaign in Post-Tiananmen China." *Communist and Post-Communist Studies* 31, no. 3 (1998): 287–302.

Zhao, Wen. "'Gongye Dang' Ruhe zai Gaizao 'Gudai' Shijie de Tongshi Gaizao Ziji: Lingao Qiming de Qimeng Xushi Shiyan" [How the "Industrial Party" Transforms Itself Through Reforming the "Ancient World": The Illuminating Narrative Experiment by Lingao Qiming]. *Dongfang Journal* no. 4 (2019): 130–41.

Zhao, Yanyan. "Qianxi Wangluo Wenxue de Kuaican Shuxing" [A Brief Analysis of the Fast-Food Attributes of Online Literature]. *Peony* no. 18 (2015): 102–3.

Zhao, Yuezhi. "The Struggle for Socialism in China." *Monthly Review: An Independent Socialist Magazine* 64, no. 5 (2012): 1–17.

Zhao, Ziyue. "'Lishi Xiezuo yu Chuanbo de Duoyangxing—Xugou yu Feixugou de Xiezuo' Luntan Jiyao" [Diversity of Historical Writing and Communication—Fictional and Non-Fictional Writing Forum Minutes]. *The Paper*, November 7, 2023. https://m.thepaper.cn/newsDetail_forward_25196253.

Zheng, Jianfeng. "Jiepo Lishi Xuwuzhuyi de 'Taolu'" [Exposing the Traps of Historical Nihilism]. *Guangming Daily Online*, April 2, 2020. https://theory.gmw.cn/2020-04/02/content_33708033.htm.

Zheng, Jianwei. "Zhongguo Wangluo Wenxue de Haiwai Jieshou yu Wangluo Fanyi Moshi" [A Study on the Overseas Reception and Internet Translation Mode of Chinese Internet Literature]. *Modern Chinese Literature and Culture* no. 5 (2018): 119–25.

Zheng, William. "China's Officials Play Up 'Rise of the East, Decline of the West.'" *South China Morning Post*, March 9, 2021. https://www.scmp.com/news/china/diplomacy/article/3124752/chinas-officials-play-rise-east-decline-west.

Zhihu. "Ruhe Pingjia Wangluo Xiaoshuo Chise Liming?" [How to Evaluate the Online Novel *Red Dawn*?]. *Zhihu*, July 7, 2014. https://www.zhihu.com/question/24406194.

Zhihu. "Chise Liming Zheben Xuanchuan Makesi Zhuyi de Xiaoshuo Zenme Yang?" [What Is Your Take of *Red Dawn*, The Novel that Promotes Marxism?]. *Zhihu*, October 12, 2015. https://www.zhihu.com/question/36411398.

Zhou, Zhixiong. "Wangluo Wenxue Dasai yu Wangluo Wenxue de Fazhan" [Internet Literature Contests and the Development of Internet Literature]. China Writer Net, January 22, 2010. http://www.chinawriter.com.cn/2010/2010-01-22/81753.html.

Zoonen, Liesbet Van. *Entertaining the Citizen: When Politics and Popular Culture Converge*. Rowman and Littlefield, 2005.

Zou, Sheng. "Restyling Propaganda: Popularized Party Press and the Making of Soft Propaganda in China." *Information Communication and Society* 26, no. 1 (2023): 201–17.

Zuboff, Shoshana. *The Age of Surveillance Capitalism: The Fight for a Human Future at the New Frontier of Power*. Public Affairs, 2019.

INDEX

Page numbers in *italics* indicate illustrations.

ad revenue, for online platforms, 33, 160n26

Ali Literature (aliwx.com), 26

alter-production, 55; Hao Qun as anticensorship advocate, 53; state intervention and, 52–54

alt-history fiction, 1, 76; as ideological interpellation, 94–100; as personal fantasies, 92–94, 100, 125, 182n9. *See also* Chinese dreams, in alt-history fiction; Make China Great Again alt-history fiction

Althusser, Louis, 12, 81

amusement to death or loyalty reasoning, 10–11, 18, 35, 61, 96, 134

Amusing Ourselves to Death (Postman), 10

Animal Farm (Orwell), 9

Annie Baby. *See* Li Jie

antiprofanity campaign (2014), censorship during, 47, 52

apparatus, of state censorship, 40–41, 51, 65, 82, 135; Bourdieu on, 163n62

astroturfing, 5, 41

As You Wish (song), 131

attention economy, 104–5; in commodified field of internet literature, 29, 32, 33; in politics, of internet literature, 36

authoritarian legitimation, 3, 11, 76, 83; from authoritarian resilience to, 4–8; digital challenges to democracy, 127; nonstate actors' role in, 7; state control and, 61

authoritarian power argument, 4, 11

authoritarian resilience, to authoritarian legitimation, 4–8

authoritarian rule, 4–5; digital cultural politics and, 8–11; MCGA alt-fiction influence on, 2; pop hegemony popular construction of, 2, 125; social consent for, 125, 135

Baidu Literature, 26, 160n31

Baidu Tieba social media site, 17, 53; *Reborn as a Contemporary of the People's Republic* on, 54; Zongheng acquisition to establish Baidu Literature, 26

Baum, Richard, 124

BBS. *See* bulletin board system managers, request for keyword list
Bourdieu, Pierre, 20; on apparatus, 163n62; on society with variety of fields, 27–28
Brave New World (Huxley), 10, 101, 134
Buckley, Chris, 77
bulletin board system (BBS) managers, request for keyword list, 48
Butterfly Effect, The (film), 66

Cao Qing, 71–72, 74, 91
CCP. *See* Communist Party of China
censorship, 3, 5, 40–41, 124, 165n22, 165n25; during antiprofanity campaign of 2014, 47, 52; communism in less threatening forms allowed, 55; of *How the Red Sun Rose*, 63; keyword filtering for, 42, 54, 111; microlevel blocked words, 46; *My Heroic Husband* modification through, 47; online platforms and, 42, 48, 53; political topics for, 43–46; *Powerful Young Master of the Red Family* modification, 47; of *A Qin Bureaucrat*, 56, 74; religious topics, 45, 76, 165n29; self-censoring and, 42, 57, 76; state real-time or post hoc, 42; of *Tombstone*, 63; writers acceptance of, 54; writers lack of state contact for, 46; of Yousuu, 84; Zongheng censored message, *44*
censorship apparatus, of state, 51, 65, 82, 135, 163n62; Cyber Administration of China, 40–41; cyberspace for propaganda, information gathering, surveillance, 41, 134
Ceteau, Michel de, 4
Chen, Thomas, 53
Chen Cun, as *UBT* chief artistic officer, 23
Chen Wanning (aka Ning Caishen), 23
China: ascending global influence, 8, 128; Baum and Shevchenko on post-reform politics of, 124; cultural hegemony and, 12; high culture fever of, 12, 13, 82–83, 173n16; movement toward surveillance state, 41, 134; reforms, 81–82, 84–89, *85*, 112; significant structural changes for, 124; socioeconomic and political transformation across, 8. *See also* saving China
China Business Times, writing relay with Sina.com, 23
China Internet Network Information Center (CNNIC), 21
China Literature app, Tencent merging with Shanda Literature for, 26
China News Digest, 21–22, 159n9
China wolf-warrior diplomacy, Guobin Yang on, 8
Chinese dreams, 2; MCGA theme and, 14; state ideology of, 18; state promotion of, 77; variety of, 88–93; Xi Jingping on, 13–14, 61, 63, 93, 169n9
Chinese dreams, in alt-history fiction: CCP victories and, 89–90; challenge of state agenda of ethnic inclusivity and harmony, 91–92; on China reforms, 84–89, *85*, 112; collective nature of, 93; constructive destruction, 80, 96–100; dissatisfaction expressed in guarded fashion, 90; distribution of historic time periods, 84; economic reforms, 86; Han Chinese minorities and, 87–88; on ideology of communism, 91, 95; MCGA nationalism genre, 87; method notes on, 84; military reforms, 85; Ming dynasty reforms focus, 84–85, *85*; on minorities subjugation, 92; national revival rhetoric, 79–80; nonthreatening deviations, 94–96; on parliamentary or representative democracy, 90; political reforms, 87, 89; science and technologies advancement, 86
Chinese Revolution, 72, 75
Chise Liming, 1, 43–44, 54, 72–73, 75, 84, 91, 97, 107
citizen participation, in pop hegemony, 80–83
class dimension, in ideological interpellation, readers' perspective, 119–20
CNNIC. *See* China Internet Network Information Center
commercialization, of Qidian literature portal, 25–26
commodified field, of internet literature: attention economy in, 29, 32, 33; conflict between writers and platforms, 32; gender-specific content, 30–32, *31*; market rules of supply and demand, competition, 20, 29, 33; pay-to-read

model, 29–30, 162n51; state field of power and, 28; state regulatory role, 20
commodified political field, of internet literature, 2–3, 7, 14–17, 29, 124, 161n42; commodified nature, 27–33; Guobin Yang on multidimensional interaction, 27; politics of, 34–37
communism: Chinese dreams on ideology of, 91, 95; discourse level critical discourse analysis on topics of, 113–14; as political topic for censorship, 43–46; *Red Dawn* on, 1, 107; saving China with, 95–96
Communist Party of China (CCP), 62, 77; Chinese dreams on victories of, 89–90; discourse level critical discourse analysis on, 113; Four Cardinal Principles of, 82; legitimation of, 79; MCGA on, 75, 76; MGCA inspiration from revolutionary history of, 97–98; *Red Dawn* on, 1, 107; Sandby-Thomas on legitimacy and, 154n13
Communist Revolution, 1, 39, 43, 62, 75, 98
constructive destruction process, of MGCA, 80, 96; anti-elite and anti-intellectual inclination, 100; inspiration from CCP revolutionary history, 97–98; promotion of utilitarian attitudes, 98–99; saving China from historical crises, 98; traditional intellectuals and cultural elites power dilutes with, 99
content censorship machine, of state, 5
co-optation, 3, 41, 51, 57, 76; delegation of censorship to platforms, 48; description of, 47–48; group targets of, 48, 166n38; literature portals ratings, *49*, 49–50, 166n42; literature portals social responsibility, 48–50, *49*; SAPPRFT on guidelines, 48; United Front system symposium for celebrity writers, 50; of writers and writer associations, 50; writers state recognition, 50, 167n51
coproduction, 76, 124; alter-production to, 52–53; communism in less threatening forms, 55; state intervention as, 55–57; state-market-society interaction as, 55; state promotion of liked works, 55–56; *Unparalleled Fireworks* example, 56
COVID nationalism, Guobin Yang on, 8
Crazy Stories from Hmong Frontier, 129
critical discourse analysis, of Fairclough: discourse level, 109, 111–15; social practices level, 109, 115–19, 178n36; text level, 109–11, *110*
cultural consumerism: rise of internet literature as phenomenon of, 17; social mobilization and resistance role of, 9; state capitalization of, 130–31
cultural consumerist experiences, 126; MCGA fiction and, 88, 124; politics form of, 9, 19–20, 34
cultural hegemony, 81, 125; Gramsci and, 11, 14; Marxist theory of class dominance and, 11; to pop hegemony, 11–14; social participation in, 96
Cultural Revolution, 61, 82
Cyber Administration of China, direct report to Xi Jinping, 40–41

democracy: authoritarian legitimation and digital challenges to, 127; Chinese dreams on parliamentary or representative, 90
digital consumerism processes, ideological contestation simultaneous with, 3
digital cultural politics: China authoritarian rule and, 8–11; digital cultural consumerist experiences study, 8–9
digital media, China authoritarian and democratic politics impacted by, 127
digital monitoring and tracking practices, of state, 5, 155n20
digital propaganda strategies: astroturfing, 5, 41; ideotainment, 5, 41, 97
digital revolution, impact on ideological governance, 83–84
discourse level, of critical discourse analysis: analysis of MCGA discourse, 111–15; on CCP, 113; Chinese dream theme, 112; communism topics, 113–14; MCGA titles on political, economic and social reforms, 112; morally problematic social discourse, 114–15; nationalism theme, 112; *Never Declassify*, 113; political implications of pursuit of power, 114; proregime ideological tendency, 112–13; reader

discourse level (*continued*)
comments on MCGA compared to non-MCGA works, 111; *Rescuing the Great Ming*, 113
Dragon Sky (Ikong.com) online forum, 7, 17, 25, 84; military and alt-history genres, 122

Fairclough, Norman, 109, *110*, 111–19, 178n36
fee-free literature portals, 162n51
fields: Bourdieu on, 27–28; political, 28; state as field of power, 28. *See also* commodified field; commodified political field
First Intimate Contact, The, 19, 23, 25
First Original Internet Literature Contest, *UBT*, 23–24
F—k Qing (Cao Qing), 71–72, 74, 91
foreign policy, of Xi Jinping, 13
Four Cardinal Principles, of CCP, 82
Fry, Stephan, 66
full-attendance bonus, for writers, 162n53
Future of New China, The (Liang Qichao), 64

Gao Hua, 63
gender-specific content, in internet literature, 30–32, *31*
genre fiction, 41, 57; history and military genres, 34, *49*, 60, 122; martial arts, 34; MCGA nationalism, 87; in Qidian literature portal, 30, *31*; reality or metropolitan, 60
global implications, of pop hegemony, 139–40
global influence, China ascending, 8, 128
Gramsci, Antonio: on cultural hegemony, 11, 14; on hegemony, 80; on hegemony differ from dominance, 37
grass rating system, of readers, 119–20
Great Power Heavy Industry, 51–52, 76, 119–20
group targets, of co-optation, 48, 166n38
Guibernau, Montserrat, 63
Guiding Opinions Concerning Promoting the Healthy Development of Online Literature, of SAPPRFT, 48
Guobin Yang: on China wolf-warrior diplomacy, 8; on COVID nationalism, 8; internet literature defined by, 21; on multidimensional interaction, 27; multi-interactionism framework of, 20, 158n3; on politics, 9

Hai Rui Dismissed from Office (Wu Han), 61–62
Han Chinese ethnic group, 87–88
Hao Qun (aka Murong Xuechun), 23, 24; as anticensorship advocate, 53
Healers of the Republic, 52
hegemony: cultural, 11–14, 81, 96, 125; Gramsci on, 80; Gramsci on dominance differing from, 37; ideational, 3. *See also* pop hegemony
Hello Japanese Devils, We Are Game Players, 116
high culture fever, of China, 12, 82–83, 173n16; decline in 1990s, 13
historical nihilism, 43, 63, 135, 182n39
historicity of writing: Liang Qichao and, 64–65; of MCGA stories, 89–90, 128; on national revival, 64–65
history and military genres, 34, *49*, 60, 122
Hmong ethnic minority, 129–30
Hockx, Michel, 9, 21
Hongxiu (hongxiu.com) literature portal, 26
How the Red Sun Rose (Gao Hua), 63
Huanjian Shumeng (hjsm.net) literature portal, 25
Huawei tech giant, release of Mate 60 Pro flagship phone, 123
Hu Jintao (president), 92
Huxley, Aldous, 10, 101, 134
hypercommercialization, in internet literature history, 21–27

ICT. *See* information and communication technology
ideational hegemony, 3
ideological constructs, state promotion of, 51–52
ideological contestation, 119, 121–22; digital consumerism processes simultaneous with, 3; *The Last Transfer of Western Tang Empire*, 118
ideological governance, 125; digital revolution impact on, 83–84; MCGA alt-fiction influence on, 2, 41–42

ideological interpellation, 125; alt-history fiction as, 94–100; Althusser on, 81; constructive destruction, 80, 96–100; MCGA fiction facilitation of, 97; nonthreatening deviations in, 94–96; social participation in, 96
ideological interpellation, readers' perspective: on class dimension, 119–20; ideological contestation, 3, 118–19, 121–22; methods notes, 108–9; pop hegemony and, 117–21; on regime dissatisfaction, 119–20
ideological transformation, Marx on, 81
ideotainment propaganda, 5, 41, 97
Ikong.com. *See* Dragon Sky online forum
industrial party narratives, 130; *Morning Star of Lingao* as, 8
Industrial Tycoon, The, 73–74, 76, 124
information and communication technology (ICT) sector, state intertwined with, 34
information technology (IT), 26
intellectual property (IP) transactions revenue source, for portals, 26
internet: little pink regime defense, 6, 7, 130; readers active role in, 103; voluntary fifty-cent army regime defense, 6, 7, 130
internet literature, 6, 7, 15–16, 124; attention economy of, 104–5; citizens production and consumption of, 2; CNNIC on consumer numbers of, 21; commercialized industry of, 92–93; commodified field of, 20, 28, 29–33, *31*; as fan economy, 105; field of state power and, 28; gender-specific content in, 30–32, *31*; history from idyllic days to hypercommercialization, 21–27; history in contemporary politics and, 126–27; Hockx definition of, 21; pay-to-read model in, 29–30, 162n51; political field of expression, 28; pop hegemony and, 11–14; reader as driving force of, 18; relevance of history in contemporary politics, 126; rise as cultural consumerism phenomenon, 17; shaped by state, writers, readers, market forces, 20, 125; state intervention in, 18; user base and penetration rate since 2013, 21, 22; writer-reader interaction in, 33, 35, 106–8, 162n56; Yang definition of, 21. *See also* commodified political field; Make China Great Again (MCGA) alt-history fiction; state control
internet literature, commercialization to hypercommercialization: Dragon Sky, 25; Huanjian Shumeng, 25; international audience for, 27; Qidian literature portal, 25; Shanda Interactive Entertainment hypercommercialization, 26; television dramas and films from, 26
internet literature, idyllic days of, 26–27; *China News Digest* and, 21–22; commercialization of, 25; cross-border components of, 25; Netease contest, 23; Sina.com and *China Business Times* writing relay, 23; Tianya popularity, 23; *UBT*, 23–25
Introduction to Mao Zedong Thought class, 19
IP. *See* intellectual property
IT. *See* information technology

Japanese and the War, The (Lucken), 127
Jin Chu Empire, 112
Jinjiang Literature City (jjwxc.com) literature portal, 26; female readers prevalence in, 30–31
Jin Yong, 34
Johnson, Ian, 62
Joy of Life, 112, 115

keyword filtering, for censorship, 42, 54, 111

Ladder to Heaven, 51–52
Last Transfer of Western Tang Empire, The, 118
latent Dirichlet allocation (LDA) modeling, 109–11, *110*
Leave Me Alone (Hao Qun), 23, 24, 53
legitimacy: authoritarian regimes deficit of, 4; Sandby-Thomas on CCP durability, 154n13
legitimation: of CCP, 79; Sandby-Thomas definition of, 154n13. *See also* authoritarian legitimation
Li Jie (aka Annie Baby), 23

literature portals: categorization, 25–26, 161n45; co-optation and social responsibility, 48–50, *49*; co-optation ratings, *49*, 49–50, 166n42; fee-free, 162n51. *See also specific literature portals*
little pink, regime defense by internet, 6, 7, 130
Liu Zhidan, 39–40, 62
Lucken, Michael, 127

Make America Great Again (MAGA), US, 2; MCGA connection to, 18, 127, 136–39
Make China Great Again (MCGA), 1; on CCP, 75, 76; on Chinese dream rhetoric of national revival, 79–80; comic-style videos of, 77; convergence of popular narratives and state ideology, 75; democratic backsliding in digital age, 127; genre nationalism, 87; MAGA connection to, 18, 127, 136–39; national revival theme, 2, 132; as popular, market and official narratives, 74–76; YouTube and, *77*, *78*
Make China Great Again (MCGA) alt-history fiction, 6; authoritarian rule influence from, 2; on China major historical junctures, 66–67; Chinese dream theme, 100; constructive destruction process of, 80, 96–100; cultural consumerist experiences and, 88, 124; expansionist tendency of, 97; *F—K Qing*, 71–72, 74, 91; historical nationalism in, 129; historicity of writing, 64–65, 89–90, 128; history, present and future of nation connected through, 18, 59, 61; history and national identity impact, 60, 63; on ideal China, 14, 134; ideological governance influenced by, 2, 41–42; *The Industrial Tycoon*, 73–74, 76, 124; male readers main target audience of, 93; mediated by market dynamics, 77, 88; meritocracy and, 133; *Morning Star of Lingao*, 8, 70–71, 74, 98, 104; most distinctive words in comments, *150–51*; nationalist quest for China revival in, 2, 132; past, present future in, 127–31; *Pointing South*, 1, 69, 74, 75, 90–92, 94, 97–98; political nature of, 2, 59; politics of writing history, 61–64; popularity and political implications of, 66; *A Qin Bureaucrat* as, 56, 74; *Red Dawn*, 1, 54, 72–73, 74, 75, 84, 88, 97, 107; *Ruling Under the Heaven*, 68, 74, 90, 100, 114–15; *Tang Cavaliers*, 67–68, 74; technology- and market-mediated process of, 2; theme of saving and reviving China, 18, 61, 66, 75, 83, 89, 93, 98; *Usurping Ming*, 70, 74, 91, 97, 100, 108; words frequently used in comments, *146–48*, 177n24
Making History (Fry), 66
Mao Zedong, 7; *Hai Rui Dismissed from Office* criticism of, 61–62; *How the Red Sun Rose* on, 63; on literature, 39; Wu Han criticism and imprisonment by, 62
market: commodified field and rules of supply and demand, 20, 29, 33; internet literature shaped by, 20, 125; state control of internet literature through, 36; state negotiations with, 37
market and digital media platforms, pop hegemony role, 15, 17
market dynamics: in internet literature politics, 36; MCGA fiction mediated by, 77, 88
martial arts genre, 34
Marx, Karl, 81
Marxist theory of class dominance, cultural hegemony and, 11
Mate 60 Pro flagship phone, of Huawei tech giant, 123
MCGA. *See* Make China Great Again
microlevel blocked words, in censorship, 46
Milner, Helen, 137
Ming dynasty (1368-1644), 7–8, 25, 61, 70–71; Chinese dreams alt-history fiction focus on, 84–85, *85*
minjian intellectuals: prominent role of, 13; Veg on, 3, 102
minorities: Chinese dreams Han Chinese, 87–88; Hmong ethnic, 129–30; subjugation of, 92
Monument to the Heroes of the People quote, 65
Morning Star of Lingao, 8, 70–71, 98, 104
multi-interactionism framework, of Guobin Yang, 20, 158n3
Murong Zuechun. *See* Hao Qun

My Country, My Parents (film), 130–31
My Heroic Husband, 47, 106–7; writer-reader interaction with, 33

nationalism: discourse level theme of, 112; social practices level on dimension of, 118–19; Guibernau on, 63; Guobin Yang on COVID, 8; MCGA alt-history fiction on China revival, 2, 132; MCGA alt-history fiction on historical, 129; MCGA genre, 87; in pop hegemony, 132; of state, 4, 82; state challenge of extreme, 126; in Three Principles of the People, 133, 178n32; turn of Xi Jinping, 13
National Press and Publication Administration (NPPA): "Publication Project of Excellent Realistic and Historical Genre Internet Literature Works," 57; writers and works recommendations by, 51, 167n53
national revival: Chinese dreams MCGA alt-history rhetoric, 79–80; historicity of writing on, 64–65; MCGA alt-history fiction on quest for, 2, 132
Netease internet literature contest, 23
Never Declassify, 113
NewSmth (newsmth.net) online forum, 17
1984 (Orwell), 9, 10, 101
Ning Caishen. *See* Chen Wanning
non-MCGA works: discourse level critical discourse analysis of reader comments on, 111; frequently used words in comments on, *142*
nonstate actors: agency in internet literature politics, 36; role in authoritarian legitimation, 7
nonthreatening deviations, in ideological interpellation, 94–96
NPPA. *See* National Press and Publication Administration

obscene and pornographic censorship targets, 42, 164n19
One Generation of Favors. See *Powerful Young Master of the Red Family*
online platforms, 16, 17; ad revenue for, 33, 160n26; conflict between writers and, 32; delegation of censorship to, 48; state participation in intervention of, 56; strong incentive to comply with censorship, 53; taboo word lists of, 46; writer advice to avoid censorship, 42; writer income and contracts with, 160n27; writers full-attendance bonus, 162n53. *See also specific online platforms*
Orwell, George, 9, 10, 101

patriotic movies, for PRC seventieth anniversary, 130–31
pay-to-read model, in internet literature, 29–30, 162n51
People's Liberation Army (PLA), 52, 77
People's Republic of China (PRC): founding of, 65, 75; patriotic movies for seventieth anniversary, 130–31
people's rights, of Three Principles of the People, 133, 178n32
personal dream, of becoming writers, 92, 174n30
personal fantasies, of alt-history fiction, 92–94, 100, 125, 182n9
PLA. *See* People's Liberation Army
platform-writer-reader relationship, 40
Pointing South (Zhinan Lu), 1, 69, 74–75, 90–92, 94, 97–98
political field of expression, in internet literature, 28
political topics, for censorship: *Red Dawn* censorship, 43–44, 84, 91; *Red Flag over the Wasted Land* censorship, 44–45; SARFT on time-travel dramas, 43; *Talented Martial Arts Girl* censorship, 44; writings on communism, 43–46
politics: of commodified political field, of internet literature, 34–37; everyday experiences engagement in, 3; form of cultural consumerist experiences, 9, 19–20, 34; Guobin Yang on, 9
politics, of internet literature, 37; amusement to death and, 10–11, 18, 35, 61, 96, 134; attention economy rules and, 36; discursive struggles and ideational contestation of, 34; history and military genres as political, 34; market dynamics and nonstate actors agency, 36; martial arts genre and, 34; state ban of erotic and political content, 35; state intertwined with ICT market sector, 34; state time- and place-sensitive controls, 35, 40

politics, of writing history: Communist Revolution redefined, 62; *Hai Rui Dismissed from Office* example, 61–62; Johnson on, 62; *Liu Zhidan* example, 62; on regime legitimacy, 63–64; state attempts to censure and manage alternate memories, 63; state control over past in, 63–64
pop hegemony, 3, 18, 117–21, 123–24, 127–30; authoritarian rule constructed under, 2, 125; citizen participation and, 80–83; cultural hegemony to, 11–14; global implications of, 139–40; improved governance component, 132; internet literature and, 11–14; limited participation and, 132–33; market and digital media platforms role, 15, 17; nationalism in, 132; social actors role, 15–16, 17, 100–101; state role, 15, 17, 126
populism, 2, 136, 138–39; Milner on, 137
Postman, Neil, 10
Powerful Young Master of the Red Family, renamed *One Generation of Favors* through censorship, 47
Practice of Everyday Life, The (de Certeau), 4
PRC. *See* People's Republic of China
Prison Notebooks (Gramsci), 11
promotion, 41, 57, 76; of Chinese dreams by state, 77; of core socialist values and main melody works, 51; of *Great Power Heavy Industry*, 51–52; of *Ladder to Heaven*, 51–52; of liked works by state, 55–56; of state ideological constructs, 51–52; of utilitarian attitudes, 98–99; by writers and their works awards, 51
proregime discourses: ideological tendency of, 112–13; little pink, 6, 7, 130; voluntary fifty-cent army, 6, 7, 130
prosumption, readers in age of, 103–5, 112
Provisional Methods for Evaluating Social Benefits of Online Literature Publications Service Platforms, of SAPPRFT, 48–49
"Publication Project of Excellent Realistic and Historical Genre Internet Literature Works," NPPA, 57

Qidian (qidian.com) literature portal, 17, 104, 106; attempt to revise writer contracts, 32; commercialization of, 25–26; free and VIP categories of, 25–26, 161n45; genre fiction in, 30, *31*; history genres on, *49*, 60; Shanda Interactive Entertainment acquisition of, 26
Qin Bureaucrat, A, censorship of, 56, 74
Qin Revolution, 91

Raimondo, Gina, 123
ranking scores, of Yousuu literature commentating portal, 72–73, 173n46
readers, participation in MCGA, 102, 106–22; as internet literature driving force, 18; in prosumption age, 103–5, 112. *See also* critical discourse analysis, of Fairclough
reader-writer interaction. *See* writer-reader interaction
reality or metropolitan genres, 60
Reborn as a Contemporary of the People's Republic, as alt-history fiction, 54
Record Within the Pillow (Shen Jiji), 59
Red Dawn (Chise Liming), 72–73, 74, 75, 88, 97; censorship of, 43–44, 84, 91; on communism, 1, 107; online availability of, 54
Red Flag over the Wasted Land censorship, 44–45
regime dissatisfaction, 119–20
religious topics, censorship of, 45, 76, 165n29
Republic Against the Epidemic, 52
Rescuing the Great Ming, 113
resistance, cultural consumerism role in, 9
Return of the Condor Heroes, The (Jin Yong), 34
Rise of a Great Writer in Republic Era, The, 115, 165n22
Ritzer, George, 103
Ruguanism narrative, 130, 156n28; anticipation of China replacing US, 7; on pursuit of international great power, 8; US seen like Ming dynasty, 7
Ruling Under the Heaven, 68, 74, 90, 100, 114–15

Sandby-Thomas, Peter, 154n13
SAPPRFT. *See* State Administration of Press, Publication, Radio, Film and Television

SARFT Television Drama Management Department, 43
saving China: with communism, 95–96; social practices level critical discourse analysis on, 115–16; from historical crises, 98; MCGA alt-history fiction theme of, 18, 61, 66, 75, 83, 89, 93, 98
self-censoring, 42, 57, 76
Shanda Interactive Entertainment, 26
Shanda Literature, Tencent IT giant formation of, 26
Shen Jiji, 59
Shevchenko, Alexei, 124
Sina.com, writing relay with *China Business Times*, 23
SMTH online forum, 24, 25
social actors, pop hegemony role, 15–16, 17, 100–101
social consent, for authoritarian rule, 125, 135
social mobilization: cultural consumerism role in, 9; of internet and digital media, 4
social participation, in cultural hegemony, 96
social practices level, of critical discourse analysis, 178n36; *Hello Japanese Devils, We Are Game Players*, 116; nationalism dimension, 118–19; on saving China from hardships, 115–16; sociopolitical practices, 115–17; *Spy Stories*, 116–17
social welfare, of Three Principles of the People, 133, 178n32
SonicBBS online forum, 7, 104
Southern Song dynasty (1127-1279 CE), *Pointing South* on, 1, 69, 74, 75
Spy Stories, 116–17
state: ban of erotic and political content, 35; capitalization, of cultural consumerism, 130–31; censorship apparatus of, 40–41, 51, 65, 82, 135, 163n62; Chinese dream promotion, 77; as coproducer of internet literature, 3; coproducing digital experiences, 124; digital monitoring and tracking practices, 5, 155n20; as field of power, 28; Hockx on culture regulation by, 9; internet literature active engagement, 3; internet literature regulatory role, 20; market and society negotiations, 37; nationalism of, 4, 82; political internet literature strong control by, 20; pop hegemony role, 15, 17, 126; procontrol tendency, 134; real-time or post hoc censorship, 42
State Administration of Press, Publication, Radio, Film and Television (SAPPRFT): *Guiding Opinions Concerning Promoting the Healthy Development of Online Literature*, 48; *Provisional Methods for Evaluating Social Benefits of Online Literature Publication Service Platforms*, 48–49; recommended works of, 51, *141–45*; words to introduce recommended works of, *141*
state control, of internet literature, 134–35; alt-production and resilience to state control, 53–54; authoritarian legitimation and, 61; through market and social actors, 36; on past, 63–64; permissible boundaries patrol, 37–38; regulation and exploit of online expression, 13; reliance on intermediary actors for, 36; time- and place-sensitive controls, 35, 40; writers frustration for, 52–53
state intervention, 18, 42–51; alter-production and, 52–54; as coproduction, 55–57; cultural elites struggles with, 39; cultural products careful management, 39; innovative propaganda and social control tactics, 40; *Liu Zhidan* controversy over publication, 39–40; Mao at Yan'an Forum on Literature, 39; platform-writer-reader relationship and, 40; sophisticated censorship apparatus and, 40–41; Xi Jinping on cultural realm of literature, 39. *See also* censorship; co-optation; promotion
Story of the Ming Dynasty, The, 25
surveillance, China movement toward state of, 41, 134
sustainability, of writers, 107, 177n15

taboo word lists, of online platforms, 46
Talented Martial Arts Girl, censorship of, 44
Tang Cavaliers, 67–68, 74

Tangjia Sanshao. *See* Zhang Wei
Tencent Literature IT giant, 26, 32
text level, of Fairclough critical discourse analysis: frequent word analysis, 111; topic analysis using LDA modeling, 109–11, *110*
Three Principles of the People, of nationalism, social welfare, and people's rights, 133, 178n32
Tiananmen movement (1989), 12, 62, 76, 82, 102
Tianya (now expired) online forum, 17, 23–25
time- and place-sensitive control, by state control, 35, 40
tipping income, for writers, 106, 177n14
Toffler, Alvin, 103
Tombstone (Yang Jisheng), 63
topic censorship, 164n18; of obscene and pornographic material, 42, 164n19
Trump, Donald, 136

Under the Banyan Tree (*UBT*) internet literature site, 23–25
United Front system: symposiums for internet writers, 50; writers as part of, 51
United States (US): *The Butterfly Effect* in, 66; MAGA, 2, 18, 127, 136–39; Ruguanism narrative on Ming dynasty like, 7
Unparalleled Fireworks, 56
US. *See* United States
Usurping Ming, 70, 71, 74, 91, 97, 100, 108

Veg, Sebastian, 3, 102
voluntary fifty-cent army, internet regime defense by, 6, 7, 130

Warrior Wolf 2 (film), 77
WeChat Reading App, 17, 46, 56, 91, 105
words: censorship microlevel blocked, 46; frequently used in MCGA comments, *146–48*, 177n24; frequently used in non-MCGA comments, *142*; to introduce SAPPRFT recommended works, *141–45*; most distinctive in MCGA comments, *150–51*
writer-reader interaction, 106–8, 162n56; commenting, recommending roles for, 105; interactive experiences of, 35; of *My Heroic Husband*, 33
writers, 33, 105, 160n27; censorship acceptance of, 54; conflict between online platforms and, 32; co-optation and state recognition, 50, 167n51; NPPA recommendations for works and, 51, 167n53; as part of United Front system, 51; personal dream of becoming, 92, 174n30; promotion of works awards by, 51; state censorship lack of contact with, 46; state control frustration, 52–53; sustainability of, 107, 177n15; tipping income, 106, 177n14
Wu Han, 61; Mao criticism and imprisonment of, 62

Xi Jinping (president), 7, 50, 62, 92; assertive foreign policy of, 13; on Chinese dream, 13–14, 61, 63, 93, 169n9; on cultural realm of literature, 39; Cyber Administration of China direct report to, 40–41; nationalism turn of, 13; populism of, 137

Yan'an Forum on Literature, Mao at, 39
Yang Jisheng, 63
Yousuu (yousuu.com) literature commentating portal, 17, 60, 84, 108; historical accuracy and, 122; ranking scores of, 72–73, 173n46
YouTube, 77, *78*

Zhang Wei (pen name Tangjia Sanshao), 27, 50
Zhihu social media site, 17
Zhinan Lu, 1, 69, 74–75, 90–92, 94, 97–98
Zongheng (zongheng.com): Baidu merge with to establish Baidu Literature, 26; censored message from, *44*; *Red Dawn* publication on, 43

www.ingramcontent.com/pod-product-compliance
Lightning Source LLC
Chambersburg PA
CBHW032133020426
42334CB00016B/1147

* 9 7 8 0 2 3 1 2 2 0 5 5 2 *